STANDING FOR THEIR FAITH

(A history of churches of Christ in Tennessee, 1900-1950)

William Woodson

J & W Publications
203 North Ave.
Henderson, Tennessee 38340

Williams Printing Co.
Nashville, Tennessee

For
Jeanne,
Melissa, Bill and Allison

PREFACE

This work presents a history of the churches of Christ in Tennessee from 1900 to 1950. It originated in a doctoral study but has been revised and edited for presentation in this form.

During the months of research and writing, the aid of numerous individuals has been sought and enjoyed by the author. Adequate thanks cannot be given, but some word of appreciation seems appropriate. The writer acknowledges the kind assistance of Mrs. Jane Miller and and her library staff who provided easy access to the many volumes in the Freed-Hardeman College Library and who assisted in securing needed research materials elsewhere. Mrs. Lois Rhodes assisted in the research, writing, and various revisions in so many ways that it is only the statement of the fact, with grateful appreciation, to state that her assistance was most valuable, thorough, and cheerfully given in often trying circumstances. My wife Jeanne, and our children Melissa, Bill, and Allison have been patient and understanding, and most supportive, as the weeks became months and years. Their interest and encouragement sustained me in the process. Also, a deep expression of gratitude is due to the administration, faculty, and student body of Freed-Hardeman College for much assistance and encouragement through the years.

This work is sent forth with a desire to help understand the heritage which earlier Christians in Tennessee and elsewhere have bequeathed to those of us who have come after them. May it be said of us when our generation has passed, as this book seeks to say of those whose names and deeds are remembered here, that we were standing for our faith as those in earlier times were standing for theirs. Without those who went before this story could not have been told. May its telling, with those limitations I know so well, be a source of encouragement and admonition to all who read it.

November 20, 1978   William Woodson
Henderson, Tennessee

TABLE OF CONTENTS

INTRODUCTION

In 1971 Herman A. Norton published his work on the history of the Christian Church (Disciples of Christ) in Tennessee. He traced the story of the restoration movement in the state from the early years of the nineteenth century until the division between the Christian Churches and churches of Christ in the later years of that century and early years of the present century.[1] In the remaining section of his work he discussed the history of the group known as the Christian Church.[2] While most valuable in recounting the events prior to 1906, the work does not discuss the churches of Christ in Tennessee after 1906. This work by Norton points up the absence of a treatment of churches of Christ in Tennessee after 1906.

It was the lack of treatment of churches of Christ in this century, as distinguished from the Christian Churches and Disciples of Christ, which stimulated the interest of the writer to prepare the following study. In this discussion of churches of Christ in Tennessee an analysis and general history of these brethren from 1900 to 1950 is presented. Accordingly, an analytical treatment of churches of Christ in Tennessee is provided with major emphasis placed on events after rather than before 1906.

The significance of developments in Tennessee for the history of churches of Christ in America can hardly be over estimated. The following study will briefly indicate the significance of early men and churches. The issues which resulted in division around the turn of the past century found both advocates and opponents in the state. Many leading men whose work or views shaped the course of restoration history in this century spent the major portion of their productive years in Tennessee. The single most influential paper among churches of Christ for more than one hundred years has remained, since its origin in 1855, in Nashville. The most significant controversies which were encountered by the group either took place in large measure in the state or had leading participants who worked primarily in the state. A strong publishing house, several colleges, and a rapidly increasing membership with well developed churches and energetic programs of missionary and educational activities made it clear that progress was being made in the state. These and related developments among churches of Christ in Tennessee in the period studied make it clear that to understand the fortune and progress of the cause of churches of Christ in this state is, in large measure, to understand the broader and more comprehensive progress of brotherhood. It is this crucial position which churches of Christ sustained in Tennessee that gives significance to their history. The following work provides an analysis and synthesis of their progress.

The primary purpose of the work will be to investigate thoroughly the sources of the period under study and to isolate and synthesize those elements of growth which made possible the development and influence of churches of Christ in Tennessee both within the state and in the brotherhood at large.

The secondary purpose will be to investigate approximately fifty years of history during which time the churches of Christ in Tennessee identified themselves, become stable and made adequate progress to guarantee their continuance as a viable religious force in the state.

These two purposes will merge at almost every turn of events and consequently may be viewed as different sides of the same coin. The primary purpose will consider broad doctrinal and brotherhood concerns and the secondary purpose will show how these broad areas of development were actually working themselves out in the progress of the churches in the state.

Three particular limitations have been applied to the study so as to allow it to conform to acceptable space requirements.

First, the study has been limited to roughly fifty years of development in the state. By approximately 1950 the churches of Christ in Tennessee and elsewhere had entered a new phase in their growth. Specifically, they had entered into a period when they launched a major effort to address themselves, affirmatively and negatively, to opportunities and problems which were posed by the post World War II situation at home and abroad. This positive and negative attempt to confront problems and opportunities resulted in a major controversy with a resultant division of significant proportions. Also, by virtue of significant efforts at home and abroad, major strides of progress were made after 1950 in such areas as evangelism, mission work, religious education, publishing activities, educational institutions, erection of church buildings, and use of various techniques and resources which were made possible by expanding technology and economy. To attempt to analyze such developments after as well as before 1950 would force either a cursory treatment or a study far in excess of proposed limits. Accordingly the year 1950 was set as roughly the chronological limit.

Second, an indepth study has not been made of the involvement in and response to such social, economic, and political events as World War I, the modernist controversy of the 1920's, the great depression, and World War II. To be sure, some notice will be given to such areas of context and concern, but the purpose of this study has been to focus primarily on those factors of brotherhood development which provided the inner dynamic of the progress discussed. These several factors were in operation during these major events which affected the nation at large, as well as Tennessee itself, and the churches of Christ in the state were neither isolated from nor uninvolved in these affairs. However, these developments provided more of a context in which to relate and react than a dynamic or vehicle by which relation and reaction were to be sustained. Accordingly, while attention is paid in some measure to these and other developments of this general period in American history, these developments are not, for this study, major areas of concern. Instead, attention will be directed to those brotherhood concerns and activities which made possible the development of churches of Christ in the state into a unique and viable group of religious people.

Third, a lengthy discussion of major figures as to their lives and contributions has been omitted. The lives of some outstanding men have been sketched in varying degrees of completeness, but attention has primarily been called to the specific contribution of these men at particular times and places of concern. The lives of the leading men, while interesting in themselves, have not been considered germane to the purposes of this study and have been reduced to the barest of essentials or omitted entirely.

The literature concerning churches of Christ, Disciples of Christ, Christian Churches and the movement they variously represent is enormous. This literature, in periodicals, formal histories, and books of various kinds, has been worked through in various ways by writers in the respective groups. Each of these writers has surveyed the literature from his own perspective, sometimes reflecting and sometimes indicting the perspective of the group he personally represents.

The general history of the restoration movement and the specific history of the groups involved have usually been merged in the published works concerning the respective churches. Garrison and DeGroot, from the perspective of Disciples of Christ, presented a broad survey of the movement and discussed developments among the Disciples of Christ after 1906.[3] James DeForest Murch did much the same for the Christian Churches from their perspective.[4] From the perspective of churches of Christ the discussion of events after 1906 has been meager in the extreme. Earl Irvin West gave seventeen of eight hundred fourteen pages to his discussion of events after 1906.[5] Homer Hailey gave eight pages to his discussion of the same period.[6] The recent work by David Edwin Harrell, Jr. concluded his discussion of the history with events in 1900.[7] These works, and others by men of similar perspective, have not attempted a full discussion of the history of the churches of Christ after the year 1906. It is hoped that writers in the future will supply this desired general history, but the present work seeks to present such a history for the movement as a whole only as it relates to the significant events which were occurring in Tennessee.

The various groupings and sub-groupings within the movement as a whole and the controversial nature and course of their history have supplied the historians with a welter of problems for analysis and interpretation. The historiographic stance has varied from writer to writer and this variation would seem to require that some consideration be given to the stance taken by the present writer. A major concern of the historians of the movement has been their statement of the cause or causes of the division made public in 1906 and on this subject the variations have been extensive. Some attention will be given to these variant explanations of the cause or causes of the division as they impinge on the background of the rupture in fellowship to be discussed in Chapters Two and Three in this work, but detailed attention to alternative views of the cause(s) and effect(s) of the division is not deemed necessary at this point in the study.

Following the direction of Barzun and Graff concerning the need to uncover the conditions which attend the emergence of historical events,[8] the writer seeks to express the conditions in which the division between churches of Christ and Christian Churches emerged. Along with West,[9] the writer believes that the most basic condition contributing to the emergent division was a profound difference of viewpoint or attitude toward the nature and application of the Bible to the life and work of the church.

This difference of viewpoint or attitude toward the Bible and its application to the church was present in and, no doubt, affected to some degree by varying social, economic, sectional, personal, and political conditions obtaining in the state at any one time or place. But it is the view of the writer that the major point of concern to and among the participants in the emerging division was doctrinal in nature. As they saw it, one group of participants believed that the perspective they held toward the Bible and its application to the church was both called in question and subverted by developments they saw emerging over several decades. The other group of participants either denied the legitimacy of the former attitude toward the nature and application of the Bible to the church or else refused to agree that said application was being subverted by themselves. In this battle over the proper viewpoint and/or its application to the church irreconcilable differences emerged and division ensued. The former participants came to be designated the churches of Christ in Tennessee and the major part of this study will discuss how they identified themselves, stabilized their movement, and made progress in the first fifty years or so which followed the division.

The primary sources for a study of churches of Christ before and after 1906 are to be found in the weekly and monthly religious papers which, generally, arose and died in a few years. A leading exception to this short lived journalistic productivity was and is the *Gospel Advocate*. Since 1855 this paper has recorded the events which affected the men and the movement in Tennessee and elsewhere. Here the leading writers practiced their craft in efforts to instruct, encourage, direct, and refute. Here controversies began, swirled, and ended. Here a man would rise to leadership, a city would become prominent, a book would be declared as urgently needed, and a school would be supported by appeals for assistance. The history of the work and impact of the *Gospel Advocate* among churches of Christ, if ever written, will surely make clear the twin functions of the editors and writers of this paper in reflecting the concerns, problems, and achievements of brethren in the state and gently but firmly nudging the people in the direction deemed best at a certain time. This reflecting and nudging, this reacting and molding, supplies the primary source material for the following study.

The pages of the *Gospel Advocate* provide the most reliable, in some instances the only, source of information for interpreting the development of churches of Christ in Tennessee from 1900 to 1950. It was to this source, through many volumes, that constant reference was made at every point of progress. Other materials—books, monographs, theses, dissertations, personal papers, and related written works—were used more as corroborative and supportive interpretations than as primary sources. Consequently, the work of the writer has been to collect, analyze, synthesize, and interpret the events and developments recorded in the pages of this paper which had and maintains a continuous history both before and after the limits set for this book. The fact that the paper not only survived but increased in reception and support throughout the period makes it clear that its columns were, in all significant areas, a reflection of and stimulus to churches of Christ in the state and elsewhere. Other papers flourished for a time but this paper, serving the needs and supporting the advancement of churches of Christ in the state, endured and thereby became and remains the chief, if not the only, source for the historian of churches of Christ in Tennessee until 1950, and, indeed, beyond that date until the present.

An analytical approach has been adopted for this study. Such an approach was suggested in part by the work of William Banowsky [10] and Stephen Eckstein [11] respectively. Banowsky discussed developments among churches of Christ in general as they were reflected in the lectureships of Abilene Christian College, Abilene, Texas, from 1918 to 1964. He isolated and integrated various doctrinal and practical concerns which were discussed in this continuing forum. Eckstein discussed the history of churches of Christ in Texas with much attention being given to their early years and particularly to their geographical expansion in the state. Attention was also called to the controversies and progress of the churches of Christ in that state. These two well done studies, with different emphases but similar interests, offer a possibly fruitful approach by means of which the history of churches of Christ in Tennessee may be interpreted.

The desire of the writer has been to reconstruct those major developments of self understanding, stabilization and progress which made possible the continuance and increase of the churches of Christ in Tennessee within the period studied. These three broad areas of self understanding, stabilization, and progress form the heart of the following work. But, it seemed necessary to present a broad background sketch of the break made public in 1906 between themselves and those generally known as the Disciples of Christ and/or the Christian Churches. This background sketch will include a short narration of the early years in the state, a discussion of the chief controversies which issued in the break, and the series of developments which culminated in the actual division in roughly 1897-1906. This preliminary background supplies the general context out of which the separate existence of churches of Christ in the state emerged. It was this emergent, separate existence which made needful the expression of self identity, the achieving of stabilization, and the continuation progress of the churches of Christ in Tennessee to 1950.

In summary, the approach will be to develop four areas of primary concern to churches of Christ in the state: The background of division, the clarification and expression of identity, the stabilization of doctrinal stance, and the continuation of progress until 1950. This broad development lies behind the progress of the discussion in the separate chapters of this book. In summary, this work shows that in the period 1900 to 1950 churches of Christ developed a pattern of clarification of identity, stabilization of doctrinal position, and continuity of progress. In this way they overcame the shock of division as it had emerged from a context earlier made manifest and a course earlier followed by leaders and members alike.

REFERENCES

[1] Herman A. Norton, *Tennessee Christians* (Nashville: Reed and Company, 1971).

[2] *Ibid.,* pp. 217-77.

[3] Winfred Ernest Garrison and Alfred T. DeGroot, *The Disciples of Christ: A History* (St. Louis: The Bethany Press, 1948).

[4] James DeForest Murch, *Christians Only* (Cincinnati: Standard Publishing Company, 1962).

[5] Earl Irvin West, *Search for the Ancient Order,* I (Nashville: The Gospel Advocate Company, 1949); II (Indianapolis: Religious Book Service, 1950). See Vol. II, pp. 449-63.

[6] Homer Hailey, *Attitudes and Consequences in the Restoration Movement* (Rosemead, California: Citizen Print Shop, Inc., 1952), pp. 239-47.

[7] David Edwin Harrell, Jr., *A Social History of Disciples of Christ,* Vol. I: *Quest for a Christian America: The Disciples of Christ and American Society to 1866* (Nashville: The Disciples of Christ Historical Society, 1966); Vol. II: *The Social Sources of Division in the Disciples of Christ, 1865-1900* (Atlanta and Athens, Georgia: Publishing Systems, Inc., 1973).

[8] Jaques Barzun and Henry F. Graff, *The Modern Researcher* (New York: Harcourt, Brace & World, Inc., 1970), pp. 169-71.

[9] West, *op. cit.,* I, p. xiii.

[10] William S. Banowsky, *The Mirror of a Movement* (Dallas: Christian Publishing Company, 1965).

[11] Stephen Daniel Eckstein, *History of Churches of Christ in Texas, 1825-1950* (Austin: Firm Foundation Publishing House, 1963).

CHAPTER ONE

EARLY YEARS IN TENNESSEE

The restoration movement in Tennessee dates from early in the nineteenth century. No one knows for certain when the first preachers came, the first converts were made, and the first churches were established. The most one is able to say with assurance is that early in the nineteenth century the work of the restorationists began.

The work of Barton W. Stone was undoubtably the leading influence in the early years. In 1796, while still a Presbyterian preacher, Stone and a man from West Tennessee made a trip into Tennessee. They travelled from Knoxville to Nashville where Stone met many acquaintances of earlier years. After a brief visit in Nashville Stone went to Kentucky.[1] Later years were to witness his great work in the Cane Ridge Meeting in 1801 and the subsequent events of his restoration efforts in Kentucky.

The biography of Stone indicated that after the death of his wife, Eliza, on May 30, 1810, he and a companion, Reuben Dooley, conducted an extensive preaching tour. Of this trip he stated: "We preached and founded churches throughout the Western States of Ohio, Kentucky and Tennessee." Later he moved from Kentucky to Tennessee and remained for some two years. Charles Ware estimated these years to have been from November 1812 to November 1814. During this time Stone lived at the Mansker Creek settlement in Sumner County, twelve miles from Nashville.[2] Because of home duties he was not able to evangelize as much as he desired. Of this period he stated: "While I was in Tennessee my field of labors in the Word was very much circumscribed, and my manual labors took up much of my time in fixing for living comfortably." [3] Nevertheless, there was apparently time for some evangelistic efforts, because in 1860 T. M. Allen told of meeting some people in Rutherford County, Tennessee who had been immersed by Stone some fifty years before.[4]

From this personal work of Stone and the efforts of those influenced by Stone, the restoration efforts began. In 1891 David Lipscomb traced the work among the churches of Christ to the efforts of Stone and those whom he had influenced. He stated:

A movement of this kind ["turning to the word of God and excluding all the opinions and inventions of men, practicing only what is plainly required in the Scriptures of truth", WW] began in Kentucky under the lead of Barton W. Stone, assisted by Rogers, Johnson, Morton, the Creaths and others. Starting from different standpoints the rule laid down brought them to see alike and made them one people. Those connected with the Stone movement first came into the mountain districts of Kentucky and Tennessee . . . These started a good distance apart, but following the same rule, they came together as one brotherhood in Christ.[5]

An interesting account of work done by Barton Stone appeared in a report of an interview which E. A. Elam conducted with Mr. Charles Ragan of Sumner County. J. W. Grant included the report in his sketch of the reformation in Tennessee. The report stated:

> Barton W. Stone preached first in the fifth civil district of Sumner County in 1811,* on the farm of H. P. Jones. From there he went immediately to the place where the little village of Roganna now stands, and preached on Bledsoe's creek, at the mouth of Dry Fork Branch. The preaching was done under an Elm and Oak . . . Stone was accompanied here by the brethren Craighead and Dodridge . . . From this place they went to where Hopewell now stands, and preached under a Beech Tree, covered with Summer Vine. Mr. Ragan says there were additions at both places, but he does not know how many . . . Mr. Ragan . . . remembers what he heard his father relate concerning this.[6]

The records do not indicate the exact time when the first churches were established. The earliest account seems to be that of the Post Oak church in Roane County. Of this church, now a Christian church, J. H. Roulhac stated that it was established by "Brother Smith and Brother Randolph" in 1813 or 1814.[7] Further details have not been preserved. The Bethlehem church in Wilson County was established in 1815[8] or 1816.[9] John Hill gave a brief history of this church in a 1903 article in the *Gospel Advocate*.[10] In the same year A. B. Cathey gave a history of the Cathey Creek church. He stated that the church was eighty or more years old, thus placing the date as 1823 or earlier.[11] Other early churches include the Liberty church in Marshall County (1823), the Roans Creek church in Carroll County (1825),[12] a church in Nashville in Davidson County (1828), a church in Adamsville in McNairy County (1829) and a church in Dyersburg in Dyer County (1829).[13]

West[14] and Norton[15] refer to several churches established in the early years. From these and others, known and unknown, the work of restoration continued. Garrison and DeGroot estimated the number of members in 1827 as 1800,[16] though their source was not given. Norton listed thirty-two churches in sixteen counties of the state in 1832. He also indicated that there were scattered churches in all three major districts of the state—West, Middle and East Tennessee.

Because of the central and strategic position of the city in political affairs and the great influence of churches and individuals within it, the cause of the restoration in Nashville deserves a brief discussion. In 1820 Jeremiah Vardeman and James Whitsett established what was known as the "Baptist Church of Nashville." This church became a member of the Concord Baptist Association but later withdrew. The first preacher, Richard Dobbs, died in 1825.[17] The next preacher was to be of significance for the restoration movement.

In 1879 P. S. Fall looked back to his early work in Kentucky and in Nashville and in these reminiscences made available much material about the work in Nashville. Fall, while a Baptist preacher in Louisville, came to know the work of Alexander Campbell in the debates with Walker and

McCalla. He also read some issues of the *Christian Baptist*. Through these works he came to be open to conviction about baptism but he was not yet ready to surrender his views. Alexander Campbell came to Louisville in November 1824 and a discussion between the two men occurred. Fall began to preach from the Bible, abandoning "the textuary system," and stood against "the doctrines of any theological school." The church in Nashville sent an invitation to Fall and, when a teaching opportunity at the Female Academy was also presented, Fall accepted it. The church was found to have members who had begun "to question the scripturalness of their denominational position, and were ready for a change." This change entailed a departure from the Concord Association because there was no authority for it in the New Testament.[18] Along with the departure from the Association there was a series of discussions about the proper course for the church to pursue. The result was a decision to reconstruct the church in accordance with the New Testament. After two years, five members, who formerly had agreed to reconstruct the church, organized themselves into a separate body and became the nucleus of the Baptist Church in Nashville. Fall remained with the larger, reconstructed membership until 1831 when his health failed and he returned to Kentucky.[19]

During Fall's first ministry in Nashville, Alexander Campbell came to the city. On Christmas Day 1831 Campbell debated Obadiah Jennings, a Presbyterian preacher, after which thirty people were baptized. Later Campbell wrote about the church in Nashville:

> This congregation is so far advanced in the reformation as to meet every Lord's day, to remember the Lord's death and resurrection, to continue in the Apostles' doctrine, in the fellowship, breaking of bread, and in prayers and praises. From its location, in the capital of the state, this society has already exerted, and is likely still to exert, a happy influence over the whole state. Like the congregation in Rome in that Empire, may their faith and piety be spoken of throughout, at least, the whole state of Tennessee.[20]

This desire for continued influence by the Nashville church was, in spite of various problems, to come to be a reality in the following years as this centrally located group of brethren preached, wrote, debated, and supported the cause in various parts of the state and elsewhere.

The growth of the cause in Tennessee was steady through the 1830's and 1840's. Norton gave a list of eighty churches in the state by 1842.[21] West gave a similar indication of progress in his treatment of the early years as he traced the work until 1848.[22] By the end of the 1840's the work was so well established that continued growth was assured.

The earliest systematic register of churches and preachers was *The Christian Register Containing a Statistical of the Christian Churches in Europe and America*, edited by Alexander Hall of Loydsville, Belmont County, Ohio in 1848. In this year a report on the Tennessee churches, as to location, number of members, and preachers, was submitted.[23] In forty eight counties of the state there were one hundred forty one churches listed. The largest number of members was five hundred in

15

Nashville, with many churches indicating a total of less than twenty. The total membership reported in the respective churches was 9,664. The preachers listed were thirty two in number.

This brief survey indicates that by 1849 the cause was well established in the state. In addition to the number of churches and members—likely more than indicated due to the inefficient methods of research and the indifference, resistance, and even opposition of many people to the whole idea of collecting statistics—the summaries by Norton,[24] Garrison and DeGroot [25] and West [26] call attention to capable preachers, religious journals, and two early colleges which greatly influenced the movement. Such men as John Mulkey, Joshua Kennerly Speer, Jesse L. Sewell, W. C. Huffman, and Tolbert Fanning carried the message through the state and into surrounding areas. In 1836 John R. Howard founded the *Christian Reformer* in Paris, Tennessee although it lasted only one year. *The Bible Advocate* was published from 1842 to 1846 by John R. Howard in Paris, Tennessee when it was moved to St. Louis.[27] In January, 1844 the *Christian Review* began in Nashville with W. H. Whorton, J. C. Anderson, and Tolbert Fanning as editors; it continued as a monthly paper until 1847.[28] In 1848 the *Christian Magazine* was begun by Tolbert Fanning and Jesse B. Ferguson. It served as a state paper until 1853 when it was terminated as a result of a controversy between Ferguson and numerous other men in the state and elsewhere, although Ferguson published the paper independently until 1855. The two educational efforts were Franklin College (1845-1866), and Burritt College (1849-1939). Franklin College [29] was founded by Tolbert Fanning and his wife, Charlotte Fall Fanning, on their farm near Nashville. More than fourteen hundred students attended the school. The Bible was taught as a textbook along with literary and practical subjects, the college program being divided into the physical, intellectual, and moral sections to accommodate such efforts. Several of the graduates were to become great leaders in the subsequent history of the church in Tennessee, but the most illustrious were to be David Lipscomb and E. G. Sewell. Burritt College [30] was begun as a civic enterprise in response to the demand for more education in the area of Spencer, Tennessee. Bible study was soon instituted by William Davis Carnes, president from 1850 to 1858 and from 1872 to 1878. The school was coeducational under Carnes and stressed scientific physical culture. The curriculum was modeled after the state university at Knoxville, along with vigorous religious and moral instruction. Various problems plagued the school, but its influence was to be felt in the training of preachers as well as civic and educational leaders.

In the year 1849 events elsewhere set in motion concerns and controversies which soon impinged on brethren in the state of Tennessee. When these problems came they were faced with strength and determination. By the year 1849 it was clear that the cause was to grow in the state, although the rigors of growth and clarification of the grounds and principles upon which growth would occur were still to be faced.

REFERENCES

[1] James R. Rogers, *The Cane Ridge Meeting-house* to which is appended the Autobiography of B. W. Stone (Cincinnati: The Standard Publishing Company, 1910), p. 191.

[2] Charles Crossfield Ware, *Barton Warren Stone* (St. Louis: The Bethany Press, 1932), p. 200.

[3] Rogers, ibid., p. 192.

[4] T. M. Allen, "Progress of Reform," *The Millennial Harbinger* 3 (August 1860):478-79.

[5] David Lipscomb, *Life and Sermons of Jesse L. Sewell* (Nashville: Gospel Advocate Company, 1891), p. 81.

[6] J. W. Grant, *A Sketch of the Reformation in Tennessee*, p. 7. This is an unpublished manuscript, the original of which is in the Tennessee State Archives. A copy was prepared by Carroll B. Ellis in 1968 and from this copy this reference is cited. [*The date 1811 may be a mistake; Ware concluded the period was 1812-1814. W.W.]

[7] J. H. Roulhac, "Tennessee," ed. John Brown, *Churches of Christ* (Louisville: John P. Norton and Company, 1904), p. 282.

[8] Herman A. Norton, *Tennessee Christians* (Nashville: Reed and Company, 1971), p. 11.

[9] Earl Irvin West, *The Search for the Ancient Order*, 1 (Nashville: Gospel Advocate Company, 1949), p. 251.

[10] John M. Hill, "History of Bethlehem Church, Wilson County, Tennessee," *Gospel Advocate* 45 (April 30, 1903):279.

[11] A. B. Cathey, "The Church at Cathey's Creek, Maury County, Tennessee," *Gospel Advocate* 45 (March 12, 1903):176.

[12] A more recent search has indicated that the Roan's Creek church likely began in 1820. William M. Pinckley, *The Story of Roan's Creek Church of Christ* (Jackson, Tennessee: Privately Published, 1975), p. 4.

[13] Norton, ibid., pp. 17, 278-79.

[14] West, ibid., pp. 251-57.

[15] Norton, ibid., pp. 278-80.

[16] Winfred Ernest Garrison and Alfred T. DeGroot, *The Disciples of Christ: A History* (St. Louis: Christian Board of Publication, 1948), p. 287.

[17] West, ibid., p. 258.

[18] West, ibid.

[19] P. S. Fall, "Interesting Reminiscences," *Gospel Advocate* 21 (May 15, 1879):310.

[20] Alexander Campbell, "The Church in Nashville," *Millennial Harbinger*, II (March 7, 1831), pp. 121-22.

[21] Norton, ibid., pp. 278-80.

[22] West, ibid., I, pp. 251-54.

[23] Alexander Hall, *The Christian Register* (Loydsville, Ohio: The Compiler, 1848), pp. 36-39.

[24] Norton, ibid., pp. 19-44.

[25] Garrison and DeGroot, ibid., pp. 287-89.

[26] West, ibid., I, pp. 251-68.

[27] Edgar Carlisle Riley, "A Classified and Annotated List of the Periodicals of the Christian Church (Disciples of Christ) Prior to 1900," (unpublished Master's Thesis, The University of Kentucky, Lexington, 1941), p. 12.

[28] Ibid., p. 33.

[29] M. Norvell Young, *A History of Colleges Established and Controlled by Members of the Churches of Christ* (Kansas City, Missouri: The Old Paths Book Club, 1949), pp. 34-52.

[30] Marion West, "Pioneer of the Cumberlands: A History of Burritt College," (unpublished Master's Thesis, Tennessee Technological University, Cookeville, 1971), pp. 2-5.

CHAPTER TWO

THE MISSIONARY SOCIETY CONTROVERSY

In 1849 an event occurred in Cincinnati, Ohio which was to be momentous for the movement to restore New Testament Christianity. In that year a missionary society was established which appealed to the churches and individuals for support in its projects of evangelism. This development presented problems of major proportions for the group and was to be one of the two most significant factors in a split which became public and final by 1906. The details of the origin and controversy which followed almost immediately have been told by various historians of the restoration movement.[1] The definitive study of the missionary society controversy, by Bill J. Humble,[2] has thoroughly detailed the background, proceedings, controversy, respective positions, and prelude of division to 1875.

The society, with a money membership fee and rather limited support from churches, began to function in 1850 by sending Dr. James T. Barclay to Jerusalem as a missionary. This was not a permanently successful effort because of the difficulty of gaining converts in Jerusalem, the indifference of support, and the opposition of determined editors and preachers. Other efforts were to prove equally disappointing for many years.[3]

The organization of the society generated a serious controversy. The arguments pro and con on the subject were to occupy the interest of the brotherhood for many years.

Defense of the Society

The case for the missionary society was argued very strongly. Three advocates, representative of others, were Alexander Campbell, W. K. Pendleton, and J. A. Minton. Alexander Campbell defended the idea of the society in the *Millennial Harbinger* from 1841 to 1848. In 1849 he began a series of articles which was to climax in the establishment of the society.[4] W. K. Pendleton delivered what was probably the most definitive defense of the society in a convention address in 1866.[5] Late in the century J. A. Minton, of Bells, Tennessee, engaged in a lengthy exchange with E. A. Elam concerning the propriety of the Tennessee missionary society.[6] In all of these defenses the same general arguments were to be found. The basic case contended that the society was merely an expedient by means of which the gospel could be preached. The propriety of expedients was demonstrated and accepted by brethren, according to the argument, by and in the use of religious papers and was clearly seen to be acceptable to God under the general authority he had given to preach the

19

gospel to the world. There was no violation of Bible authority because there was no specific plan or pattern to be followed in evangelism; consequently the principles of the Bible could not be used against the missionary society unless one argued from the silence of the scriptures. This prohibitory use of the lack of specific authority for various matters was to be a frequently repeated issue in years to come. A further defense of the society argued that it was but the implementation of the universal church in the same way that the sending of a preacher was an expression of recognized responsibility on the part of the local church. The moneyed basis of membership was a constant problem, but it was deemed necessary for fund raising. Because of opposition this basis of membership was suspended on occasion, but it was later restored. These threads, in essence, were the defense of the society.

As the years passed, the advocates of the society felt their case had been made. C. S. Loos contended in 1866 that the whole matter "was no longer a doubtful question among us," but instead it was "decided and accepted." The few who opposed had "by the unsanctified bitterness and rudeness of their attacks, given full evidence of the causes of their opposition." These causes he listed as "a lack of knowledge, of an enlightened piety or a true spiritual nature." Such men would be difficult to teach as he noted, "To attempt to teach such men is well-nigh useless, as it is almost hopeless." [7] Later in the decade appeals were made by Thomas Munnell [8] and W. K. Pendleton [9] that opponents as well as friends forget past mistakes, make any necessary changes, and all work together for more effective evangelism.

In the period from 1849 to 1875, the society advocates felt they had made their case for the scripturalness of the society. There had been some limited success, much bitter opposition, and some rather serious mistakes; but the principle or principles on which the effort rested had been, to the satisfaction of those in favor of the societies, sustained from the Bible, the history of the movement, and practical wisdom. This attitude was to bear fruit in the following decades.

Objection to the Society

There had been opposition to missionary societies in the days of the *Christian Baptist*, edited by Alexander Campbell from 1823 to 1830. Humble noted that in the first volume of the *Christian Baptist* there were seven significant articles against the societies of the prevailing religious groups.[10] Accordingly, it was no surprise that in later years much use was made of Campbell's earlier arguments against the missionary society of which he had become the first president.[11]

In the 1830s and 1840s there was considerable opposition to the societies among the denominations as well as to cooperative meetings among brethren as noted in detail by Humble.[12] In 1836 T. M. Henley of Virginia presented the plan of cooperating through a local church.[13] This plan entailed the determination to send an evangelist, the cooperation of other interested churches, oversight by the elders of the church which initiated the plan, and the freedom of all churches to assist as they desired. This plan was to be utilized in the following years as an alternative to the cooperative meetings and societies.

The strongest opposition to the society was led by Tolbert Fanning, a Tennessee preacher and editor. Although he worked in various cooperative efforts in Tennessee from 1842 to 1855, Fanning later stated that he had doubted the practical results of such efforts in the state and elsewhere but had yielded to brethren of age and experience. He indicated a change in his thinking by saying, "I should be willing to yield longer, could I conclude it would be to the honor of God." [14] His initial statement of demurrer followed a long period of questioning even while he was participating in various cooperative efforts. In 1842 he attended a meeting which had terminated with the agreement that human organizations in evangelism could not be defended. [15] In 1844 Fanning argued that the Bible contained a complete system of government for the church, challenged the validity of expedients as the result of the wisdom of men and not of God, and concluded that the churches of the apostolic age were capable of worship and service independently. [16] In 1866 he recalled that the original cooperative meeting in Tennessee in 1842 had concluded that the church was the only divinely authorized organization for Christian service and all other organizations tended to obscure, discredit, and subvert the reign of the Messiah. [17] It was clear that Fanning, while participating in certain cooperative efforts, was seriously questioning the principle on which these efforts rested. As this questioning became confirmed opposition the struggle over the missionary society began in earnest.

Fanning was joined in his opposition by such men as Jacob Creath, Jr. and David Lipscomb. Creath had opposed the societies as early as 1850 by charging that the societies represented an abandonment of the Bible alone as authority in religion. [18] After the war, David Lipscomb, who had participated for a time in cooperative efforts in Tennessee, came out in vigorous opposition to the society. He conducted a twenty article exchange with Thomas Munnell in the 1867 *Gospel Advocate.* He argued that the society basically usurped the place of God in the oversight of the church. [19] In the remaining years of the century Lipscomb was to become the recognized leader of the opposition to societies in the South, if not in the nation.

The opposition to the society was summed up in a meeting of preachers in Franklin, Tennessee in 1856. [20] As with the defense, the positions, once crystallized, did not vary much over the years. The first objection maintained that the society was without scriptural authority. The essential details such as president, secretaries, and life directors could not be found in the Bible either by precept or example. The second objection charged that the society was an indication of lack of respect for the adequacy of the church to do what God had given the church to do. The

21

church was to be the means of evangelizing the world and was sufficient to do this work. In short, the society depended on man's presumption of the right to substitute human plans for divine plans, i.e., the society was a substitute for the church as the God given means to evangelize the world. To the degree that the society succeeded the church was disregarded and relegated to a secondary place of influence. A third objection asserted that the society would become a giant ecclesiasticism which would jeopardize the freedom and autonomy of the local churches. The defenders of the societies retorted that this objection was not justified by principle or example of such usurpation and threat, but the opponents claimed that examples of such infringement were not only present in the workings of the society but such infringement was inherently necessary for the society to carry out its stated objectives. A fourth objection contended that the society was a virtual repudiation of the plea of the movement to follow the Bible in all matters. This corollary of the first objection gained strength by noting the changes Alexander Campbell's thought from the *Christian Baptist* days until the origin of the society in 1850.[21] The fifth objection proclaimed that the money basis of membership was such that Jesus and the apostles, as well as the average Christian, could not be a member of the group. This somewhat emotional objection had a telling effect as evidenced by the decision in 1868 to abandon for a time the money basis for membership, although this plan was later reinstituted.

The Louisville Plan

The opening of the decade of the 1870s saw an attempt by the missionary society advocates to effect a change in the society which would, hopefully, reduce opposition and secure adequate assistance. By 1869 the society situation had become most discouraging for its upholders. In a meeting in Louisville, October 19-21, 1869, a revision was made in the whole organizational structure of the society. The new proposal, called the Louisville plan, consisted of national, state, and district organizations. A general board and secretary on the national, state, and district levels were to have responsibility for oversight and fund raising. One half of the district funds were to be sent to the state board, which would retain one half received and send one half to the national board. This series of changes made necessary a rewriting of the society's constitution and ended the American Christian Missionary Society so as to create the General Christian Missionary Society.[22] No southern state, except Kentucky, was included in a list of the state conventions which by 1870 had ratified the new arrangements.[23] The period from 1869 to 1875 was one of continued opposition, particularly from Tennessee, and of lack of support. The reports over the years showed that the new plan would not succeed. The problems and uncertainties of the venture prompted David Lipscomb in 1874 to observe that in missionary work "the *Advocate* has been right from the beginning." [24] By the latter part of the year 1874 it was admitted by even its most staunch supporters that the Louisville plan had failed.

The meeting of supporters in Louisville in 1875 revised the constitution so as to allow for a foreign missionary society on the same basic pattern as that on which the American Christian Missionary Society had been established in 1849. The earlier shift from an individual to a church convention arrangement was reversed. The Foreign Christian Missionary Society also returned, after rescinding the practice for a time, to the money basis for life directors, life members, and annual members. This new arrangement proved to be most successful. The Louisville plan in its years of operation had barely raised enough to pay its overhead, but the new arrangement produced an annual excess of some $25,000 for the first eight years of its existence.[25]

This new development in the society arrangement also ushered in a new attitude toward opposition. Quoting from the *Report of Proceedings,* 1873, Humble referred to the presidential address of R. M. Bishop who observed that the opposition could not be conciliated, indeed nothing would satisfy them. Admitting that previous years had seen only limited results, Bishop contended that things had changed, every strategic point was held by society men, and there was no longer a need to wait for others to cooperate.[26] By 1875 society supporters were no longer willing to wait for their opponents of the past twenty five years to change. Instead, the Foreign Christian Missionary Society was organized and those who wished could support it, all others could do as they saw fit. The summary by Humble stated the matter clearly,

> Actually, when the Foreign Missionary Society was organized, it was an admission that compromise had failed, that the progressives were determined to brush aside the critics, and that division among the northern Christians was now inevitable. The crucible of division was filled with every essential ingredient except one—time.[27]

The course of the next quarter century which supplied the final ingredient, time, may be traced in the subsequent history as West [28] and others have done until 1906. West observed that the brotherhood was divided on fundamental issues by 1875 and the subsequent years witnessed "an era when congregations, preachers, and members were lining themselves up on one side or another." [29] This lining up on one side or the other may be traced in the movement toward division in Tennessee in succeeding chapters.

REFERENCES

[1] Earl Irvin West, *Search for the Ancient Order,* 1 (Nashville: The Gospel Advocate Company, 1949), pp. 149-227; Winfred Ernest Garrison, *Religion Follows the Frontier* (New York: Harper and Brothers publishers, 1931), p. 238; Winfred Ernest Garrison and Alfred T. DeGroot, *The Disciples of Christ: A History* (St. Louis: Christian Board of Publication, 1948), pp. 350-51.

[2] Bill J. Humble, "The Missionary Society Controversy in the Restoration Movement (1823-1875)," (Ph.D. dissertation, The State University of Iowa, 1964).

[3] West, ibid., pp. 215-17.

[4] Alexander Campbell, "Church Organization—No. 1," *Millennial Harbinger* 20 (February 1849):90.

[5] W. K. Pendleton, "Address Delivered at the Eighteenth Anniversary of the American Christian Missionary Society," *Millennial Harbinger* 37 (November 1866):494-514.

[6] Anonymous, "The Elam-Minton Discussion," *Gospel Advocate* 39 (March 4, 1897):130. The discussion continued through the rest of the year.

[7] C. S. Loos, "Ohio Missionary Meeting," *Millennial Harbinger* 37 (June 1866):274-75.

[8] Thomas Munnell, "Untying the Missionary Knot, No. I and II," *Millennial Harbinger* 39 (August 1868):459-64.

[9] W. K. Pendleton, "Remarks," *Millennial Harbinger,* 39 (August 1868):464-65.

[10] Humble, ibid., p. 39.

[11] David Lipscomb, "Solid Thoughts by Earnest Men," *Gospel Advocate* 26 (April 23, 1884):262.

[12] Humble, ibid., pp. 53-69.

[13] T. M. Henley and Robert Richardson, "Cooperation of Churches," *Millennial Harbinger* 7 (July 1836):333-34.

[14] Tolbert Fanning, "Co-Operation," *Gospel Advocate* 1 (October 1855):110.

[15] J. K. Speer, "Human Organizations and the Gospel Advocate," *Gospel Advocate* 7 (August 1860):225.

[16] Tolbert Fanning, "Church Organization," *The Christian Review* 1 (February 1844):27-28.

[17] Tolbert Fanning, "The Path of Safety," *Gospel Advocate* 8 (February 6, 1866):82.

[18] Jacob Creath, "Conventions—No. IV," *Millennial Harbinger* 7 (November 1850):615.

[19] David Lipscomb, "Discussion—Missionary Societies," *Gospel Advocate* 9 (March 14, 1866):208.

[20] J. J. Trott, S. E. Jones, and F. M. Carmack, "Report of the Consultation Meeting at Franklin, Embracing the Second Lord's Day in April, 1856," *Gospel Advocate* 2 (June 1856):182-83.

[21] Humble, ibid., p. 146.

[22] Ibid., pp. 281-87.

[23] Ibid., p. 292.

[24] David Lipscomb, "The Louisville Plan," *Gospel Advocate* 16 (November 12, 1874):1064-68.

[25] Humble, ibid., p. 322.

[26] Ibid., pp. 323-24.

[27] Ibid., p. 326.

[28] West, ibid., 2, pp. 92-112, 430-48.

[29] Ibid., p. 112.

CHAPTER THREE

THE INSTRUMENTAL MUSIC CONTROVERSY IN EARLY YEARS

Two major controversies, along with minor ones, prepared the way for the rupture of fellowship which was made public among churches of Christ in Tennessee in 1906. The missionary society controversy erupted prior to the instrumental music issue, but this latter controversy during the latter part of the nineteenth and the early part of the twentieth century has received the greater amount of attention from various writers. This greater attention was apparently due to the fact that the problems posed by the controversy were immediately obvious in the churches and the use or non-use of the instrument thereby became most urgent.

A survey of various historians makes it clear that the instrumental music controversy was of utmost significance. In his study of the grounds of division A. T. DeGroot declared that the introduction of instrumental music in worship was the chief recognizable difference between the two groups in the division of 1906.[1] Garrison and DeGroot gave much the same evaluation.[2] West devoted large sections of his two volume work to this subject.[3] Murch gave attention to the controversy,[4] though not so extensively as did West. Thrasher discussed the controversy from 1850 to 1906.[5] Herman Norton regarded the controversy as "far more relevant than the 'Society' question in Tennessee." [6] Harrell discussed the controversy in a summary chapter.[7] The following treatment reflects these studies as well as the use of articles of significance as the controversy developed.

Early Notice of Instrumental Music

In 1851 a correspondent named "W" wrote to J. B. Henshall, associate editor of the *Ecclesiastical Reformer* (Harrodsburg, Kentucky, 1848-1852) posing the question, "What say you of instrumental music in our churches?" He observed that the brethren were "far in the rear of Protestants on the subject of church music," felt that the use of such musical instruments would add greatly to the solemnity of the worship, thought that the hearts of the saints would thereby be raised to a "higher state of devotion," and admonished that it was "high time that we awaken to the importance of the subject." [8] Henshall replied that "helps to their devotion" were only necessary when men became worldly minded, had lost their fear of God, had no gratitude to God for the new dispensation of Christ, and were unworthy of the benefits available thereby.[9]

A few articles on the subject were written over the years. John Rogers wondered if the effect of a quarter of a century of work had been to introduce instruments into the worship.[10] Alexander Campbell observed that such music was as appropriate to "spiritually minded Christians" as would be "a cow bell in a concert." [11]

These articles indicated an awareness of the presence of instrumental music in religious services as well as a desire for such use among the reformers, but there was a general opposition to such practice, limited as it was, and a general resistance to its use because it was judged to be incompatible with the spirit and objective of the movement.

The Instrumental Music Controversy in Early Years

An editorial war over the instrument began after Benjamin Franklin wrote that where a church had lost the Spirit of Christ, where the preacher was incapable of commanding and interesting an audience, and where a church sought to be a fashionable society or place of amusement while abandoning all idea of religion and worship, "instrumental music would be a very pleasant and agreeable part of such entertainment." [12] In response L. L. Pinkerton indicated that so far as he knew he was the only preacher in the brotherhood in Kentucky who "has publicly advocated the propriety of employing instrumental music in some churches," and that the Midway church was the only one that had made "a decided effort to introduce it." [13] He protested against the harsh words of Franklin, indicated his disapproval of one who pronounced such condemnations "on account of a difference of opinion as to what is expedient in a community of which the denounced is a part," and affirmed his willingness to discuss the subject of instrumental music in worship "with any man who can discriminate between railing in bad grammar and Christian argumentation." [14]

In 1863 a man from St. Louis told that a church in that city had purchased a building containing an organ although it had not been used in worship. He indicated that larger churches, as in Cincinnati and New York, were using the organ, but the question had not arisen in St. Louis at that time. [15] Ben Franklin responded that the organ was advantageous where the church had lost its spirituality, the preacher was not competent, and the purpose was to entertain. Joseph Smith replied that while he did not advocate the use of the instrument in worship, he felt that the Book of Psalms allowed such use and certainly would be against the harsh tones of Franklin as revealed in his article. [16] Franklin replied that the use of Psalms would also allow dancing and polygamy and observed that the present dispensation entailed a better covenant under which worship was to be in spirit and in truth. He summed up his case in these words,

> The difference between instrumental music and singing with the human voice, in the worship of Christians, is simply that the latter is authorized in the Christian Scriptures and the former is not. We go for what is authorized and not for what is not. [17]

In March 1864 Moses Lard entered the battle. Never one to avoid plain words, Lard stated that the principle on which the movement rested was that of accepting the New Testament as the standard for "the smallest point of doctrine" and "the most trivial feature in practice." Warming to his subject, he stated, "To warrant the holding of a doctrine or practice it must be shown that it has the affirmative or positive sanction of this standard, and not merely that it is not condemned by it." In the light of this he asked, ". . . what defense can be urged for the introduction into some of our congregations of instrumental music?" He replied, "The answer which thunders into my ear from every page of the New Testament is, none." [18] He counseled that no preacher should enter a meetinghouse where an organ stood, urged that no member should unite with such a group, and declared his own intention as to "organ grinding churches." He stated, "I have no sympathy with them, no fellowship for them, and so help me God never intend knowingly to put my foot into one of them." [19]

In the latter part of 1864, J. W. McGarvey plead for a full discussion of the subject. He recalled that earlier years had seen unanimity in rejecting the use of the instrument because it was unscriptural, not in harmony with the Christian institution, and a source of corruption. But he claimed that now an attempt was being made to introduce the instrument into churches. He plead, "Let us, then, have the question fully discussed and finally settled." He then responded to the argument supporting the use of instruments from the Jewish worship. He noted the difference between the Jewish and Christian dispensations, claimed this must be respected, and concluded that this distinction would show the fault of the argument for instrumental music since it would also prove, if valid, the use of incense, candles, and priestly robes.[20] A. S. Hayden claimed McGarvey's argument was inadequate although he personally did not advocate the use of the instrument in worship. He also challenged the view that the silence of the New Testament as to instrumental music was an indication that God condemned the use of the instrument.[21] These two men continued to exchange articles on the subject for several months.

The exchanges were resumed between J. W. McGarvey and A. S. Hayden in 1868 when, after the battle had temporarily ended, Hayden wrote that expediency and progress sustained the use of the instrument. He lamented a pamphlet which sought to prove that instrumental music in the churches was a violation of the gospel by referring to Jude 3. He then stated that improvement should come in church music. His words were:

> Our church music is below the standard of the times. No one is censurable for doing the best he can, if he works in humility. Our general standard and style of tunes is too low—we have too many tunes that are light and fugitive, caught up from social circles and secular associations. They served, perhaps, well for the time. But we are fast passing on by them. A new and better taste is gaining the ascendant. Our psalmody is purified and augmented. Let our music be brought up to a corresponding degree of improvement.[22]

McGarvey read this article and stated that he found "a most painful antagonism between my soul, and the purpose for which the article named was written." He then observed that, "This question of instrumental music is becoming a serious one." After noting the cry of expediency and progress, for the instrument as well as such items as pew renting, dancing, and theatre going, McGarvey focused on this topic of expediency. His words were carefully chosen as he stated,

> . . . you know that such are the convictions of a very large number of the best and most intelligent class of your brethren, that they will resist to the very last extremity the introduction of instrumental music in the worship, and that they will never, while they live, permit it to rest anywhere in peace. Such being the case, how can you, in the light of apostolic teaching, press the innovation in the manner you do? . . . Do you say that you are under no more obligation to yield than they? You cannot, because you are urging an *innovation*, one which you confess the Scriptures do not authorize, and which, therefore, you cannot feel bound in conscience to maintain. Your only ground of defense is the expediency of it, and the assumption that our religion is flexible enough to receive it. If your religion is thus flexible, why must it all the time bend toward those corrupt parties who invented and have hitherto exclusively used the organ, yet remain as stiff as a crowbar against your own brethren who oppose it? [23]

Hayden responded that although he was not an advocate of the instrument in worship, he was troubled by brethren who sought to make the use of such music "an integral part of the great and mighty plea for the restoration of primitive Christianity." He stated his concern in these words,

> Assuming it as ranking among questions of faith and apostolic teaching, it then stands among questions of duty and of Christian fellowship. This granted, it becomes a cause of dissension and dismemberment in all our churches. Seeing all this, and as I love the purity and the peace of the churches, my back is not supple enough, nor my knee limber enough to permit willingly this high crime to come upon us through the artifices and plausibilities of specious and inconclusive logic. Now in respect to this view of the nature of this question, viz., that it belongs to the realm of the proprieties and the expediencies of the kingdom, and not to the domain of its laws,—I may be in error, and I may not. But surely Lexington is not so astute (sic) as to be unable to understand me, nor so wanting in candor as to refuse me justice. [24]

Here then the issue was clearly joined. McGarvey saw the matters involved as those of the faith and laws of the reign of God; Hayden saw them as matters of propriety and expediency which were being elevated to the sphere of law and doctrine by specious and inconclusive logic. Later years were to see those two positions expanded and argued at great length, but the positions around which the subsequent controversy would turn were present by 1870.

The Instrumental Music Controversy in Tennessee

Norton surveyed the instrumental music controversy in Tennessee in its early years. He concluded that it was a far more relevant problem in the state than the missionary society and observed that it brought vir-

28

tually every member of the church to an hour of decision.[25] In the earlier years, 1860-1869, there was little said about the instrument in Tennessee churches although the swirling controversy was not lost to the readers of the various papers which circulated in the state. In 1869, David Lipscomb indicated his awareness of the controversy when he wrote concerning some articles in the *Christian Quarterly,*

> The direct effort is to cast approbrium upon every man who contends for faithful adherence to the teaching of the Lord, and who opposes innovations such as the substitution of hired machine music for the Christian's teaching, and admonishing one another in psalms, and hymns, and spiritual songs . . . All those who protest against these things are stigmatized in the Quarterly as "fools," "Pharisees," "theological constables," and "dirty harpies," beside quite a formidable list of other ugly names.[26]

As the century progressed the developments in Tennessee were to become of more significance and the leading paper, the *Gospel Advocate,* was to be not only a state but national voice which called for opposition to the use of the instrument.

Norton dated the first use of the instrument in worship within the restoration movement in the state in the summer of 1869 in Memphis when a small organ was purchased so that services would match the new and tasteful edifice. In 1883, when a carpet was installed and cushions were added for the seats, a more expensive organ was purchased. In 1887 a pipe organ, costing $1,200, was installed.[27]

The relative absence of instrumental music among the churches in Tennessee is made evident in a report about a preaching tour conducted by J. M. Barnes. In 1875 he concluded a seven weeks' tour among churches in Tennessee. In recounting his impressions of the tour, Barnes discussed singing, congregational improvement, and the need to teach the brethren how to sing better. He indicated the absence of instrumental music in worship and expressed his disfavor of its use. Concerning the use of notes in song btoks he wrote: "Whilst I can sing any kind, I would be glad if there was but one kind of notes. Instruments I know require round notes (it is not absolutely necessary) but there is no instrument in the church of God." Also he stated the need to have clear and distinct articulation in singing. His words were:

> If singing is designed to edify, teach and admonish, it should be done so that every word may be heard distinctly. If fine sound is all that is necessary, then there would be some reason for introducing the organ or the fiddle. For God has a place for his songs, and no human inventions take their place.[28]

His position was clear, and the status of the churches was one which reflected no widespread use of the instrument in worship.

Herman Norton stated concerning the restoration movement that prior to 1890 the only churches in Tennessee which were using the instrument were Clarksville, Knoxville, Henderson, Woodland Street and the Second church in Nashville, and Memphis. However, one must note that even though the use was not widespread, the introduction of the instrument in each case had occasioned controversy.[29] The general pattern of difficulty over the instrument was one of introduction, controversy, struggle for control, and eventual separation by the losing group in the struggle. In a note concerning those who gained control of property after these disputes Norton stated the rationale for such acquisition in these words, "Of course, when a feeling existed that innovations were sinful, there was nothing else to do but withdraw."[30] This pattern of introducing the instrument and acquiring property was repeated in Tennessee in such places as Pulaski in 1902,[31] Henderson in 1903,[32] and Tullahoma in 1906.[33]

The controversy over the use of the instrument was slowly gaining intensity in Tennessee. There was a consciousness of the issue from the beginning, but the problem posed thereby was not as yet great enough for a rupture in fellowship.

REFERENCES

[1] Alfred Thomas DeGroot, *The Grounds of Divisions Among the Disciples of Christ* (Chicago: Privately Published, 1940), p. 91.

[2] Winfred Ernest Garrison and Alfred T. DeGroot, *The Disciples of Christ: A History* (St. Louis: Christian Board of Publication, 1948), pp. 343-48.

[3] Earl Irvin West, *Search for the Ancient Order,* 1 (Nashville: The Gospel Advocate Company, 1949), pp. 306-17; 2 (Indianapolis: Religious Book Service, 1950), pp. 73-92, 430-48.

[4] James DeForest Murch, *Christians Only* (Cincinnati: Standard Publishing Company, 1962), pp. 8157-63.

[5] Byron Thrasher, "A History of the Instrumental Music Controversy During the Nineteenth Century Restoration Movement," (M.A. thesis, Harding College, 1956).

[6] Herman A. Norton, *Tennessee Christians* (Nashville: Reed and Company, 1971), pp. 157-64.

[7] David Edwin Harrell, Jr. *A Social History of Disciples of Christ,* 2 vols. *The Social Sources of Division in the Disciples of Christ, 1865-1900* (Atlanta and Athens, Georgia: Publishing Systems, Inc., 1973) 2:3-16.

[8] "W" and J. B. Henshall, "Instrumental Music," *Ecclesiastical Reformer* 4 (March 15, 1851):171.

[9] Ibid.

[10] John Rogers, "Dancing," *Millennial Harbinger* 1 (August 1851):467-68.

[11] Alexander Campbell, "Instrumental Music," *Millennial Harbinger* 1 (October 1851):582.

[12] Ben Franklin, "Instrumental Music in Churches," *American Christian Review* 3 (January 31, 1860):19.

[13] L. L. Pinkerton, "Instrumental Music in Churches," *American Christian Review* 3 (February 28, 1860):34.

[14] Ibid.

[15] W. H. P., "Answer to a Query of a Young Disciple in St. Louis," *American Christian Review* 6 (November 24, 1863):185. Quoted by Thrasher, ibid., p. 28.

[16] Joseph Smith, "Review of Franklin's Article on Instrumental Music," *American Christian Review* 6 (October 6, 1863):158. Quoted by Thrasher, ibid., p. 29.

[17] Ben Franklin, "No Title," *American Christian Review* 6 (October 6, 1863):152. Quoted by Thrasher, ibid., p. 30.

[18] Moses E. Lard, "Instrumental Music in Churches and Dancing," *Lard's Quarterly* 1 (March 1864):330-31.

[19] Ibid., p. 333.

[20] J. W. McGarvey, "Instrumental Music in Churches," *Millennial Harbinger* 7 (November 1864):510.

[21] A. S. Hayden, "Instrumental Music," *Millennial Harbinger* 36 (January 1865):38-40. Quoted by Thrasher, ibid., p. 42.

[22] A. S. Hayden, "Expediency and Progress," *Millennial Harbinger* 39 (March 1868):135-44, 141,142.

[23] J. W. McGarvey, "Bro. Hayden on Expediency and Progress," *Millennial Harbinger* 39 (April 1868):217.

[24] A. S. Hayden, "Reply to Brother McGarvey," *Millennial Harbinger,* XXXIX (June 1868, p. 330.

[25] Norton, ibid., p. 157.

[26] David Lipscomb, "Christian Quarterly," *Gospel Advocate,* 11 (April 29, 1869):394-95.

[27] Norton, ibid., p. 160.

[28] J. M. Barnes, "Away up in Tennessee. No. 12," *Gospel Advocate* 17 (April 15, 1875):367,368.

[29] Norton, ibid., p. 164.

[30] Ibid., p. 215.

[31] E. A. Elam, "More of Myhr's Work," *Gospel Advocate* 45 (February 26, 1903):129.

[32] E. A. Elam, "A Meeting at Henderson, Tennessee," *Gospel Advocate* 45 (February 5, 1903):81-82.

[33] Anonymous, "Miscellany," *Gospel Advocate* 48 (January 4, 1906):5.

31

CHAPTER FOUR

PROGRESSION OF DAVID LIPSCOMB TOWARD DIVISION

The two controversies over the missionary society and instrumental music in worship contained the elements of division from the beginning. At first some were aware and some were not aware of this potential separation. As early as 1856 James Warren observed, "It appears to me that a foundation is laying by some of the brethren that may finally produce a division among us." [1] In 1861 William Lipscomb gave his view that, ". . . our brethren are still united and must remain so as long as they are content to adhere faithfully to the simple order of Heaven. . . . Attempts at consolidation alone can give any place for division." [2] These foreshadowings, with the fact of and conditions requisite for division set forth, were to become most significant as the century continued. In spite of such denials of the possibility of division as Moses Lard gave,[3] an eventual rupture was to come.

The process of division has been frequently discussed among historians of the movement. The standard histories by Garrison and DeGroot, Murch, and West have been noted previously. More recent historians, such as Norton, Harrell, and Murrell[4] have also been concerned with this area of study. It is worthy of note that two somewhat valuable contributions have been made by the more recent historians. First, while Harrell noted that "the division resulted from a profound theological rupture in the movement," he also called attention to such related factors as sectional, economic, and social conditions which in varying degrees provided something of a context in which the issues were discussed.[5] Second, Murrell called attention to the fact that the leading advocates of the views held by churches of Christ frequently were moderate and patient in this period of intense controversy.[6] The sharp exchange of views often hid from readers the fact that in spite of the differences there was a long period of editorial reluctance and resistance which transpired before the break eventually came. One may disagree as to the relative extent of each of these two factors, but the literature shows that both of these elements are of significance in the emerging division. The present work reflects an awareness of these historical works and seeks to utilize insights gained from each.

In Tennessee the same brotherhood elements were at work as elsewhere, both of cohesion and rupture, and the course of division may be traced in the state as well as the nation. In the gradual process of division it became increasingly apparent that extremists of either side of the issues were not to dominate the thinking of most Tennesseans. Instead, the dominant position was one of patience, caution, and reluctance. It was also evident that at some point, when patience and appeal offered no further hope of unity, there was to be a firm but reluctant acceptance of the fact of irreconcilable differences which made further unity impossible. This torturous path of gradual recognition and acceptance of inevitable division may be traced in the progress of David Lipscomb toward division.

David Lipscomb (1831-1917), one of the five most prominent leaders in the restoration movement in the last third of the nineteenth century,[7] became prominent in the early years after the Civil War as the organizer of a major effort to assist churches and individuals in the South to recover from the war.[8] He steadily progressed in influence as the editor of the *Gospel Advocate,* reissued in 1866 after an interruption during the war, and by this editorship became the most influential leader in Tennessee immediately before the division which was made public in 1906. In his writings during this period a steady progress can be traced in reacting to the missionary society, instrumental music, and what he considered related issues.

In all his efforts, David Lipscomb sought to be honest and hold to his convictions, but he came to his convictions slowly. In the process of such development of convictions he regarded exchanges with opposing positions as valuable and necessary, but observed that differences and controversies should not necessarily alienate brethren.[9] Looking back in 1903 he observed that he had changed over the years as he had thought about music and the societies but regarded this as the rightful course for a thinking man.[10] He was a man who thought deeply before taking a position, but once reached, the position became a stubbornly defended view to be given up only after full response and exposure as erroneous. This attitude characterized his views on the society and instrumental music problems, and was to be reflected in his editorial labors and personal conduct toward fellowship in the latter part of the century.

David Lipscomb was convinced the society was not proper by 1866 and argued against it in a series of ten exchanges with Thomas Munnell of Kentucky in the *Gospel Advocate* of 1867.[11] As noted perviously, he had protested in 1869 against the slurs cast by instrumental music advocates upon those who objected. But, he was not prepared to draw lines of fellowship on the issues in 1871. In that year he commented on the editorial policy of the *American Christian Review* and *Apostolic Times* which urged brethren to withdraw and not worship where the organ was used. He stated,

> While we condemn the organ certainly as wrong, unauthorized and corrupting, we have never decided it is a Christian's duty to go to this extremity . . . so we hesitate, while we heartily and earnestly condemn the innovation as at once the outgrowth and promoter of evil.[12]

In the 1870s David Lipscomb became more convinced that what was being done by the societies was not right and that instrumental music should not be accepted. Of the Louisville Plan, noted previously, he stated, "We feel sure that thousands of good brethren all over the country feel just as I do, that it is anti-scriptural, in organization, subversive of the work and organization of the churches, inefficient in operation and corrupting in influence." [13] Later in the same year, in commenting on a statement of Moses Lard that the plan should be given a chance on the basis of expediency, Lipscomb made clear his concern for authority rather than expediency. His note also indicated the similarity between instrumental music and the society, an equation to be most significant later.

> It is seen there the ground upon which the Louisville Plan is placed by him. "It is wholly unknown to the New Testament." It is neither required or sanctioned! We confess our surprise to see Brother Lard accept an institution in the kingdom of God on such ground. He opposes instrumental music. It rests on precisely the same ground. It is neither required or sanctioned by the New Testament. [14]

In 1878 David Lipscomb came out forcefully against the instrument in worship. [15] Admitting that he had said little on the subject during the controversy over the years, he remarked that he had not been indifferent to the issue but had "wished to weigh" the matter well before he spoke. He recognized the appeal of the instrument in worship and admitted that if judgement alone were enough to adopt the practice he would not object. However, noting the use of instrumental music in the Old Testament and the absence of it in the New Testament he concluded that the use of the instrument was an indication that the "heart worship of Christ" had to be given up for the "formalism of Judaism" in order to allow for instruments in worship. The nature of worship in the respective periods was such that instrumental music was not present in the New Testament period and should be omitted in subsequent worship of the church. This was to remain his basic position and its application became most important in later years.

As was noted earlier, in 1879 Lipscomb gave an indication of the intensity of his feeling when he commented on a difficulty which had arisen in Bowling Green, Kentucky over the introduction of the instrument. The lengthy quotation gives clear evidence of all major elements of the problem and serves as an index of Lipscomb's thought.

> Men who have nothing, save what they receive from God will have no grounds or occasion for difference. But when men introduce what they did not receive of God, into the church then they give occasion of difference, introduce strife and originate parties in the church of God. They do it contrary to the word of God.
>
> A man who by introducing something not required by God, drives out from the church of God men and women willing to do the whole will of God—divides that church simply by refusing to be led by God, to walk by his law, his rule, by giving offence contrary to the word of God. Such a man is a schismatic—a producer of schism and strife in the church of God. He is a heretic, a schismatic. Heresy is the foundation of schism and division. A heretic is a promoter or causer of division.

Now, regard the question of the introduction of the organ as you may, unless it be regarded as an absolute requirement of God and a sin to leave it out of the worship, he who by introducing it, causes a division, a strife, a party in the church of God, drives off brethren that are willing to do the whole will of God, tramples under foot the prayer of the Savior, turns a deaf ear to all the admonitions, warnings, entreaties of the Holy Spirit and divides those whom he died to make one. He in this despises the blood of Christ—he prefers the gratification and triumphs of his own views of expediency and his pride of position to the unity of the body of Christ. He causes division and strife contrary to the tradition received from Paul or the Holy Spirit. He is a heretic. The sin here is unmistakable. It is not a question of the right or wrong of instrumental music. We might worship with a man, who believes this admissible. But when a man is willing to sunder and divide the church of the living God upon what he claims, to be only an admissible human expedient, the crime against the church of God, and against God himself is greatly increased in enormity. . . . No man ever received a tradition or commandment from the Apostles to introduce an organ into the church of God, and he who divides the church of God for the sake of it, walks disorderly, and Christians are commanded to withdraw themselves *from every such brother.*

Leaving out of question then the admissability of instrumental music in the worship of God, if there is a coloring of truth in the report given of the proceedings of the church at Bowling Green, the preacher has been guilty of causing divisions in the church of God, not in order to sustain any truth or ordinance of the Lord. It is as high crime against God as man can commit. It is the duty of Christians there and elsewhere to avoid, to withdraw themselves from him while causing these divisions. If we intend to be Christians, we must acknowledge the laws and authority of God by obedience to his commandments and institutions.

We have written lengthily on this question as given above. We know of the ADVOCATE. We have tried patiently and faithfully to see and point out the wrongs of the church and the preacher, that brought about the difficulty. There are others that we have not mentioned, but those we present seem to us the chief and leading wrongs.[16]

The missionary society issue became more intense in 1879 when the church in Knoxville gave five dollars to the Foreign Christian Missionary Society, the first contribution to a society by a church in the state.[17] The following years saw more and more of the churches participating in the support of the Foreign Christian Missionary Society. In 1884, out of $26,601 received by the society, Tennessee churches gave $223; in 1888, $775 out of $62,767 to the society came from Tennessee churches. By 1889 all of the urban churches, except one in Nashville and one in Chattanooga, had endorsed the society.[18] It was becoming apparent that the society advocates were gaining some ground in the state in the decade of the 1880s.

It was also apparent, as noted previously, that by the early 1880s the society advocates had resolved to go on with their plans regardless of the objections by others. This attitude and the success attendant on the efforts in the period by society personnel made it clear, in Tennessee as

36

well as elsewhere, that two ideas were present in the brotherhood and that they could not long remain in close fellowship. In 1880 John F. Rowe summarized the situation in a clear fashion,

> We are grieved to say that the line of separation is becoming more distinct every day. There are two classes among us—those who represent "The Ancient Order of Things" and those who represent "The New Order of Things." It is manifest that these two parties are not only not acting in sympathy, but that the men of the New Order of Things are determined to crush down, if possible, the Ancient Order of Things.[19]

As the decade closed, E. G. Sewell contended that if the society advocates wanted to get started in Tennessee, they should go into new areas of the state and establish churches rather than seeking to obtain support for the societies among churches which had been established earlier without society help. He charged that the alternative of invasion was causing discord, confusion, and strife.[20]

By the year 1890 there was a serious problem of contention and strife over the society, and to some extent over the use of the instrument in worship. The next few years were to trace the last steps to divison, but the factors which would produce inevitable separation were already present. During this period of the 1880s the churches had enjoyed steady growth as noted by Norton. He observed that there were 106 congregations with 12,285 members in 1860, but the number increased to 203 congregations with 19,425 members by 1870 while in 1890 the number was 41,125 members in 322 congregations.[21] These numbers were arranged, according to Norton, in opposing camps but they had not yet gone down separate roads.[22] No doubt, David Lipscomb was aware of these developments, but he was not yet willing to see the churches in Tennessee become divided over the issues in controversy. He was to await further developments before becoming embroiled in the dreaded rupture of fellowship.

REFERENCES

[1] James R. Warren, "The Sufficiency of the Church," *Gospel Advocate* 3 (February 1857):50.

[2] William Lipscomb, "The Duty of the Hour," *Gospel Advocate* 8 (March 1861):82-85.

[3] Moses E. Lard, "Can We Divide?" *Lard's Quarterly* 3 (April 1866):335.

[4] Arthur Van Murrell, "The Effects of Exclusivism in the Separation of the Churches of Christ from the Christian Church" (Ph.D. dissertation, Vanderbilt University, 1972).

[5] David Edwin Harrell, Jr., *A Social History of Disciples of Christ*, 2 vols. *The Social Sources of Divison in the Disciples of Christ*, 1865-1900 (Atlanta and Athens, Georgia: Publishing Systems, Inc., 1973) 2:7.

[6] Murrell, ibid., pp. 121-22; 167-78; 209-22.

[7] William E. Tucker, *J. H. Garrison and Disciples of Christ* (St. Louis: Bethany Press, 1964), p. 18.

[8] Earl Irvin West, *The Life and Times of David Lipscomb* (Henderson, Tennessee: Religious Book Service, 1954), pp. 113-19.

[9] David Lipscomb, "Differences Between Brethren," *Gospel Advocate* 12 (November 18, 1869): 1065-67.

[10] David Lipscomb, "Lipscomb Squelched by the Lawyers," *Gospel Advocate* 45 (July 2, 1903):424.

[11] Bill J. Humble, "The Missionary Society Controversy in the Restoration Movement (1823-1875)" (Ph.D. dissertation, The State University of Iowa, 1964), pp. 252-61.

[12] David Lipscomb, "Piece of News," *Gospel Advocate* 13 (March 23, 1871):277.

[13] David Lipscomb, "Mississippi and Louisville Plan," *Gospel Advocate* 13 (January 12, 1871):38.

[14] David Lipscomb, "Louisville Plan," *Gospel Advocate* 13 (September 15, 1871):845.

[15] David Lipscomb, "Instrumental Music in Worship," *Gospel Advocate* 20 (August 29, 1878):551.

[16] David Lipscomb, "Church Difficulty," *Gospel Advocate* 21 (May 1, 1879):277-79.

[17] Herman A. Norton, *Tennessee Christians* (Nashville: Reed and Company, 1971), p. 174.

[18] Ibid., p. 175.

[19] John F. Rowe, "The Old and the New Order," *American Christian Review* 23 (March 30, 1880):100.

[20] E. G. Sewell, "A False Charge," *Gospel Advocate* 31 (November 6, 1889):711.

[21] Norton, ibid., pp. 147, 187.

[22] Ibid., p. 165.

CHAPTER FIVE

OTHER DEVELOPMENTS AND ISSUES LEADING TO DIVISION

While it was true that the two leading factors which contributed to the emerging rupture in fellowship were the missionary society and the use of instrumental music in worship, it was also the case that other issues of significance were in dispute. Allusion was made to these in the preceding chapter. The present chapter will set forth certain major developments and relevant issues which indicated the imminent presence and advanced the progress of an emerging division in the state.

The year 1897 was to prove to be eventful for churches of Christ in Tennessee. In spite of his reluctance during the previous years, by 1897 David Lipscomb had become convinced that a rupture of fellowship was unavoidable between the two groups in the state. Early in the year M. C. Kurfees stated that in view of the admission that both the society and the instrument were untaught in the Bible and were divisive, the users thereof should be admonished to relent, and if not they should be marked and avoided.[1] Later Lipscomb stated that one must make a clear distinction between truth and error. If one could not remove the error, in this article the instrument, "he must withdraw from the error, or he practically destroys the distinction between truth and error." [2] As the year was closing, Lipscomb distinguished between those who served God and those who sought to obey him. He reasoned that those who used the instruments and societies, the Catholics, and "the denominations one and all" were guilty of seeking to serve God but not being willing to obey him in fulness. In view of this distinction, those introducing the society and the organ were to be admonished and if they persisted they were to be withdrawn from by those who sought to obey God.[3] The year was, therefore, of major significance for the cleavage which was to be made public in 1906. In the year 1907 David Lipscomb looked back over the years and summed up his conclusions by stating concerning the two groups, "But here are two distinct bodies, guided by diametrically opposite principles, travelling in opposite directions, but calling themselves by the same name." [4] By a long and difficult path the two groups had finally become completely separate and were never again to be united. This chapter will summarize the events between 1889 and 1897 which led to this final parting of the ways.

The Sand Creek Address and Declaration

Since 1873 the Sand Creek church, in Shelby County, Illinois, had annually been conducting fellowship or homecoming gatherings on the church grounds. These gatherings, attended by members and interested brethren, gave opportunity for renewing acquaintances and, as will become obvious, for other activities as well. On August 18, 1889 there occurred a meeting which was a significant milestone in the movement to restore first century Christianity. Both West[5] and Morrison[6] discussed this event in some detail, although each wrote from slightly different perspectives. The event was significant in that it projected to the forefront Daniel Sommer, who had succeeded Benjamin Franklin as editor of the *American Christian Review;* provided a platform for division; and gave stimulus to the uniting of churches north and south in turning against innovations they respectively opposed.

The Address, some 900 words or so in length,[7] was signed by "officers" of five churches. Apparently it was written by Peter Warren,[8] and followed a sermon by Sommer attacking innovations and departures. The address observed that there were those who practiced things which were unauthorized by the New Testament such as church festivals, instrumental music, a select choir, the missionary societies, and the one man pastor system. Also, the address continued, there were those better informed brethren who opposed all such false teaching and corrupt practice. Consequently, the document stated that the latter group must indicate their inability to tolerate such practices further without becoming "blamable" for such tolerance. The address closed with the statement,

> . . . We are impelled from a sense of duty to say that all such as are guilty of teaching or allowing and practicing the many innovations and corruptions to which we have referred, after having had sufficient time for meditation and reflection, if they will not turn away from such abominations, that we cannot and will not regard them as brethren.[9]

Alfred Ellmore sensed that the address was an effort to effect a "full separation in this great body," but recognized it would take more time.[10]

In 1892 the same church issued a further statement which urged all those who opposed the society and the instrument, in buying church property, to insert a clause in their deed which would restrict such "innovations" from ever being used on the premises. This recommendation occasioned great controversy. The advocates of the instrument and the societies cried that this meant a creed was being placed in the deed. The opponents claimed they were merely guaranteeing the property would be used for the purposes intended.[11]

There were those who were hesitant or opposed to the 1889 and 1892 activities in the Sand Creek proclamations. For example, R. B. Neal lamented the 1889 Address and Declaration by stating that it was "to be regretted and earnestly and kindly condemned." He felt that the "tests" were not "gospel tests" and stated his judgment that such actions would "tend more to weaken the efforts of conservatives and to strengthen innovationists than years of earnest faithful work can atone for." He felt that congregational worship was involved and congregational fellowship might be withdrawn over such use, but "christian fellowship" should not, he reasoned, be broken thereby. He opposed the idea that "the rank and masses of our brotherhood" . . . "will or ought to take action as a mass," but felt that "as congregations they will speak and act."[12] In addition, J. C. McQuiddy spoke his mind about "Sand Creekism" and related ills in an article in 1892. He said:

The Sand Creek manifesto was manifest folly and the ADVOCATE emphatically denies any sympathy with Sommerism—whatever that is— Sand Creekism, Sand Lotism, Sansculottism, Standarism, or any other partyism in religion. The ADVOCATE is for Christ and his Church (chosen ones), and is in ardent sympathy with all who are drawing their lives from him who is the true vine. If it be true that Daniel Sommer "has abandoned apostolic ground," as the *Standard* states, he has already gone "to his own place," as the *Standard* desires; but if it is shown that he has only abandoned the "teaching of the Fathers," the ADVOCATE "cares for none of these things." It is not trying to build a church on the teachings of the *Standard's* Fathers, nor is it following any other body's Fathers. Moreover, when the ADVOCATE wants to read a man out of the party with which it is identified, instead of calling for a concensus of party opinion on the case, it proceeds to quote scripture to him showing him that he has abandoned apostolic ground; which thing the *Standard* throughout its long editorial and adendum signally failed to do.[13]

In July 1892 David Lipscomb responded to a plea by the *Christian Standard* that the *Gospel Advocate* indicate whether the work of Daniel Sommer in the Address and Declaration would have its sympathy. Lipscomb stated that he thought Sommer had been misrepresented by the *Standard* and showed that the main points of Sommer's objection had earlier been opposed, at least in part, by such men as Isaac Errett, Alexander Campbell, and Benjamin Franklin. He stated further that his hesitancy about the restrictive deeds, on which his conscience was "tender," was due to his concern that such an effort seemed to be maintaining if not propagating the faith by means of human laws. Of the call for withdrawal of fellowship from Sommer, Lipscomb stated,

The command is to withdraw from those who introduce these questions of strife and occasions of stumbling into the church of God. Judged by authorities the *Standard* quotes, both human and divine, it is the guilty party. Then the case presents itself thus: The *Standard* and its friends introduce things into the churches of God, based on the opinions of men, not required by God. The *Standard* dare not affirm one of the things opposed by Sommer is required in the scriptures, and because Sommer opposed things not required, the *Standard* calls for his exclusion.[14]

These differences of judgment as to the propriety of the Sand Creek activies were obvious in the period, but the ultimate result was to be that the *Gospel Advocate* writers were later to reflect much if not all of the emphases of the Address and Declaration. David Lipscomb had long been reluctant to engage in mass meetings which issued declarations purporting or tending to be binding on others. He also objected to the use of anything which seemed to entail the use of civil power to uphold or propagate spiritual truth. One wonders if a visit by Daniel Sommer to David Lipscomb—related by Daniel Sommer in the *American Christian*

Review (June 17, 1941) [15]—had anything to do with the making up of the mind of Lipscomb, but no answer is available to the historian. Nevertheless, Lipscomb did offer words of clarification and defense in behalf of Sommer. In 1906 he expressed support for a major stumbling block in the 1892 proceedings when he wrote in support of the restrictive clause.[16] The succeeding years had brought some changes in his thinking.

As one looks back, it seems that the 1889 and 1892 developments in Sand Creek sought to provide a firm platform which gave a rationale and plea for division and recommended a legal procedure which hopefully would guarantee a distinction between those who opposed and those who favored the practices in dispute. Also, it gave a clear indication that the movement which earlier had pled for unity was rapidly coming to a parting of the ways. The result was to be that many brethren were feeling more and more obliged to sever all ties from those whom they regarded as in violation of God's will. The Address and Declaration was a reflection of and possibly a contributor to this development.

The Missionary Society in Tennessee

Since the 1842 discussion involving Tolbert Fanning and the early issues of the *Gospel Advocate* the missionary society question had been discussed by Christians in the state. There had been many anxious years in which the issues pro and con had been discussed in the papers and, apparently, among the churches; but with few exceptions very limited actual influence and activity of a missionary society as such were known in the state. The cry of missionary society advocates had been that the churches in the state which did not rally to the societies were either not making progress in reaching converts or not willing to cooperate to spread the gospel or both.

In 1875 E. G. Sewell responded to these charges in a lengthy article on "Co-Operation." J. H. Gregory asked about the design and use of the American Christian Missionary Society. Sewell replied in an article concerning the nature of the society and, for good measure, responded to the oft heard charge that opponents of the missionary society were opposed to all cooperation. His words were as follows:

> We have never been in any way connected with it, nor had anything in the world to do with it. But from what we have seen regarding it, those who framed it, designed it as a system of co-operation through which many churches and States may co-operate together in the use of their means to spread the gospel of Christ, and extend the kingdom of God, and they claim to use it for that purpose. . . . We, know, however, that in opposing missionary societies as such, we are often accused of opposing the co-operation of Christians and churches entirely, and that we oppose and hinder paying preachers in any way. No greater mistake or misunderstanding was ever made. We believe most firmly in the co-operation of Christians and churches in every good word and work, wherever and whenever such co-operation will further the cause of God. All the churches in the United States which are blessed with plenty, can co-op-

42

erate in sending aid to the needy of any particular locality, as in the case of the Kansas sufferers recently, or the sufferers South a few years ago. But all this can and may be done and has been done without any Society, outside of the church, without any salaried officers, or any concentration of money or power. And upon the same principle, any number of churches may certainly co-operate together as churches in sending out preachers, and sustaining them, without any sort of organization in the world except the churches of the Living God as such. These churches in adjacent localities can understand each other and work together without any president, or corresponding secretary, as in the case of societies; while in this case, all the means paid by the members, goes directly for the work to be done, instead of a large portion of it being consumed in paying officers to manage it, as in the case of societies. Nor is there any necessity that all the churches in a large section or State or number of States should attempt to confer together, so as to do things in a body. If sufferers in a certain section of country are to be relieved, let each congregation go to work at once, without waiting to see what others will do. And whenever a number of churches engage in a work of this kind, they are co-operating scripturally, whether they understand each other's movements at the time or not. Or if the gospel is to be preached in a new or destitute place, the church or churches nearest by, should attend to that matter. And to do this, there is no need of any outside plan through which to accomplish it. If one congregation be not able to accomplish the work, let them call upon the ones nearest to them to assist in the work, and so on till it is done. And if all the churches everywhere would act in this way, all the work would be done that they are capable of doing, and no trouble about plans, nor would any part of their means be consumed in paying the expenses of societies. All that brethren pay, would go directly to the work for which they designed it. In this way, a vast amount more of good can be accomplished with the same amount of means, and no trouble or detention in calling boards together, or waiting their tardy action, to say where, when, and by whom the work should be done.

From these considerations, and many others which might be given, we are constrained to conclude that the existence of such a society as the one named above, is a non-essential, and stands in the way of the work of God as such, and has a tendency to exalt human wisdom above the wisdom of God. We can never honor God, except by doing everything by his authority and direction. He has given no directions, either how to establish missionary societies, or how to carry them on, when established. We long to see the time come when the church of God shall be exalted to the work to which God ordained it, and when human wisdom, and human expedients, shall all be yielded up for the wisdon of God; then, and not till then, will the church fill its proper mission in this world.[17]

In spite of the objections by such men as Fanning, Lipscomb, and Sewell, there were some missionary society or quasi-society activities which had been practiced through the years. For example, there were cooperative meetings which involved the activities of various committees and secretaries. A case in point was the proposal in 1879 of S. J. Gohagen, following an earlier "co-operation meeting at Jackson,

Tenn.," that the forty-four churches in West Tennessee wake from a long sleep of inactivity, meet at Brownsville at a mutually agreeable date, and "put our minds *and money* together, and send out a live worker, to stir up the churches and build up the waste places." [18] In June he told of a forthcoming meeting at Brownsville on Saturday before the first Lord's day in July next and designated himself the "Corresponding Secretary." [19] One is probably able to understand that more than inconvenience of travel kept David Lipscomb from attending this meeting as indicated by the rather abrupt statement of the editors of the *Gospel Advocate* when they said, "It is not probable that Brother D. Lipscomb will be able to attend the meeting." [20] Later months revealed little significance attached to this or other similar meetings though they continued to be conducted occasionally.

In addition to these cooperative meetings there were more formally organized activities, a few of which may be noted. In 1867 the American Christian Evangelizing and Educational Association was organized among several Negro churches. This meeting, in Nashville, produced the first such organizational instrument beyond the local churches among the Negro brethren. In 1880 an Annual Missionary Convention was organized with Thomas Bayless as state evangelist. This work was not very successful in Middle Tennessee, but did quite a bit better in East Tennessee.[21] A Ladies Aid Society was organized in Clarksville in 1865. A national organization for women, The Christian Woman's Board of Missions, was organized in 1874. An organized work among women began in Memphis in 1875. In 1882 a woman from Memphis became state secretary for the national organization. In 1888 an organized women's work of missions began in Chattanooga.[22]

The conflict over the society focused on events which took place primarily in Nashville in the Woodland Street church in the late 1880s and early 1890s. An account of the developments at this church was preserved by E. G. Sewell.[23] E. G. Sewell and others started this church in the early part of 1871. He had preached there, on occasion, for six years. Then he served among weak churches in the surrounding areas for two years. During those eight years the church had built a meeting house and Sewell was asked to do more preaching at Woodland Street. He began to sense that something was wrong as evidenced by declining attendance and interest, and feeling that a change in preachers was in order resigned at the close of 1882. In 1883 W. J. Loos began preaching at Woodland Street. A better idea of what was taking place was possible after Loos returned from a convention in Cincinnati and eagerly promoted the missionary society. Sewell opposed this development, but many members and at least two of the four elders were in favor of it. Soon the differences were the occasion of disagreement and the problem quickly became a public concern.

When Loos terminated his work, R. M. Giddens came as the preacher. Giddens also wanted the missionary society to be supported by the church; consequently, the issue became more heated. In October 1887 Andres Ivarson Myhr, an ardent missionary society advocate, conducted a gospel meeting at Woodland Street. Shortly thereafter R. M. Giddens and a number of ladies in the church organized a Home Mission Board. This group sent several hundred letters to Tennessee churches in an effort to secure additional support. Interest was gained from ladies in the church in Chattonnooga, but little support was present elsewhere. In November 1889 Myhr came to Tennessee from Missouri and travelled among the churches. His report encouraged the belief the time was right to begin organized work. The Woodland Street elders were urged to take charge of the work and employ someone to continue the work begun by Myhr. Three of the elders agreed, but Sewell refused because the plan "looked too much like a society." [24] Myhr was soon back in the state and began his work February 1, 1890. Sewell plead that the plan be abandoned, but the others refused. [25] The three elders in favor of the plan published a plea in the *Christian Standard* that there would be a meeting in Chattonooga of all who favored the type of organized work they upheld. The meeting was conducted October 6-8, 1890 and issued in the establishment of the State Missionary Convention of the Christian Church of Tennessee or as it was termed the Tennessee Christian Missionary Co-operation. David Lipscomb attended the meeting along with nine Tennessee preachers and three preachers from outside the state, one hundred thirty two people being present in all. Lipscomb spoke against the effort as being wrong, but to no avail. Myhr was asked to continue his work and sixteen congregations made commitments to assist. David Lipscomb observed that the churches supporting the activities were also organ using churches. [26] Myhr quickly went to work with vigor and by 1891 had organized district conventions in West and East Tennessee. [27] David Lipscomb saw the drift of the events and observed shortly after the organizational meeting, "The departures may not be very marked or flagrant at first, but once under headway they will grow with accelerating force, (sic.) we are certain this movement will affect the churches in Tennessee." [28] This insight was soon to be demonstrated to be most perceptive as subsequent events made clear.

In the wake of the effort in 1890, the General Christian Missionary Society held its annual meeting at the Vine Street Christian Church in Nashville, beginning October 18, 1892. David Lipscomb observed that of the twenty five hundred white Christians in the city less than 100 desired the convention. Also, he noted, no Tennessee preacher, native to the state or "identified in faith and feeling with the disciples in Tennessee," desired the meeting. [29]

During the meeting C. M. Wilmeth proposed a meeting between the advocates and opponents of the society, but this was declined by the organizers of the sessions because of a lack of time. A paper, signed by Wilmeth, David Lipscomb, E. G. Sewell, James A. Harding, M. C. Kurfees, and given in full in the *Gospel Advocate*, [30] was prepared to be read at the convention. It charged that of some forty thousand members in the state less than one thousand were in sympathy with the society and appealed for consideration of the conscience of those who opposed the society. The document appealed that the society be abandoned and the energies be expended through the churches, "under the direction of their heaven-appointed officers." This would remove "a cause of wide spread division," and bring about "that union and cooperation in which there is strength and which will enable us to make more rapid conquest of the earth for Christ." [31] This was read to the group, but J. W. McGarvey referred it to committee. Nothing came of the effort favorable to the "memorial." West observed that J. H. Garrison, a prominent editor, made a joke of the whole affiar.[32] Lipscomb later gave the background of the writing.[33]

Lipscomb and others had attended and observed the proceedings. Their impressions were not for good. Lipscomb observed the applause and "old Fourth-of-July spread-eagle" enthusiasm, the appointment of women to the several boards, the transferring of authority from elders to the committee ,[34] and the use of women to make speeches before large audiences.[35] Of particular concern was a proposal, restrained by "wiser heads," to express the convention position as to prohibition. This showed Lipscomb that some in the group were ready to not only legislate on religious questions and thus forsake the Bible, but they were also ready to enter the field of partisan politics.[36] Lipscomb summarized his feelings in these words,

> If that Convention was not an open, defiant rejection of God and his holy Word, I would not know how to reject God and set aside the authority of his word. I do not think delicious speeches or animal enthusiasm manifested by constant cheering and hand-clapping applause compensate in any way for the violated will of God. Nor do I think its being for a worthy cause helps the cause or palliates the sin.[37]

Of the purpose and effect of the meeting, an anonymous article from the *Firm Foundation* was quoted in the *Gospel Advocate*. The author was convinced that the choice of Nashville was due to the fact the *Gospel Advocate* was published there and the purpose was to marshall the "hosts of 'progression' " so as to "snap their fingers and shake their fist" in the face of David Lipscomb who had "exposed their sophistries and laid bare their fallacies about missionary societies." The result was stated in clear terms,

> We have lost our last lingering hope that any of the leaders of "progression" will ever give up the dictates of their "sanctified common sense" and return to the way ordained of God. We think now they have crossed the Rubicon and burnt the bridges behind them. The safe way to regard them now is as enemies of the cross of Christ, bent on a rapid construction of another popular sect.[38]

Lipscomb summed up his reaction by noting that not a single man among Tennessee preachers, known to him, had failed to be strengthened in his conviction that "these things are all wrong and lead men to division and strife, and gradually school men to neglect the Bible." [39]

It was clear by 1892 that the missionary society advocates would not listen to the call of Tennessee preachers to cease and desist. It was also clear that, in spite of support for the foreign mission work by a national society, the majority of people in the churches of the state, along with preachers, were not in favor of the society being established and actively functioning in the state. As had been apparent to society advocates previously, it was now apparent to society opponents in Tennessee that no change in purpose and practice would be forthcoming. Another step toward divison was apparent.

Open Membership

The subject of the relation of the restorationists to the various religious bodies about them had been disputed through the history of their work.[40] Some, led by the thinking as such men as W. T. Moore, had begun to accept those who had received sprinkling for baptism. Missouri preachers had been instructed along this line in 1890 although controversy resulted. Even Thomas Munnell, who had discussed the society question with David Lipscomb in the late 1860s, proposed treating immersion as an opinion to be waived in an effort to promote union.[41]

David Lipscomb observed these developments and warned that they represented the logical implication of the society position since the same authority which changed the organization of the church could, if it desired, change the faith.[42] Later years were to see the development of a specific resolution which illustrated and confirmed, to Lipscomb and others, the point they were making. In 1902 a convention in Omaha adopted a resolution to the effect that churches of the restorationist persuasion were not to disturb or convert the existing denominational groups in the respective towns.[43] This resolution became the center of a storm of controversy, but for this study the chief significance lay in the fact that it was regarded as the logical outcome of the society arrangement. Lipscomb argued that those who passed such resolutions were presuming to make laws for God's people and, if they chose, they could make or change other laws.[44] E. A. Elam saw the development as an attempt to manage the churches and claimed that the society efforts in Tennessee had resulted in the introduction of instrumental music with discord, strife, and division following in the wake.[45]

In the mid 1890s David Lipscomb was watching the developments of the open fellowship proposals of various leaders of the society efforts. He saw, apparently, that the position would entail a reduction of uniqueness and pose a threat to establishment of the churches he loved to see growing all over the state and elsewhere. His suspicions were later to be confirmed in 1902 when the federation proposals began to be voiced. The society, he charged, had begun by rejecting one aspect of truth in order to exist; the federation was of the same kind and no less blameworthy. Those who upheld the former but denied the latter were inconsistent.

To David Lipscomb and others the federation was one of the signs of the progressive evil inherent in the society. The time was coming when a break would have to be final. This, along with Sand Creek and the society developments in the state pushed David Lipscomb, and through him many others in the state, to a realization that further fellowship would be almost if not completely impossible in the state between groups now separated by attitudes and activities from which neither would or could desist.

Rationalism and Modern Critical Approaches

The general development of what is termed modernism or liberalism cannot be treated in this account. The standard works in the period, such as the study by Ahlstrom,[46] and the specific work by such writers as Ash[47] may be consulted for the general period. The problem of rationalism was known among the restorationists since the early leanings in this direction by L. L. Pinkerton in 1869[48] and the concern had grown until the late 1880s and early 1890s. In these years certain preachers in Missouri became the focal point of a significant controversy.

For several years there had been concern about the soundness of the teaching by some Missouri preachers when an episode involving R. C. Cave of St. Louis erupted. On December 1, 1889 Cave preached that in inviting people to come to God by Christ he did not mean to come by virtue of any sacrifice that Christ had made to appease the wrath of God, but that they should come to Christ as a teacher, guide and example. He declared in a sermon on December 8 that men should come to Christ as they understood him even if they did not believe in miracles or even in the Bible. A meeting which was conducted the next Sunday presented a series of resolutions upholding Cave but a protest meeting on December 27 resulted in his resignation. Later he organized a church congenial to his views where he served as the preacher.[49]

When Lipscomb heard of the incident he wrote an article on "Sad Apostasies." In this article he stated that he was not surprised since he had heard for some time that Cave doubted the inspiration of the Bible and questioned the miraculous conception of Jesus and other truths of the Bible. Lipscomb knew that Cave had gone to Missouri after serving as the preacher at the Church Street congregation in Nashville. He stated he might have more to say on the incident later.[50]

F. D. Srygley alluded to the matter and connected the development with the "pious unimmersed" idea which some had fostered. He stated, "We have been lavish of our sympathy for the pious unimmersed. What, now shall we do with the pious unbeliever?[51] He followed by twitting J. H. Garrison, a St. Louis editor who upheld the society but opposed Cave. He noted Garrison's lament that the church was divided because Cave had insisted on doing as he had done and observed that Garrison's editorial policy had "all over this broad land and Texas too" produced division by pushing things many brethren had opposed such as "this

48

society and organ question." The conscientious objections to the society and organ were of small moment, but the conscience of Garrison had to be respected.[52] Obviously an *ad hominem* argument, Srygley's observation focused on the point which Lipscomb and others were to press more and more, namely that respect for the Bible in the fullest sense of the term entailed not only respect for it as an inspired volume, but also entailed respect for its teaching as to evangelism, worship, means of membership and other matters. Srygley, sensing he had a live issue, followed this line of thought in a subsequent article. He quoted an editorial in Garrison's paper which stated, "We should not deny a man christian faith who could not bring himslelf to believe in the divine inspiration of the song of Solomon, or the book of Esther, or some other book or parts of the Old Testament." Concerning this he asked, "If there can be no definite line drawn indicating what part of Bible a man may reject without denying the faith or forfeiting fellowship, why may he not reject the whole thing?" [53]

To bring the matter home David Lipscomb penned a series of articles involving the state evangelist, A. I. Myhr. Lipscomb argued that Myhr was in sympathy with leading rationalists and had defended the high degree of spirituality of such Missouri rationalists as Alexander Proctor and George W. Longan.[54] He then showed that E. B. Cake, a liberal Missouri preacher, had been in Nashville in company with R. M. Giddens, the preacher who had brought Myhr to the state and who encouraged the work he, Myhr, was doing.[55] He then observed,

> The man who defends these men or their teaching, whether he intends it or not aids and abets the spread of rationalism in the land. For a man . . . to defend and cherish the men who advocate them, as brethren, shows a sectarian spirit, or moral cowardice that unfits for membership in the church of God. . . .[56]

Lipscomb was arguing basically two positions in his articles. First, the attitude toward the authority of the Bible manifested by the upholders of the society and the organ was at bottom the same attitude of disrespect which rationalism was manifesting. Those who upheld the former were, unintentionally, preparing the way for the latter. Second, those who aided and abetted the defenders of rationalism, namely Giddens and Myhr were also the men who were actively advancing the society cause in Tennessee. In Lipscomb's mind the two were connected together, and he was becoming more fully convinced that the society, organ, and rationalism complex were of the same piece of cloth and were moving to a point of no return.

As the years passed, Lipscomb felt the bits and pieces of society support were falling into a pattern which, as it became clearer, was forcing a decision concerning fellowship. Some were following a course which, he believed, would turn men from the arrangements of God. This insight was not as clearly seen by him in the 1870s and 1880s as it was in the 1890s. By the mid 1890s the pattern was clear to him and the course to be followed was also becoming clear. He had seen this in 1892 when he noted that the society question was being pursued longer than he personally desired, but felt such teaching was necessary because most people learn slowly. He stated of the process he envisioned,

... despite all statements to the contrary there is a tendency toward solid ground on which all who honor God can stand. The grounds are shifting, men are more and more seeing they do violate the divine order and besides that God's ways are wiser. This work will go on until the line will be drawn, and two parties, one accepting the Bible as the only authoritative and perfect will to guide men, the other placing human wisdom and ordinances above the Bible. Let us be firm but patient, and God will work his own ends.[57]

Lipscomb was to see, as the last half of the 1890s passed, that this line was being drawn and two irreconcilable groups were present. The final phase was at hand.

REFERENCES

[1] M. C. Kurfees, "The Fight of Faith," *Gospel Advocate* 39 (February 11, 1897):92.

[2] David Lipscomb, "Truth and Error," *Gospel Advocate* 39 (May 20, 1897):308.

[3] David Lipscomb, "Serving God, Not Obeying Him," *Gospel Advocate* 39 (November 11, 1897):708.

[4] David Lipscomb, "The Church of Christ and the Disciples of Christ," *Gospel Advocate* 49 (July 18, 1907):457.

[5] Earl Irvin West, *Search for the Ancient Order*, 2 (Indianapolis: Religious Book Service, 1950), pp. 430-36.

[6] Matthew Clifton Morrison, "Daniel Sommer's Seventy Years of Religious Controversy" (Ph.D. dissertation, University of Indiana, 1972), pp. 135-65.

[7] Given in fullness by West, ibid., 2, pp. 430-32.

[8] Morrison, ibid., p. 137.

[9] P. P. Warren, "Sand Creek Address and Declaration," *Christian Leader* 3 (September 10, 1889):2. Quoted by West, ibid., 2, p. 432.

[10] Alfred Ellmore, "Wheat and Chaff," *Christian Leader* 3 (December 17, 1889):4. Quoted by West, ibid., 2, pp. 433-34.

[11] West, ibid., 2, pp. 434-36.

[12] R. B. Neal, "Neal's Notes," *Gospel Advocate* 31 (November 6, 1889):709.

[13] J. C. McQuiddy, "Miscellany," *Gospel Advocate* 34 (June 30, 1892):408-09.

[14] David Lipscomb, "Our Response," *Gospel Advocate* 34 (July 7, 1892):429.

[15] Morrison, ibid., pp. 163-64.

[16] David Lipscomb, "The Creed in the Deed," *Gospel Advocate* 48 (January 11, 1906):25.

[17] E. G. Sewell, "Co-Operation," *Gospel Advocate* 17 (May 27, 1875):515-517.

[18] S. J. Gohagan, "To The Church of Christ in West Tenn." *Gospel Advocate* 21 (May 22, 1879):328.

[19] S. J. Gohagan, Cor. Secretary, "Meeting of West Tenn. Brethren," *Gospel Advocate* 21 (June 12, 1879):377.

[20] Ibid.

[21] Herman A. Norton, *Tennessee Christians* (Nashville: Reed and Company, 1971), pp. 135-36.

[22] Ibid., p. 154.

[23] E. G. Sewell, *Gospel Lessons and Life History* (Nashville: McQuiddy Printing Company, 1908), pp. 261-304.

[24] Norton, ibid., pp. 189-91.

[25] David Lipscomb, "The Work of Strife," *Gospel Advocate* 32 (September 3, 1890):566-67.

[26] David Lipscomb, "Convention Notes," *Gospel Advocate* 32 (November 5, 1890):710.

[27] Norton, ibid., pp. 193-99.

[28] David Lipscomb, "Convention Notes," *Gospel Advocate* 32 (October 22, 1890):678.

[29] David Lipscomb, "Card of Invitation," *Gospel Advocate* 34 (October 6, 1892):629.

[30] Anonymous, "The Anti-Society Memorial," *Gospel Advocate* 34 (November 3, 1892):700.

[31] Ibid.

[32] West, ibid., 2, p. 360.

[33] David Lipscomb, "Notes on the Convention," *Gospel Advocate* 34 (November 10, 1892):709.

[34] David Lipscomb, "Convention Items," *Gospel Advocate* 34 (October 27, 1892):676.

[35] David Lipscomb, "Convention Thoughts," *Gospel Advocate* 34 (November 10, 1892):709.

[36] David Lipscomb, "Convention Items," *Gospel Advocate* 34 (October 27, 1892:676.

[37] David Lipscomb, "Convention Thoughts," *Gospel Advocate* 34 (Noevember 10, 1892):709.

[38] Anonymous, "He Gives Them Up," *Gosepl Advocate* 34 (December 8, 1892):770.

[39] David Lipscomb, "Convention Items," *Gosepl Advocate* 34 (October 27, 1892):676.

[40] Anonymous, "Do the Unimmersed Commune?" *Lard's Quarterly* 1 (September 1863):41-53.

[41] Winfred Ernest Garrison, *Religion Follows the Frontier* (New York: Harper and Brothers, 1931).

[42] David Lipscomb, "How It Was Treated," *Gospel Advocate* 27 (July 29, 1885):470.

[43] Anonymous, "What is Church Federation?" *Gospel Advocate* 44 (November 27, 1902):756.

[44] David Lipscomb, "That Federation Resolution," *Gospel Advocate* 44 (April 2, 1903):217.

[45] E. A. Elam, "Two Different Things," *Gospel Advocate*, 48 (May 3, 1906):273.

[46] Sydney E. Ahlstrom, *A Religious History of the American People* (New Haven: Yale University Press, 1972), pp. 763-824.

[47] Anthony L. Ash, "Old Testament Studies in the Restoration Movement," *Restoration Quarterly* 10 (1967):89-98. See also, Anthony L. Ash, "Attitudes Toward Higher Criticism of the Old Testament 8Among the Disciples of Christ," (Ph.D. dissertation, University of Southern California, 1966).

[48] Winfred Ernest Garrison and Alfred T. DeGroot, *The Disciples of Christ: A History* (St. Louis: Christian Board of Publication, 1948), p. 390.

[49] West, ibid., pp. 260-62; 266-71.

[50] David Lipscomb, "Sad Apostasies," *Gospel Advocate* 32 (January 15, 1890):32.

[51] F. D. Srygley, "From the Papers," *Gospel Advocate* 32 (January 15, 1890):32.

[52] F. D. Srygley, "From the Papers," *Gospel Advocate* 32 (January 29, 1890):65.

[53] F. D. Srygley, "From the Papers," *Gospel Advocate* 32 (February 5, 1890):79.

[54] David Lipscomb, "Bro. Myhr's Work," *Gospel Advocate* 32 (February 12, 1890):103, and David Lipscomb, "A Criticism," *Gospel Advocate* 32 (March 12, 1890):166-67.

[55] David Lipscomb, "Is Rationalism Rife in Missouri?" *Gospel Advocate* 32 (March 19, 1890):183.

[56] Ibid.

[57] David Lipscomb, "Be Firm but Patient," *Gospel Advocate* 34 (January 7, 1892):5.

CHAPTER SIX

A SIGNIFICANT YEAR

In the first issue of the 1897 *Gospel Advocate,* David Lipscomb stated,

I am fast reaching the conclusion that there is a radical and fundamental difference between the disciples of Christ and the society folks. These desire to build up a strong and respectable denomination. To do it they rely on strong and moneyed societies, fine houses, fashionable music, and eloquent speeches too often devoid of gospel truth.[1]

In the same issue, E. Snodgrass remarked that a new denomination was in formation which would soon become a reality. He asserted this was obvious to anyone who regularly read the papers published by the society advocates. He noted a statement from the *Christian Standard* which declared, "Tennessee is the key to our enlargement throughout the Central South, and for this cause, as well as for its own sake, must be secured for aggressive New Testament Christianity." All this had convinced Snodgrass that a new denomination was being formed to exclude those who opposed the societies and that this effort was focusing on winning Tennessee to its position.[2] These two articles underscored the fact that to the *Advocate* supporters such a fitting of pieces together was present that the radical and fundamental differences between two formerly united groups were becoming obvious. The details of this awareness of such differences may be traced in this year of 1897.

The year witnessed a lengthy exchange between J. A. Minton and E. A. Elam concerning the propriety of the missionary society, particularly in Tennessee. Elam plead for the all sufficiency of the church and scored Minton for admitting this truth but upholding the society as an experiment although it was working successfully. Elam had challenged Minton to affirm the Tennessee Missionary Society was scriptural and therefore necessary to the evangelization of the state, but Minton had declined. Elam agreed to further negotiation for a debate on condition that a paper favoring the society also carry the exchange, but felt David Lipscomb and J. W. McGarvey were better qualified to discuss the issues.[3] Minton replied that he would not ask concerning Lipscomb and McGarvey and a debate, but he stated his readiness to deny that there was a plan clearly set forth in the Bible by which to do missionary work in the church. He also refused to supply a paper to publish his side of the exchange since, he charged, the *Advocate* had begun the dispute.[4] Elam promptly denied the *Advocate* had so initiated the discussion as Minton claimed and agreed to an oral debate or a written "one sided" debate in the *Advocate,* but claimed that fairness would have the debate in papers of the respective positions.[5]

While Elam and Minton were discussing the society, instrumental music in worship was also gaining attention. In April 1897 W. K. Homan wrote James A. Harding, of Nashville, concerning the possibility of a debate on instrumental music between Harding and J. B. Briney. One of the conditions of the debate, to be published in a Texas paper, stated that the participants were to "treat each other with Christian courtesy, and to recognize each other as members of the body of Christ." Harding responded by recasting the proposition he was to affirm so that it read, "the use of a musical instrument in the church, as such instruments are used in Dallas and elsewhere, is a sin that justifies the withdrawal of Christian fellowship by those who oppose from those who use it." Harding then indicated his decision as to the condition noted previously by stating, "I do not regard myself as belonging to the same religious body with Brother Briney." He expalined, "I am not a member of the same religious body with any man who persists in advocating and using instrumental music in the church after he has been properly admonished. . . ." Again, he indicated that he regarded Briney as a scholar and a gentleman, but stated, "I certainly do not regard him as a member of the body of Christ." [6] Homan was distressed with this development and withdrew the offer to print the debate. Harding denied any change in his position, indicated that he and Briney were "once members of the same body," but that the instrument had forced a parting of the ways and claimed that the users of instruments were to be marked and avoided.[7] The issue was to recur during the year, but Harding had drawn the line of fellowship over the instrument.

E. G. Sewell, in an article on unity, stated that those who sought the unity required by the Bible could not run with the organ and were not quietly to submit and participate in the innovation without resistance. He concluded, "But the truth in the matter is that those who introduced the organ have already broken up the unity of the Spirit and dissolved the bond of peace." [8] Those who were present for such introduction were obliged "to either withdraw or become parties to the innovation, but they do not need to get into any bad temper or do any rash thing . . ." [9] As the year was closing, Lipscomb observed that while one was seeking to learn and do God's will he ought not to be rejected but helped. But, if the mistake is persisted in, the duty became clear, "While all forebearance and long-suffering should be exercised, still if they refuse to turn from sin, they should be rejected." [10]

It was clear that the *Gospel Advocate* staff, with the active participation of David Lipscomb, was now convinced that the society and music "folks" were of a different religious body from themselves and the time for "rejection," "wintdrawal," "marking" and "avoiding" was present.

Along with the missionary society and music question, other points of difficulty were discussed during the year. The "federation" issue was opened again by F. D. Srygley in response to a proposed "Union of Two Denominations," in St. Louis, namely the Christian Church and a Congregational Church.[11] This was taken by Srygley to mean that the missionary society group was willing for such union to occur. He also noted a proposal for an interdenominational council and concluded that the proposal admitted the group favoring such activities was itself a denomination and that this meant all should work together as denominationalists, without any disagreement or criticism of a denomination, " . . . regardless of its departure from the New Testament in doctrine and practice." [12] J. H. Garrison, of St. Louis, though not denying the report, resented the implication and requested the *Advocate* no longer be sent to him. Lipscomb, Sewell, and Srygley observed concerning this development, "If we must suppress convictions we consider sacred . . . to receive the Christian-Evangelist . . . and remain on friendly terms with Brother Garrison, we make a sacrifice and stand by our convictions. . . ." [13]

In July F. D. Srygley was conducting an exchange with an Alabama preacher concerning Srygley's charge that the Christian Church, of which the Alabama preacher was a part, was "driving at a denominational organization pure and simple." [14] By August Srygley was saying of the State Evangelist of Alabama, "He may not know this; but it is, nevertheless true. He belongs to the Christian Church, or Disciples of Christ, which is as clearly defined and fully organized a denomination as can be found anywhere." [15] The essential point was that it had become clear that the group now being called the Christian Church or Disciples of Christ, was considered a denomination by *Advocate* writers who thought it was to be treated in the same way as other denominational groups.

A vital development came in August 1897 when, again, F. D. Srygley opened an exchange with J. W. McGarvey over his lack of consistency in arguing that the instrument was wrong and claiming one should not have fellowship where it was used while persisting in working with the society men who introduced and used the instrument. [16] This placed McGarvey in the position of upholding by practice what he denied by profession. It also inseparably connected the society and music issues so that one could not, consistently, oppose one and accept the other. McGarvey, after reaffirming his opposition to the instrument in worship, responded to Srygley that he had never proposed to withdraw fellowship simply because of the use of the instrument. [17] Soon the battle was on in earnest. McGarvey contended that he could bear with the instrument—while refusing to preach where it was used and regarding its inrtoduction as high-handed wickedness— and yet not withdraw fellowship. [18] Srygley quoted from old writings of McGarvey in 1881 where he had stated that he would withdraw, but observed that the question was really whether McGarvey's stand was right in admitting the instrument was wrong but refusing to withdraw fellowship. [19] The controversy continued for sometime, but the point of emphasis was to the effect that no middle ground was possible. One could not consistently argue the instrument was wrong and then refuse to withdraw from those who persisted in such activity.

As a related issue to the Srygley-McGarvey exchange, a serious dispute arose over the charge that the society advocates were generally the ones who introduced and upheld the instrument in worship, and therefore, to hold to one was, in effect, to open the door to the other. Srygley cited examples in Kentucky, Georgia, Texas and in Nashville, Chattanooga, and Union City, Tennessee to prove his point.[20] McGarvey denied this, as quoted by Srygley,[21] but M. C. Kurfees came forward with an article citing examples of this procedure which he had observed.[22] Srygley charged that everyone knew this to be the case in spite of the denial by some.[23] The point being made was that the society sent out agents who introduced the instrument and those who upheld the societies were supporting the introduction of the instruments regardless of their convictions and wishes to the contrary.

A major development of the year 1897 was that in this year all the threads of argument, alienation, and accusation were being gathered together by the respective groups. Two articles make this clear. David Lipscomb penned a significant article on what he termed "The Vital Point."[24] In this he referred to the pious unimmersed, the repudiation of the need of faith in Christ by Cave, confederation, societies, instrumental music, and the establishment of denominational agencies. All these were regarded as a few of "numerous examples" readily available which sprang from the same source, a departure from God. The man who departed from one point weakened his disposition to cling to God in another. He reasoned that to open the door for one departure was, in effect, to open the door for a thousand. In this article Lipscomb was tying together the threads which he had watched being woven through the past decades in Tennessee and elsewhere. The departures in the 1860s had led to others, and no means was at hand to resist what followed in the wake of the first departure except the repudiation of man's wisdom and the insistence on obedience to the express will of God. The die was now cast. Lipscomb had finally accepted the fact that division was a reality, due to irreconcilable conflict of principle, and must be admitted. To depart from God's law was to be unfit for the service of God.

In the next month, F. D. Srygley indicated the need to not only tie the threads together, but to take the next step of open repudiation of fellowship. Because of departure, the offenders must be "marked" and "avoided." Of the process he stated,

> . . . it seems to me an easier and faster way would be to lump the whole business, mark all denominational institutions and organization and follow the plain teaching of the New Testament in all matters of religious work and service.[25]

The path to division had now reached its destination. The year 1897 may be regarded as the year when the final tapestry of division was completed. David Lipscomb, the writers of the *Gospel Advocate*, and the churches and individuals in sympathy with the editorial efforts of the paper were at the final moment in the long struggle. From this year the division was a reality. It began and closed on the note of mingled sadness and relief; sadness that the break had come through a torturous path, but relief that now at last the break was made and the pieces could begin to be sorted out and at last a new road could begin to be followed.

In the closing decade of the nineteenth century the strands were finally woven together which issued in the reality of division. Instrumental music in worship and the use of the missionary society had paved the way. The Sand Creek Address and Declaration had formally stated the appeal and the urgency of division. The coming of the society and the convention in the state had convinced David Lipscomb and others that the society advocates would not be persuaded to desist. The coming of A. I. Myhr, along with his friendship with rationalistic society advocates, further convinced Lipscomb and others that the society in Tennessee meant, in spite of disaproval, that the floodgate was open and there was no way to avoid, on these principles, the infidelity becoming apparent in Missouri and elsewhere. By 1897 the fabric was complete. Beginning with a fully expressed acceptance of Bible authority and arguing that the society, instrument, and related matters were wrong, it was concluded that the advocates of such arrangements were no longer members of the same religious body. Instead, they must be marked and avoided. At most, respective champions might meet for a debate of issues, but they could not meet as members of the same group as in the past. The path of division had come to a fork and never again would the movement in search of unity walk in unity and brotherhood.

REFERENCES

[1] David Lipscomb, "The Churches Across the Mountains," *Gospel Advocate* 39 (January 7, 1897):4.

[2] E. Snodgrass, "Foreign Mission Column," *Gospel Advocate* 39 (January 7, 1897):13.

[3] E. A. Elam, "Brother Elam to Brother Minton" *Gospel Advocate* 39 (January 14, 1897):19.

[4] J. A. Minton, "Brother Minton to Brother Elam," *Gospel Advocate* 39 (January 28, 1897):62.

[5] E. A. Elam, "Brother Elam to Brother Minton," *Gospel Advocate* 39 (February 4, 1897):68-69.

[6] James A. Harding, "The Instrumental Music Question—A Correspondence between W. K. Homan and J. A. Harding," *Gospel Advocate* 39 (May 29, 1897):323.

[7] Ibid.

[8] E. G. Sewell, " 'Endeavouring to Keep the Unity of the Spirit in the Bond of Peace,' (Eph. 4:3)," *Gospel Advocate* 39 (September 9, 1897):565.

[9] Ibid.

[10] David Lipscomb, "Serving God, not Obeying Him," *Gospel Advocate* 39 (November 11, 1897):708.

[11] F. D. Srygley, "From the Papers," *Gospel Advocate* 39 (March 11, 1897):144-45.

[12] Ibid.

[13] David Lipscomb, E. G. Sewell, and F. D. Srygley, "No Title," *Gospel Advocate* 39 (May 27, 1897):323.

[14] F. D. Srygley, "From the Papers," *Gospel Advocate* 39 (July 15, 1897):433.

[15] F. D. Srygley, "From the Papers," *Gospel Advocate* 39 (August 19, 1897):513.

[16] F. D. Srygley, "From the Papers," *Gospel Advocate* 39 (August 5, 1897):481.

[17] J. W. McGarvey, "Editors of the Gospel Advocate," *Gospel Advocate* 39 (August 19, 1897):518.

[18] F. D. Srygley, "From the Papers," *Gospel Advocate* 39 (September 16, 1897):577-78.

[19] Ibid.

[20] F. D. Srygley, "From the Papers," *Gospel Advocate* 39 (September 23, 1897):593-94.

[21] F. D. Srygley, "From the Papers," *Gospel Advocate* 39 (October 28, 1897):673.

[22] M. C. Kurfees, "Response to Brother McGarvey's Call for Proof," *Gospel Advocate* 39 (November 18, 1897):722-23.

[23] F. D. Srygley, "From the Papers," *Gospel Advocate* 39 (December 23, 1897):801.

[24] David Lipscomb, "The Vital Point," *Gospel Advocate* 39 (August 19, 1897):516.

[25] F. D. Srygley, "From the Papers," *Gospel Advocate* 39 (September 28, 1897):593.

CHAPTER SEVEN

THE CENSUS REPORTS

The divergence of views which foreshadowed division has been traced to the year 1897. James A. Harding had seen this divergence in 1884 when he wrote, "It is an undeniable fact that there are two wings to this reformation, and that they are drifting apart." [1] In 1901 an article by A. E., a regular contributor to the *Advocate*, claimed that there were two groups, one of which was "trying to be faithful" to the divine principle of "observing all things commanded" while the other was following the principle of "observing all things not forbidden." Of the situation he observed that "there is among us practically a division, and ought to be a separation." [2] Jesse P. Sewell stated in the next year, "That the disciples of Christ are divided needs but to be stated, and with sad hearts we are forced to concede the situation." [3] By 1906, David Lipscomb stated, "But here are two distinct bodies, guided by diametrically opposite principles, traveling opposite directions, but calling themselves by the same names." [4]

Division was present and had been for several years, but how were the groups to be distinguished, how were they to recognize themselves and in turn be recognized by others? All aspects of such recognition were not to be clarified for several years, but at the time of these statements and later there was a group consciousness of respective identities and this consciousness was beginning to express itself in publications of the two groups. These expressions were designed to indicate which churches and preachers were regarded as being within the respective groups.

The first general register of churches and preachers was published in 1848. [5] In Tennessee one hundred forty one churches were listed and many preachers were designated as being related to the churches. The list included such men as Tolbert Fanning, Jesse B. Ferguson, B. F. Hall, and J. K. Spear. [6] Later years were to see the inclusion of other men and churches in the yearbooks. In 1900, for example, M. C. Kurfees of Kentucky, E. A. Elam, James A. Harding, Brodie Hardeman, David Lipscomb, E. G. Sewell, F. D. Srygley and others of Tennessee were listed in the yearbook. [7] All of these men were to be prominent among churches of Christ in later years, but in 1900 they allowed the listing of their names along with such men as R. M. Giddens, R. P. Meeks, and A. I. Myhr, all of whom were to be on the opposite side of the various questions in dispute. Before the end of the decade, however, a separate book was to show the preachers in the group designated the churches of Christ. In 1910 the Christian Church Yearbook noted "the defection of the anti-society brethren, in the South particularly" which had become more and more obvious and was accounting in part for the apparent loss in membership as reflected in the publication. [8] In that year M. C. Kurfees of

Kentucky was listed as well as E. A. Elam, David Lipscomb, and others,[9] but the strain was apparent. By 1912 the names of E. A. Elam, David Lipscomb, and E. G. Sewell were omitted, and M. C. Kurfees was omitted shortly thereafter. In a real sense, the preacher lists had spoken by 1912 and the men in the respective groups were becoming known. The men were aware that a difference was present and they did not desire their names to be placed in lists with those with whom they disagreed on what they regarded as essential matters.

Before the completion of reports for the Bureau of Census in 1906 there had been some interest in the record of the churches in the state but not to the degree to be noted in 1906 and the following years. A request for statistics in the state had appeared as early as 1856 in the *Gospel Advocate*.[10] Reflecting an attitude which Hall had observed in 1848,[11] David Lipscomb in 1869 questioned the propriety of securing church statistics lest one sin as had David in numbering Israel.[12] But David Lipscomb was not unmindful of the statistics of the movement in Tennessee. In 1881 he commented on a report from the General Missionary Society concerning the approximate number of churches and members in the state, reportedly 275 churches, 195 preachers, and 38,900 members. Lipscomb had declined to assist in gathering the information, but he thought the estimate to be much too low. He stated that he could name 12 counties with an aggregate of 150 churches and he was sure that there were 35 other counties with an average of 5 congregations each. His estimate was at least 350 churches, "claiming to be churches of Christ." He ended his article by noting that though he was opposed to gathering statistics, he felt obliged to use them to show the inaccuracies of others.[13] It was becoming obvious to Lipscomb that the reports, statistics, and lists of preachers and churches might not only be inaccurate, but might also be used to mislead and confuse his readers.

In 1902 a group of preachers, attending a debate in Kentucky, collected a list of preachers opposed to the organ annd the society. This list increased in number as it became better known. John R. Williams, of West Tennessee, spent quite a bit of time compiling the list. He quoted T. A. Smith as saying, "I see a number of preachers gave their names as opposed to the use of the organ and societies . . . You know where I stand; put me down for the truth." Williams reported that men from Georgia, Kentucky, Mississippi, Arkansas and Oklahoma were sending in their names. To young preachers requesting help in finding places to preach he wrote, "Send in your names and let the congregations know where you stand; then it will be no trouble for you to get work to do." [14] It was apparent by 1902 that a desire was present to determine where preachers and churches stood on the problems then facing the churches of the state. The use of a list of preachers was one way to begin such determination.

Several events in 1906 called attention to the effort to identify the churches in the state which were alike in faith. J. W. Shepherd told of his plan to write a history of the churches in Tennessee and requested readers to assist with reminiscenses of early days.[15] This history was, apparently, never completed due to work of another nature to be noted shortly. David Lipscomb published a brief history of the work in Nashville,[16] and later a work on the churches in five counties of the state.[17] The latter article was significant in that it compiled information obtained at the request of Lipscomb, asked for "correct statements of churches in all the counties," and was followed by several articles of similar nature. The article indicated 23 churches in Maury County, 16 in Wilson, 13 in Humphreys, 18 in Warren, and 12 in Lincoln counties respectively. Warren County had increased in some 50 years from 3 churches with about 400 members to 18 churches with more than 1400 members. Lipscomb repeated his request in a list of 9 other counties with a total of 110 churches.[18] Later he indicated his wish for "the list of all the churches claiming to take the word of God, loyal and disloyal, and the churches of colored brethren also." He published a list of 50 churches in Davidson County including 7 colored churches and marked those who did not "worship and work as the Lord directs," a total of 4 white and 2 colored churches. Sixty one other churches in 6 other counties were indicated, and 8 additional churches were added to the list of counties discussed previously.[19] By the middle of the year he had a record of 502 churches in the various counties. Six counties in Middle Tennessee had not reported, 6 counties in West Tennessee had indicated 43 churches, and 5 counties in East Tennessee had reported 19 churches.[20] In this list also Lipscomb noted churches reported as "digressive" although their names were included. In October Lipscomb published the names of 143 churches in West Tennessee, with 18 indicated as "digressive." [21] In the same year J. W. Shepherd requested "every loyal gospel preacher" to send his name and address to him so that a list he had presented in December 1905 might be revised and brought to completeness.[22] The collection of statistics, both of preachers and churches, was to continue through the year. The point was obvious that the churches in the state were aware of their identity by 1906 and were willing to be known by inclusion in a printed statement. Later years were to see some additions, but a large list had been prepared by 1906-1907. David Lipscomb stated that he had a list of 800 churches in the state, with 35 of the 96 counties not reported in July 1907. His estimate was 900 churches in the state with some 100 being designated "progressive." [23]

The arrival of a letter, dated June 17, 1907, started a series of events which clearly indicated a consciousness of the identity of churches of Christ in the state. S. N. D. North, director of the Bureau of Census, stated that he was charged with the responsibility of gathering the statistics of the religious groups in the nation and sought the help of David Lipscomb. He had received a preachers list published by the McQuiddy Printing Company which named the *Gospel Advocate* as representing the churches of Christ. He faced a problem because comparision with the lists in the *American Home Missionary,* a Christian church paper, showed an overlapping of individuals.

In an effort to resolve the problem North presented four questions to Lipscomb concerning whether the two groups were the same, where the headquarters and other offices of the "religious body called 'church of Christ' " might be found, what were the distinctive principles of the churches of Christ, and how a complete list of the churches might be secured. In answering the questions, Lipscomb went back to the plea of Thomas Campbell in his Declaration and Address to find the keynote of the movement. The early increase of membership was followed by a rupture which developed when many desired to be popular and sought to adopt human inventions which in earlier years had been opposed, namely missionary societies and instrumental music in worship. Because of what was regarded as subversion of the fundamental principles of the movement a division had resulted. At the time of writing the division was not complete because not all members of the groups had divided. In general, however, it was the case that those who favored the societies and instrumental music in worship were unwilling to use preachers who opposed these practices and the same was true of those who opposed these "innovations." Lipscomb answered the questions by noting several characteristics of the churches of Christ. The group known as "the churches of Christ" or "churches of God" were distinct and separate in name, work, and rule of faith from all other bodies or peoples. No general organizations of any kind were present among them due to their strict congregational and independent polity. Their aim was to unite all professed Christians in the effort of "promoting simple, evangelical christianity as God reveals it in the Scriptures." He concluded that the only way he knew to supply a list of churches was to compile one through response to a general circular. He closed his answer by stating,

These disciples have separated from the "Christian churches" that grew out of the effort to restore pure primitive christianity, by remaining true to the original purpose and the principles needful to develop it, while these churches have departed from this end and have set aside the principles of fidelity to the word of God as the only and sufficient rule of faith and practice of Christians. This seems to give us as correct an idea of the facts concerning these churches as I can give.[24]

On November 7, 1907 Lipscomb told of a visit to Nashville by S. N. D. North as a result of the article previously noted. North had requested J. W. Shepherd to assume the task of gathering the information through blanks supplied for the purpose. Lipscomb urged the compliance with this request although he had never laid much stress on the compilation of such statistics.[25] Early in the following year, E. A. Elam noted the presence of false claims by society advocates and plead that all churches assist in the effort being made by Shepherd.[26]

A difficulty soon developed in that many "conservative" churches had sent reports to G. A. Hoffman who was compiling a list of churches for the "progressives." Shepherd pointed out this confusion and appealed that those who had made this error secure another blank and send it to himself so the proper listing could be made.[27] Other complications were overcome, in part, and the results were published in 1910. The results were indicated as 631 churches and 12,451 members in the state in 1906. The statistics of other years will be noted in subsequent sections of this work, but the major result of the census report of 1906 was to mark the fact that two distinct restorationist groups were present in the state. They cherished a common heritage and had enjoyed fellowship for several decades before the turn of the century, but they were then divided over such problems as the use of missionary societies and instrumental music in worship. These two groups have remained divided over the same basic problems from 1906 to the present.

Through the years one can note the view expressed that the problem was one of appearance and not of substance. It was argued that the religious statistician and the secular press had created an impression of division when in reality there was only a serious difference of views. Also, it was contended, as Moses Lard had stated in 1866,[28] that there was no adequate cause for such division and there was no organization by means of which division could come to be. In spite of this refusal to admit reality, it was clear that a division, real and beyond repair, was present in the state by 1906. Those who objected to what they regarded as departures from the principles of the movement, called churches of Christ, were conscious of their identity and were willing to indicate such awareness by compiling, circulating and regarding as indicative of loyalty various lists of preachers annually published by writers on the *Gospel Advocate* staff. In effect the government desire for a census report only provided an occasion to make public a fact long apparent. The list of preachers was being augmented by a gathering of names of churches in the state and the census report only provided a larger forum for such publication as was already in progress. By 1906, then, the churches of Christ were conscious of their identity in Tennessee.

REFERENCES

[1] James A. Harding, "What is it that Unites? *Gospel Advocate* 26 (January 16, 1884):42.

[2] A. E., "For and Against," *Gospel Advocate* 43 (July 18, 1901): 462.

[3] Jesse P. Sewell, "Wouldn't Stand for Organ," *Gospel Advocate* 44 (December 4, 1902):771.

[4] David Lipscomb, "The Creed in the Deed," *Gospel Advocate* 48 (January 11, 1906):25.

[5] Alexander Hall, *The Christian Register* (Loydsville, Ohio: The Compiler, 1848).

[6] Ibid., pp. 38-39.

[7] Benjamin J. Smith and C. C. Smith, eds., *Yearbook of the Churches of Christ (Disciples of Christ)* (Cincinnati: American Christian Missionary Society, 1900), pp. 18, 35, 36.

[8] W. R. Warren, "Concerning Our Statistics," *The American Home Missionary* 16 (January 1910):69-70.

[9] Ibid., pp. 106, 130-31.

[10] Tolbert Fanning, "Disciples' Almanac and Statistical Register," *Gospel Advocate* 2 (December 1856):377-78.

[11] Hall, ibid., pp. 1-3.

[12] David Lipscomb, "Church Statistics," *Gospel Advocate* 11 (April 15, 1869):353.

[13] David Lipscomb, "Those Statistics," *Gospel Advocate* 22 (February 24, 1881): 114.

[14] John R. Williams, "Notes from West Tennessee," *Gospel Advocate* 44 (May 22, 1902):336.

[15] J. W. Shepherd, "Reminiscences of the Past," *Gospel Advocate* 48 (March 15, 1906):162.

[16] David Lipscomb, "Sketches in the History of the Church in Nashville, *Gospel Advocate* 48 (April 19, 1906):243.

[17] David Lipscomb, "Churches in Different Counties," *Gospel Advocate* 48 (April 26, 1906):264-65.

[18] David Lipscomb, "Churches of Christ in Tennessee," *Gospel Advocate* 48 (May 10, 1906):296.

[19] David Lipscomb, "Churches of Christ in Tennessee," *Gospel Advocate* 48 (May 31, 1906):345.

[20] David Lipscomb, "Churches of Christ in Tennessee," *Gospel Advocate* 48 (July 19, 1906):457.

[21] David Lipscomb, "Churches of Christ in West Tennessee," *Gospel Advocate* 48 (October 11, 1906):649.

[22] J. W. Shepherd, "Miscellany," *Gospel Advocate* 48 (September 6, 1906):565.

[23] David Lipscomb, "The 'Church of Christ' and The 'Disciples of Christ'," *Gospel Advocate* 49 (July 18, 1907):457.

[24] Ibid.

[25] David Lipscomb, "United States Census Church Statistics," *Gospel Advocate* 49 (November 7, 1907):713.

[26] E. A. Elam, "The Claims of the Society Work," *Gospel Advocate* 50 (January 23, 1908):49,50.

[27] J. W. Shepherd, "United States Church Census," *Gospel Advocate* 50 (February 27, 1908):133.

[28] Moses E. Lard, "Can We Divide?" *Lard's Quarterly* 3 (April 1866):330-36.

CHAPTER EIGHT

THE HARDEMAN TABERNACLE SERMONS

In 1922 a series of preaching services began to be conducted in Nashville by Nicholas Brodie Hardeman, co-founder of Freed-Hardeman College. These services were to be significant in several ways, all of which were of importance to the subsequent history of the churches of Christ in the state. These meetings—conducted in 1922, 1923, 1928, 1938, and 1942—demonstrated the consciousness of their identity by churches of Christ and may be studied in some depth as an indication of this consciousness. The entire series of sermons was evaluated in a study by Floyd E. Merritt[1] and use will be made of this study in subsequent sections.

The Speaker

N. B. Hardeman was praised by the late B. C. Goodpasture, distinguished editor of the *Gospel Advocate,* in these words, "The influence of N. B. Hardeman for good is unexcelled in churches of Christ through the English speaking world." [2] Hardeman was the subject of a biography published in 1964 [3] and much of the introductory information has been secured from this source. He was born May 18, 1874 just north of Milledgeville, Tennessee, some twenty miles from Henderson, Tennessee, the scene of much of his career. He entered West Tennessee Christian College, in Henderson, in 1890 where he remained for several years. In 1895 Arvy Glenn Freed (1863-1931) came to Henderson to serve as president of the college, known after 1897 as Georgie Robertson Christian College in honor of the daughter of an interested donor. Hardeman studied under Freed until 1896, receiving the B.A. and M.A. degrees. According to a statement by G. Dallas Smith, Hardeman was led by Freed [4] to oppose instrumental music in worship. Hardeman joined the faculty of Georgie Robertson Christian College in 1897 and served until 1905 when, because of sharp disagreement over the instrument in worship and the missionary societies, Freed and Hardeman resigned. The college property was then deeded to the Tennessee Christian Missionary Convention.[5] In 1908 Freed and Hardeman established in Henderson, Tennessee National Teachers' Normal and Business College which opened on September of that year. In 1919 the college was renamed Freed-Hardeman College and placed under a board of directors who contracted to buy the college from the founders, both of whom remained with the college for the time being.

The journal of N. B. Hardeman, cited by Powell and Powers,[6] and references in the *Gospel Advocate* show that Hardeman was quite busy in preaching, debating and teaching. At the time of the first "Tabernacle Sermons" the speaker was well known, highly influential, and fully seasoned for his work.

The Representative Stance

The meetings were explicitly intended and presented as representative of the position of the churches of Christ in the state, indications of which may be noted. In 1928, during the third of the series, an editorial writer in the *Gospel Advocate* stated during the last week of the session,

> In getting primitive christianity before the outside public, this is perhaps the most successful effort put forth in recent years. N. B. Hardeman is plainly and boldly delivering a series of sermons setting forth the position of the church of Christ that has almost literally shaken Nashville. The good of the cause demands that every Christian attend every meeting. We are in the balances! Let us close out this great meeting with record-breaking audiences and a victorious triumph that will put the truth before the world.[7]

James A. Allen, in a front page *Gospel Advocate* article, stated concerning the third series that "more has been done in the last few days to get primitive chrisitanity before the general public than has been done in the last few decades." [8] Something of the representative stance of Hardeman appeared subsequent to the third series in response to an article which appeared in a Catholic paper objecting to some of Hardeman's statements. James A. Allen, editor of the *Gospel Advocate,* challenged for a debate on any or all of twelve propositions. He wanted Hardeman to debate the issues in the proposed debate. Concerning him Allen stated, "Thirty churches of Christ in Nashville, fifty churches of Christ in Nashville and Davidson County, and one thousand churches of Christ in Tennessee will gladly indorse Mr. Hardeman as a nationally known preacher, as a scholar, and as a Christian gentleman." [9]

In this context of endorsement and influence, Hardeman looked back, in 1938, to the meetings he had held at the Ryman Auditorium and stated,

> The influence of these meetings is, I think, yet going on. As I recall, first of all, it made the brethren conscious of their strength and who they really were. I believe it told to the people of Nashville, as nothing else could have, who we were. I believe thse efforts impressed the people of Nashville and the great brotherhood far and near who earnestly accept the faith once for all delivered to the saints. And throughout the length and breadth of the land these have served as a great encouragement to the cause of Christ.[10]

It was clear to those planning and upholding the meetings and to the one preaching that the speaker was a representative of the position espoused by the churches of Christ in the state. Consequently, his work was intended and regarded as representative of the stance of the churches of Christ in the state.

Major Themes of the Series

It was apparent that three major themes were presented in the series. These were the themes of the church, conversion, and the Bible. Of a total of 127 different titles for sermons, at least twenty eight were concerned in one way or another with the church, some twenty five were concerned with conversion, and at least twenty were concerned with the Bible and its place in conversion and life in the church. These three themes may be explored in some depth to discover what Hardeman presented as major aspects of the identity of the movement.[11] Other themes may be studied later as supporting the major emphases of the meetings.

The Church

In the first series, the topic of the church was studied in some detail.[12] The church was defined as "that spiritual realm over which Christ reigns as head and in which the Holy Spirit dwells."[13] The ideal sought was to be a member of the church "about which you read in the New Testament, and at the same time, not a member of any denomination under high heaven."[14] The origin of the church was Pentecost when the material prepared by John the Baptist was brought together, when by the gospel, believers were "added to the Lord."[15]

Recounting a bird's eye view of church history, Hardeman developed the theme "Reformers and Restorers,"[16] a subject which was to occupy much of his later sermons. The orator told of the "disposition of humanity" which was in "opposition to submitting to the authority of the word" and which formed "an ecclesiasticism" to "direct the religious machinery" not according to the Bible but according to "human intelligence, personal feeling, and opinion."[17] This process resulted in blending together church and state and produced so much distress that an attempt was made by such men as Luther, Calvin, Wesley and others to effect a reformation of the church. These men, singled out for appreciative commendation, must not, however, be given undue respect, homage, and adoration.[18] Their motives, intents, and purposes were good, but they were engaged in an impossible task, the reforming of religious institutions which refused to yield to the efforts made.[19] Hardeman commended the fact that all of the reformers "taught a great many things that were true," and observed that "truth is a universal matter, not to be cornered on, nor to be monopolized by any religious sect or order."[20] He declared that the opening of the nineteenth century found the religious world in a state of chaos and confusion. Indeed, "Denominationalism, division, discord and a partisan, sectarian spirit were visible on every hand" and "The Christianity of the Bible . . . had been lost to the world."[21] Of these groups Hardeman stated, "each of them is a total stranger to God's book."[22] This meant, according to the orator, "It is not possible . . . for the world to get together upon anything of a nature like these organizations or bodies. . . ." Consequently, he declared, it is time to halt, examine platforms, and take bearings according to "His word."[23]

These historical observations were gathered into a backdrop for the study of "The Restoration."[24] The characteristics of the general religious scene in the opening of the Nineteenth Century were sketched as including: denominationalism well entrenched in the religious world, a divided church, an arrogant clergy, a beclouded theology, a proliferation of human creeds, and blatant unbelief.[25] The restoration movement, of which Hardeman spoke, had its origin in such a context. The Haldane brothers of Scotland, Thomas Campbell, Barton W. Stone, James O'Kelley, Abner Jones and Alexander Campbell were cited briefly as making various contributions to the effort to overcome the religious conditions prevailing in the period 1790-1830. The work had a solidifying document in the Declaration and Address presented by Thomas Campbell on August 17, 1809.[26] Hardeman stated that the Campbells and others did not set out to reform anything. Instead, he stated "Their purpose was to *restore* that which once existed on earth, and which had been buried underneath the rubbish of ecclesiasticism for hundreds of years." [27] This main thrust of the movement, and a theme which was to recur again and again, was expressed in this paragraph,

> They verily believed that they had the same seed of the kingdom as was planted by Peter. They also believed that the ground or soil was just the same. Therefore, said they, "If we cut loose from humanism, and from things of a worldly nature, and will put into the hearts of men and women the pure, simple, unadulterated word of God, it will spring up and make nothing on earth but Christians. And if those Christians thus formed, and thus developed will blend together, they will constitute a church like unto that we read about in the Bible.[28]

Hardeman discussed the church in terms of its establishment, unity, identity, work, worship, relation to Christ, and importance in his second series of sermons.[29] The church is a monarchy with Christ as the absolute dictator. The arrangement of the church needs no revision or amendment. The church does not save people since Christ is the Savior, but the place of salvation is in the church.[30] The church is to be united under the direction of Christ,[31] and within the limitations fixed by Christ there must be an earnest effort to achieve the unity of the followers of Christ.[32] The identity of the church entailed its being regarded as the counterpart of the church spoken about in the Bible.[33] The work of the church was stated to be: self-edification so that new members may develop to maturity,[34] benevolence in rendering physical and temporal service and help,[35] the spreading of the gospel,[36] and the worship of God.[37] Worship is to be directed to the proper object and in the right way and manner.[38] These requirements of object, way, and manner, are "positively necessary that the act may meet Jehovah's approval." [39]

Hardeman reached the climax of his treatment of the church in his summary near the end of the second volume. He stated, after alluding to Paul's plea that Agrippa become a Christian,

> That is what gospel preachers ever since that time have persuaded men to become and be; and I, for one, would not have you to be anything else. I don't want any man who has ever favored me with his presence to be anything but simply a christian—a member of the church that you read about

in the Bible. I want him then to take the Bible as his creed and discipline and confession of faith, and be faithful, loyal, and true to it the remnant of his days, go about always doing good, walking in His footsteps, practicing the principles of pure and undefiled religion. If he will do that, when at last the storms of life are all over, heaven is certain to be his home.[40]

Conversion

The theme of conversion occupied a great deal of attention in the first, second, third, and fourth volumes, but the most extensive treatment was in the first volume. Hardeman recognized the subject was highly controversial and stated that there was no theme on which there were more differences than the subject of conversion.[41] A basic position of his teaching on conversion appeared in his discussion of the sin of Adam and Eve, the prototype for the sin of man today. Hardeman discussed the sin of Adam and Eve by referring to these steps,

The Bible says that she put forth her hand and ate of the fruit of the tree of knowledge of good and evil, and gave also unto her husband, and he did eat; and as she (1) heard, (2) believed, and (3) obeyed, she became guilty in God's sight and was disinherited and driven out. Watch that just here with these steps. Step No. 1, she believed a lie; step No. 2, she obeyed a lie; step No. 3, she became guilty; step No. 4, God drove her out and closed the gates of paradise behind her. . . .

And that is the condition, my friends, that prevails tonight with reference to every man that has put forth his hand and violated the commands of Almighty God.[42]

The sinner, having become such by and because of what he has done or failed to so,[43] needed according to Hardeman, three changes to be converted. First, the heart—that part of man which reasons, understands, thinks, believes—must be converted or changed. Second, the will—with one's purposes, plans, designs, and schemes—must be changed so that the affection, love, desire, and trust of life are centered on the right ideal and conception of life and duty. Third, the state or relationship unto the government of God must be changed, that is, one must be naturalized or adopted into the family of God.[44] Hardeman discussed a plan by which the heart, will, and the relationship to God could be changed so fully that the sinner would be brought to membership in God's family. This plan of salvation involved, as Hardeman expressed it, an action of God and an action of man. He stated,

. . . in conversion, God has his hand in it all; likewise man has a part. . . . There is nothing in a conversion unless it was begun, carried out, executed, and consumated as a result of God Almighty having a hand therein.

On the other hand, there has never been a genuine conversion unless man had a part in it.[45]

The role of God in the process of conversion was summarized in these words, "God had a part in perfecting, in revealing, in making it known; and hence it was prompted purely by his love, his mercy, and his grace. . . ."[46] Later he explained, "God provided the scheme of salvation, and orders the apostles, prompted by love, to commence with man as he is and lead him back to the state or plane from which he fell." [47]

In a summary of man's part, Hardeman stated, "It is just a question of whether or not you and I believe what God said, . . . do what He requires, and then trust Him for every promise." [48] Man learns, as a sinner, of this plan in the gospel. Hardeman argued that the gospel, as it is, is adapted to man as he is. [49] According to Hardeman's analysis, man has intellect, the power to know; will, the power to do; and emotion, the power to feel. [50] The gospel consists, according to the orator, of facts which satisfy the intellect, [51] commands which relate to the will power, [52] and promises which are "fitted to" the emotions of man. [53] Accordingly, the sinner is to be taught these facts, commands, and promises to induce him to turn away from sin and come to God, i.e., to be converted.

The sermons by Hardeman expressed in various ways the conviction of the speaker and a large portion of the audience present at the service that God has revealed a plan whereby one may return to God after he has sinned. God has told him what he must do to be saved, [54] and this is to be taught to the sinner. [55] When this gospel teaching has been heard, believed, and obeyed in repentance, confession of faith, and immersion in the name of the Father, Son and Holy Spirit, one is converted.

The Bible

Attention has already been called to several indications of the significance of the Bible in the preaching during the Hardeman meetings. Hardeman summed up his view of the place of the Bible by referring to the principle of loose versus strict construction as illustrated in the federalist and antifederalist interpretation of the constitutional proceedings in the days of Alexander Hamilton and Thomas Jefferson. [56] Of the group he represented he declared,

> We have no creed, no discipline, no confession of faith, no church manual, no ritual except the Bible, the book of God divine. . . . We claim to be nothing under the shining realm except Christians—Christians only. We stand pledged to the idea of speaking where the Bible speaks and keeping silent where God's book is silent. This gives the only possible basis for Christian unity. . . . [57]

To Hardeman, and those he represented in his proclamation, the Bible, strictly interpreted, was for the religious life what the constitution, strictly interpreted, is to be for the political life of America.

The Bible has such a place of authority because of its origin and the intention of God concerning it. Hardeman claimed that inspiration meant that "God spoke every word, one by one, unto those to whom he had assigned the task of penning his will toward man." [58] This guidance by God meant "there was not a single contradiction or discrepancy regarding any of the statements thus made." [59] Hardeman was concerned to observe that inspiration did not preclude the individual style of the writers since God was able to "fit his words, one by one, suited to the method by which Paul, Peter, James or John might express them-selves." [60] Hardeman argued that the ability of the Bible to satisfy the heart of man, the demonstration of the accuracy of its laws such as the bringing forth after its kind, the proof of prophecy, and the harmony between the Bible and God's handiwork in nature conclusively prove the Bible is the word of God.[61] He sought to establish the thought that the Bible is the inspired, inerrant word of God and can be defended against attacks which would reduce it to a lower level of origin and value.

This understanding of the origin of the Bible and its role in conversion and life underlay the view of Hardeman and his audience concerning the work of the Spirit in conversion. Hardeman contended that there were only two possible ways the Holy Spirit could operate, directly or indi-rectly. If the operation is direct, without means, then the Holy Spirit "directly, straightforward, immediately, separate and apart from every-thing else, with nothing intervening" [62] effects conversion by a direct touching of the soul of man in order to conversion. If, on the other hand, the work of the Spirit in conversion is by means, then conversion is effected by an instrument, the word of God. The speaker referred to the former position as "the unreasonable, the unscriptural, and the wholly foreign idea of a direct or immediate operation of the Holy Spirit." [63] He referred to the latter as entailing "the truth that the Holy Spirit operates upon the heart of the sinner through a medium, and that medium is the book of God!" [64] This conviction that the Holy Spirit operates in con-version in and through the Bible and not apart from it underlay the urgency of preaching because in preaching the gospel was to be taught and the sinner was brought to faith and obedience as previously noted. Because God uses the Bible as the means to produce faith and because preaching is the God given means to be used to kindle the interest of the heart of man to faith, the preacher must recognize the sufficiency of the Bible and proclaim its message with conviction and power.[65]

A significant concern of Hardeman in reference to the Bible was the practical approach of the individual to the Bible as a means to its effec-tive use. In moving from the high view of Scripture to practical results, Hardeman followed a general hermeneutic or approach which may be traced briefly. He contended that the Bible, unstudied and unsearched, is like a mine unworked and undeveloped.[66] In obtaining the teaching of the Bible, the orator observed, "How does God teach us? First, by direct statement. Second, by appropriate example. Third, by a *necessary* inference. And now it is mine to demonstrate these three methods. . . ."[67] The first means of teaching was shown by reference to repentance (Acts 17:30), the need to assemble (Hebrews 10:25), and the need to contribute in support of God's work (1 Corinthians 16:2). The second means of teaching was shown by the example of observing the Lord's Supper on the first day of the week in Troas (Acts 20:7). The third means of teach-ing required more careful expression. Hardeman state that there were some things the Bible teaches but one cannot read them in so many words and one cannot find a direct example of such things. The ground of such belief as to Bible teaching was "a necessary deduction or inference." This type of authority, the orator admitted, forced one to be careful, but it could be developed along a certain model. The distinction was drawn between inferences which are logical and reasonable and inferences which are necessary. He illustrated the former by raising the question of his means of transportation from Henderson to Nashville. It would be logical and reasonable, but not necessary, to infer he came by train, bus, private car, mule, or walking. As to each of these inferences, one could see their reasonableness, but not one of them could be said to be necessary to explain how he came to Nashville. He illustrated what he meant by a necessary, as contrasted with a logical and reasonable, inference in several ways. In Genesis 13:1 it was said that Lot went with Abraham and Sarah out of Egypt. It was said that Abraham and Sarah went into Egypt in Genesis 12, but nothing was said about Lot's going into Egypt. Accordingly, Hardeman reasoned, there was a "necessary inference" that Lot went "into" Egypt though the Bible did not say he did so. The significant statement was made, "I am forced to the conclusion, therefore, that he must have gone down into the land else the statement of the Bible that he came out of it could not be true." [68] It was the view of Hardeman that given all the relevant statements of the Bible on a certain subject, there was an inference one could draw from these verses which was not only reasonable and logical, but also necessary to be drawn. This inference was such that, given the truth of the Bible, one could not hold to the truth of the Bible and deny the necessary inference.

Hardeman applied his insights concerning a necessary inference in two significant ways, as a negative and as an affirmative instrument. In a negative application he showed that the inference from the baptism of Lydia's household (Acts 16) that infants were baptized, while not a "silly" inference, was not "necessary for the statement of God's word to be true . . ." Accordingly the inference that babies were baptized in the conversion of Lydia "is a dangerous conclusion and not necessarily so." The reason, "The facts of the Bible can exist"[69] without such an inference being drawn. In an affirmative application Hardeman referred to the establishment of the church on Pentecost. He admitted there is no clear statement or example which indicates this to be true, but he noted several verses (Mark 9:1, Luke 24: 46-48, Acts 1:8, Acts 2:1-4) which he concluded, "forced" him to the conclusion the church was established on Pentecost.[70] This instrument of clear statement, command, and necessary inference was developed in great detail in a sermon on "The Teaching of God's Word" [71] and undergirded the effort of Hardeman at every turn of Bible teaching. If sustained by this instrument, a certain doctrine or practice was regarded as authorized by the Bible, but if not so sustained it was regarded as not authorized by the Bible and was to be rejected.

A final concern of the orator was to discuss the vital theme of "Essentials and Non-Essentials." [72] He explained that he did not mean that one was free to disregard any part of the Bible and treat it without respect since "There's not a syllable in the Bible applicable to man, but there is meaning attached to it, and upon our acceptance or rejection, depands our eternal destiny." [73] Instead, he was concerned about the ways and means of carrying out commands and responsibilities to God and the study of what was termed "generic" and "specific" authority. Taking his illustration from the Great Commission (Matthew 28:19-20), he referred to three words: Go, teach, baptize. Each of these was a command of God, and each word entailed the doing of a certain thing or action. But each also entailed "a lot of things, preparatory to that act." [74] In baptism, for instance, a burial and coming up out of the water are requisite, thus "essential," but the temperature, place containing the water, the position of the one baptized, and related matters are not essential to the doing of the act itself and may be fulfilled in different ways at different times; thus such aspects are "non-essential." He concluded that "the thing" that God commands must be done, but an expedient which aids in the doing of what God commands is not of equal rank with the commanded "thing" and should be regarded as a non-essential and subject to variation. A pressing problem was to avoid making an essential into a non-essential, and reversing the process so that a non-essential was made into an essential. Hardeman clearly indicated his conclusion in a discussion of faith versus opinion.

> We ought to stand as a solid phalanx on matters of faith. If God has declared a thing and we can read it from His word, I would not move one-thousandth of an inch; I could not compromise one idea of faith taught by God's word, but if it be merely a matter of opinion, let me have it, but let me hold it to myself. I have no right to force my opinion upon anyone else. . . . Let's hold that opinion as private property. And then, in all things, let there be charity, and let brotherly love prevail as long as there is not a sacrifice of faith demanded. [75]

It was clear that Hardeman sought to weave together the strands of Bible teaching concerning the church, the plan of conversion, and the Bible. These major themes constituted the heart of the series and, in view of the representative stance assumed and supported, are to be regarded as central to the identity of the group known as churches of Christ in Tennessee. The failure to accept one or all of these central themes as developed in summary form by Hardeman would, apparently, be equal to one's being regarded as outside the group. Thus, one may see the consciousness of identity as portrayed in this series of important sermons.

Supporting Themes

The previous study has called attention to the heart of the series, but some supporting themes may be noted briefly. Hardeman taught that revelation, as was received by chosen men in the first century, is not being received today; [76] consequently, the claim of miraculous powers does not make one a child of God. [77] Instead, the Bible alone is the guide in all matters of Christian faith and service.[78] The church is to possess today all the lines of demarcation which were set forth in the first century.[79] In line with these two emphases on the Bible and the church, such unauthorized practices as washing feet[80] and instrumental music[81] must not be tolerated. Indeed, one should realize that the cause of much trouble was the introduction of the instrument into worship, in the wake of which came many other departures and the loss of property in spite the protests of those who sacrificed to build the meeting houses.[82] This error and others, should be opposed with vigor; however, the opposition should not be to persons but rather to the practices and principles involved.[83] In such defense and declaration one should proceed without a shadow of a doubt, standing "four-square for the defense of the truth." [84] To be sure, he counseled, one should not be a crank or a hobbyist in his proclamation of his faith[85] but having learned the truth he should uphold it with vigor.[86]

Two main themes, with which other parts of this study will have to do, were unity and premillennialism. These served as unspoken problems against the background of which some of the series originated. These twin problems called forth a clarification of the nature of the movement so as to be certain what was involved in and constituted elements of the proper unity to be enjoyed; premillennialism, in particular, was seen as subverting the plea of the movement by employing false principles of interpretation, reaching erroneous conclusions, and by valuing associations with fellow premillennialists more than the brotherhood in general. Such belief and practice opened the door to compromise by the entire movement.[87] Hardeman, reaching what he termed "brass tacks," indicated he could not recognize one who had not "obeyed the gospel," particularly "he that believeth and is baptized shall be saved," as a Christian, would not "play 'buddy' " with him, and would not call upon him to invoke God's blessings upon what he did not believe.[88] In contrast, the type of unity desired—to which three special sermons were devoted[89]—was to be obtained by speaking and doing wholly the things spoken in the oracles of God and not fastening upon others any personal theories or philosophies alien to this teaching.[90] Consequently, the indifference of many should be removed and all together should stand for the old principles which had sustained the movement through its history.[91]

N. B. Hardeman had lengthy and significant preparation behind him when he began this series of sermons in 1922. As the years passed he gained an even greater influence as an educator as well as preacher and debater. In the years of the Tabernacle Sermons he occupied a unique place among churches of Christ in Tennessee. In his work the threads of thought from early leaders in the movement, writers and teachers he had known, and his own studies were gathered together. In his work, therefore, the movement reached a high water mark in its consciousness of its identity. By references previously cited it was evident that his work was regarded as representative of the movement at large. Consequently, one may regard the main thoughts of the movement known as churches of Christ as having been gathered, clarified and explained in the work of this man.

REFERENCES

[1] Floyd E. Merritt, "An Institutional Study of the Hardeman Tabernacle Meetings," (Master's thesis, The University of Kansas Graduate School, 1964).

[2] James Marvin Powell and Mary Nelle Hardeman Powers, *N. B. H. A Biography of Nicholas Brodie Hardeman,* with an Introduction by B. C. Goodpasture (Nashville: Gospel Advocate Company, 1964), p. 1.

[3] Ibid.

[4] G. Dallas Smith, "A Statement Concerning Brother A. G. Freed," *Gospel Advocate* 65 (March 12, 1903):171.

[5] Herman A. Norton, *Tennessee Christians* (Nashville: Reed and Company, 1971), p. 182.

[6] Powell and Powers, ibid., pp. 157-68.

[7] Anonymous, "Read This!" *Gospel Advocate* 70 (March 29, 1928):294.

[8] James A. Allen, "N. B. Hardeman," *Gospel Advocate* 70 (April 5, 1928):314.

[9] James A. Allen, "Will They Debate?" *Gospel Advocate* 70 (May 17, 1928):458.

[10] N. B. Hardeman, *Hardeman's Tabernacle Sermons,* IV (Nashville: Gospel Advocate Company, 1938), p. 9.

[11] N. B. Hardeman, *Hardeman's Tabernacle Sermons,* 5 vols. (Nashville: Gospel Advocate Company, 1922-1942). For convenience only the separate volumes will be noted along with the page(s) cited.

[12] I, 219-32.

[13] I, 224.

[14] I, 228.

[15] I, 256.

[16] I, 256-74.

[17] I, 257.

[18] I, 260-61.

[19] I, 261.

[20] III, 111.

[21] I, 261.

[22] III, 107.

[23] Ibid.

[24] III, 110-23.

[25] III, 111-12.

[26] III, 117.

[27] III, 122.

[28] III, 123.

[29] II, 164-251.

[30] II, 176.

[31] II, 181.

[32] II, 184.

[33] II, 188-90.

[34] II, 201-02.

[35] II, 205.

[36] II, 208.

[37] II, 213-30.

[38] II, 220.

[39] II, 215.

[40] II, 249.

[41] I, 89.

[42] I, 96-97.

[43] IV, 243.

[44] I, 92-93.

[45] II, 90.

[46] I, 91.

[47] I, 97.

[48] IV, 189.

[49] IV, 60-70.

[50] IV, 66.

[51] IV, 69.
[52] IV, 69.
[53] IV, 70.
[54] I, 176-85.
[55] IV, 46-59.
[56] I, 76-87.
[57] I, 80.
[58] IV, 39.
[59] I, 68.
[60] IV, 38.
[61] I, 18-31.
[62] IV, 208.
[63] IV, 209.
[64] IV, 209.
[65] I, 27,66; IV, 100, 211, 213.
[66] I, 29.
[67] IV, 52.
[68] IV, 55-56.
[69] IV, 57.
[70] IV, 57-58.
[71] IV, 46-59.
[72] IV, 99-107.
[73] IV, 100.
[74] IV, 103.
[75] IV, 229.
[76] I, 30.
[77] I, 138.
[78] IV, 30.
[79] IV, 132.
[80] IV, 54.
[81] IV, 59.
[82] IV, 143.
[83] IV, 121.
[84] IV, 167.
[85] IV, 105.
[86] IV, 35.
[87] IV, 81-82, 86, 137-38, 149-66.
[88] IV, 121.
[89] III, 124-63.
[90] IV, 73.
[91] IV, 142.

CHAPTER NINE

UNITY MOVEMENTS
THROUGH THE YEARS

The division in the ranks of the restoration movement in Tennessee became a reality in the period 1897-1906. In these years the churches, preachers, and papers were separating into distinct groups with well-known characteristics, and were seeking to stabilize themselves for separate existence. It was only natural that those who had so many points of belief and practice in common, while admitting various points of difference as well, should seek to restore the highly cherished unity they once had known. There was in heart, head, and hand a desire for unity. What was sought was a way, a plan, a means. Over the years different attempts were made to effect the unity desired. Three of these attempts, during the early, middle, and late decades of the period studied, may be considered in brief summary. These three efforts underscore the desire for unity, the inability to find a plan, and the consciousness of identity which would not be sacrificed to achieve the unity so ardently and genuinely sought among alienated brethren.

Early Efforts

In the presence of much difficulty and conscious of the seriousness of their effort, ten men conducted a rather unique unity meeting in Nashville in 1909. Working from a memorandum book of M. C. Kurfees, who was one of the participants, P. W. Stonestreet told of the incident in 1941.[1] According to M. C. Kurfees five men in favor of the society and the organ met with five men who opposed the use of the society and the instrument. A stenographer was present to record the session. The meeting was held Thursday, February 18, 1909, at the home of John B. Cowden from 10:00 A.M. to 4:00 P.M. The purpose of the meeting was to find, if possible, "common ground accepted by all and on which all could work and worship in harmony." J. B. Briney, an advocate of the instrument, proposed a plan which would have two preachers, respectively serving churches which did and did not use the society and the instrument, unite to establish a new work in a place of mutual choosing. Such a work, he proposed, should not have the instrument and use the society so as to insure unity. This non-use of the society and instrument would supply a common ground. M. C. Kurfees agreed that the leaving off of the society and instrument would resolve the problem. He encouraged the acceptance of the proposal since it removed "the barrier to union and cooperation, and leaves us with common ground where all can work and worship in harmony." Briney then objected that his proposal extended only to a new work such as he had indicated and would not apply to an established work where an organ or society was already being used. Kurfees stated that he was willing to accept the common ground proposed for the new work and pressed to know why, if such terms of agreement were acceptable for a new work, they would not be acceptable in an established work. This point at issue was not resolved and the meeting adjourned without effecting unity. Kurfees stated that he and his brethren were willing to accept the proposal made by Briney, but he noted that under scrutiny the proposal would not be accepted by Briney and his brethren. He concluded, "The conference adjourned with their rejecting the common ground suggested by themselves, and with our hearty acceptance of it." Stonestreet, commenting on the incident, observed that the document was just as appropriate in his day as when it was written. He concluded by saying that "no better ground for unity" had been presented than the proposal in "that historic meeting." While this meeting was only a meeting of interested persons, it indicated the desire for unity and faced the sticking point in the path to unity.

Efforts in the Early 1920s

Following the Nashville discussion in 1909 there were several significant developments which prepared the way for a resumption of efforts to restore unity among the estranged brethren. In 1911 M. C. Kurfees published a volume on instrumental music in worship [2] in which he discussed "Making Tests of Fellowship and Causing Division." [3] He argued that the users of the instrument, in doing what was not authorized, were responsible for "the deliberate creation and perpetuation . . . of division in the body of Christ" and were doing this in spite of the fact that "according to their own admission" they "could prevent such division and still maintain a pure conscience before God and before men." [4] His conclusion was to be seriously challenged in later days, but Kurfees was seeking to lay the blame on the users of the instrument. It was clear that an attempt was being made by a writer on the *Gospel Advocate* to argue the scripturalness of the issue and assess guilt and innocence. A second incident of importance was the establishment of a Commission on Unity in Tennessee by E. H. Koch, Secretary of the Tennessee Christian Missionary Society (1914-1919). In 1917 this commission was organized and began sending out tracts to "conservative brothers, with a view to bringing about a better understanding and eventually bringing about union." [5] John B. Cowden, a participant in the 1909 meeting, took an active part in this work. In 1919 a book was published by O. E. Payne on *Instrumental Music in the Worship*. This book was intended as a reply to Kurfees' book, previously noted. In the book Payne took the position that the Greek verb *psallo* is such that the instrument "unavoidably inheres" in the term and is "mandatory." [6] His words were regarded as extreme even by sympathizers and were to become a serious point of contention in later years as the next chapter will make clear.

These three events—Kurfees' book, the Commission on Unity, and

Payne's book—began to be of major significance in 1922. In 1921 the Commission on Unity sent a copy of the book by Payne to F. B. Srygley, an editor of the *Gospel Advocate,* for his consideration. The next year the Commission asked for the return of the book. In response Srygley challenged the Commission on Unity to defend the propositions on church music stated by Payne in the book being circulated by the Commission.[7] On June 7 Cowden responded that the State convention would meet in Ovoca the following week and he would bring the proposal for a debate before the group. The next week Srygley quoted Cowden, showing his [Cowden's, W. W.] understanding of the relation between the debate and unity, in these words:

> . . . but this question has become so involved with the question of fraternity, which we do regard worth contending for, that we are disposed to accept your proposition as a doubtful yet possible step toward the restoration of fraternity between those that use and those that do not use instruments in the church. We have tried everything else without bettering the situation; and, for my part, I am ready to try this. However, there are many that doubt the wisdom of any such discussions, who must be considered. I have shared this view in the past, but I am now inclined to think otherwise with respect to the church-music question.[8]

As the summer passed, it became apparent that the Commission on Unity was not particularly anxious to debate the issue of instrumental music in worship. In early August Srygley surmised the debate would likely not take place because of difficulties in defending Payne's book.[9] The next week Srygley told of a letter from John B. Cowden declining to defend Payne's book in a public debate and then chided the Commission for circulating a book it would not defend. Srygley reluctantly accepted Cowden's statement that Payne would have to defend himself.[10]

Further developments transpired in the rest of that year and the following year. S. H. Hall debated J. J. Walker in Ryman Auditorium in a brief exchange on instrumental music in worship.[11] M. C. Kurfees continued to plead that those who circulated Payne's book should either defend it or repudiate it as not representative of their position.[12] In spite of considerable confusion over the wording of propositions[13] during the next year N. B. Hardeman debated Ira M. Boswell (May 31-June 5, 1923) on the proposition: "Instrumental Music in Church Worship is Scriptural."[14] Though of interest in a subsequent study, the debate which ensued need not be further considered at present.

The early 1920s witnessed a second major development in polarization in the two groups alleging to be embodiments of a restoration ideal. Previous years had seen the break made public and had witnessed the failure of efforts to heal the breach, but the events just narrated showed a new dimension. A serious effort to effect unity had emerged, several exchanges of significance had occurred, and rival books setting forth the opposing views had appeared. Now the people could turn to representative men and representative defenses of conflicting positions. A new level of development had been reached. An issue of major difference had finally been crystallized into a single proposition which could be debated by capable representatives of the opposing camps. No longer would a brief meeting by a few chosen men suffice; now a clear cut issue was present in a short statement which could be accepted or refused. The achieving of unity could not come without an all out fight on this single point which was regarded as not only intrinsically important but symptomatic of other equally serious differences. Debates which developed around this point served to underscore the reality of division and the impossibility of removing such division without resolving this crucial difference. The identity of the group known as churches of Christ was becoming more obvious and rigid. Now a basic position had been clearly expressed, capable defenders were present, and no quarter would be asked or given. The consciousness of identity was most apparent.

Efforts in the Late 1930s

Early in 1937 John T. Hinds, editor of the *Gospel Advocate,* commented on an article concerning a proposed union between Congregationalist and Disciples of Christ groups in Massachusetts. The merger recognized differences on baptism and the Lord's Supper but sought to adjust these by a "freedom of choice" arrangement which meant "each church was willing to adjust that the United church might be formed. . . ." He concluded his report with words which were to be prophetic of an attitude to prevail in succeeding months,

> By no sort of twisting can such union be made unto the likeness of the "unity of the Spirit" demanded by Paul. If people are not willing to respect Bible teaching on unity, any efforts at union must be a failure from the start. Any kind of union that omits unity must be a compromise of vital truths and a disgrace to its advocates . . . Such unions are nothing less than plain compromises.[15]

In a few months a series of unity efforts were to focus attention on the truth or falsity of the attitude expressed by Hinds. In 1934 at the Des Moines International Convention of the Disciples of Christ a Commission on Restudy of the Disciples of Christ had been established by means of which a major effort was made to find a way to reunite the various segments of the divided restoration movement.[16] In the same year a unity effort by James DeForest Murch and Edwin R. Errett of the *Christian Standard,* called "Christian Action," had also been set in motion. By early 1937 this latter effort was promoting unity meetings between equal numbers of men from the churches of Christ and the Christian Churches. Meetings in Cincinnati, Akron, Los Angeles, and other places showed the national dimension of the intended effort.[17] It was this series of meetings which generated the concern to be noted among the churches of Christ in Tennessee.

In April 1937 a report was given in the *Gospel Advocate* concerning meetings between preachers from the two groups in Cincinnati and Indianapolis. The leadership of the group among the churches of Christ was being taken by Claude F. Witty, a preacher in Detroit. Witty was quoted as being convinced that "good might come of it" and as having presented a speech in support of the continuance of the meetings.[18] Later Witty's speech was reprinted in part. He used the illustration of a kicking mule to indicate that some would object to anything in the approach to unity.[19] D. H. Hadwin, a former member of the Christian Church but now "affiliated with the church of Christ" and a personal friend of Murch, had been invited to the meetings. He felt that it was a hopeless effort to conduct such meetings. The presence of fine, conscientious people did not "mean that we can reform the Christian church" any more than Martin Luther could reform the Roman Catholic Church.[20] Witty was soon to respond that he was willing to be scorned, held up to ridicule, and even despised in an effort to restore peace "among those who should be one body and one spirit."[21] Later Witty was to claim his brethren were poorly informed as to his intentions and regard for truth. He felt that the sentiment of leading men was on his side and that the time was right to go on with the efforts for unity.[22] As the charges and counter charges were being passed in 1937 it became apparent that the proposals by Murch and Witty were being stubbornly resisted by the *Gospel Advocate.* Both on a state and a national level there was to be resistance to the proposals for unity which did not deal with and/or resolve what were regarded as major points of difference. The year closed with the issues being clearly drawn and with prospects of a sharp encounter when an opportunity presented itself.

In 1938 there was at last an occasion for the type of confrontation many desired. F. B. Srygley began the year with a charge that James DeForest Murch was premillennialist,[23] and Claude Witty attempted to focus the issues in a speech entitled "Can We Walk the Wire?" He claimed that nine issues were the causes of alienation and these nine issues were segments of a wire across which the participants in the unity effort had to walk on the way to unity. The nine items were: instrumental music in worship, missionary societies, Ladies Aid societies, the organized Sunday school, the pastor system, fund raising by means of suppers and entertainment, the use of choirs and special songs, and the use of the name Disciples' Church or Christian Church. He proposed to have sessions to discuss these differences, have the reasons for and against stated and distributed, and to have each congregation decide for itself what it wished to do on these items.[24] W. E. Brightwell responded that this proposal omitted the essential question of the right or wrong nature of instrumental music and placed such use in the realm of judgment, an essential point not to be begged. He claimed the proposal meant, in effect, that Witty had no real convictions against the instrument and could not properly "represent" those who had convictions in the exchanges necessary to be conducted. He observed that debates had already been conducted on the issues and nothing of significance was yet to be said. Also, he observed that the topics other than instrumental music and missionary societies were not of the same substantive importance and were attempts to "belittle" churches of Christ because of what others regarded as trivialities. Further, he indicated congregations had already spoken on the issues and the lines were already drawn. Of the prospects he stated,

The people whose fellowship you have enjoyed for many years will not compromise. You can do nothing more than create a disturbance, and possibly lead away a few weak members who are a liability to whoever receives them.[25]

In February H. Leo Boles argued that the present generations of Christian Churches and churches of Christ had never had fellowship and could not "restore" what had never been. In fact, the two groups are "at the extremities of two widely divergent lines." As to the proposals being offered, he stated,

It is futile to attempt any effort toward bringing these two groups of people together in fellowship with each other and with Christ without removing the differences . . . Any effort toward unification with them that ignores the causes of the separation is neither logical nor scriptural; any effort that would take the churches of Christ over to the "Christian church" is a betrayal of Christ and must be condemned by every faithful Christian.[26]

In early March G. C. Brewer told of an invitation he had received to attend and speak at a conference on unity in Detroit in May, but he indicated that he would not attend the meeting. Also, he indicated that there was no good to be derived from a lamentation over the evils of division. The sticking point was that the two groups held mutually exclusive positions and no third position was possible without compromise which neither group would make. He stated,

We cannot use instrumental music and not use it at the same time. It will either be a case of having once used it and quit, or of having once not used it, but took it up; or else it will continue as it is—one group using it and another group not using it. So of the missionary societies.[27]

In a further article Brewer recounted Tennessee history to show that in the 1920s other men had promoted a series of efforts to effect unity. This effort and related developments resulted in the dividing of churches in Columbia and Sparta, Tennessee. This evidence was used to give "some idea of what some of these digressives mean when they talk about unity." [28]

On May 3 and 4, 1938 a meeting was held in the building of the Inglewood Christian Church, 57 North Rual, Indianapolis, Indiana. The meeting was to consist of songs, prayers, and speeches on the theme of unity. During the week of the meeting John W. Kurfees stated that his brother, M. C. Kurfees, who had attended the meeting to discuss unity in 1909 and had written extensively on all phases of the division, would not be interested in the type of unity proposed by Witty and Murch.[29] It was becoming more evident each week that stubborn resistance was being offered by the writers in the Tennessee based *Gospel Advocate*.

During this meeting in Indianapolis H. Leo Boles (1874-1946) spoke to the group on "The Way of Unity between 'Christian Church' and Churches of Christ." [30] Boles' biographer stated that B. C. Goodpasture had been asked to speak on that occasion, but he had recommended Boles.[31] Boles spoke for one hour and thirty one minutes. He indicated that he was no delegate or representative and that he had not been sent by any church or group of churches. He spoke as an individual and he alone was responsible for his words.[32] He reviewed the history of the movement from the days of Barton W. Stone and the Campbells, noting that serious departures from the principles of the movement began in 1849.[33] He listed three significant departures: the missionary society,[34] the use of instruments in worship,[35] and the fact that the "Christian Church" had become a denomination.[36] The cause of the separation was stated to be making "opinion" equal to the word of God.[37] This was to substitute opinion for faith, and put such expressions as "areas of silence," "liberty of opinion," and "realm of expediency" on a par with the teaching of the New Testament.[38] Instead of the opinion standard, Boles plead for all to "exalt the supremacy of the word of God and keep opinions private," to lay aside all "opinions, ways, inventions, devices, practices, organizations, creeds, confessions, names, manner of work, except those plainly presented and clearly required in the New Testament." [39] Of this course he stated,

> Brethren, this is where the churches of Christ stand today; it is where unity may be found now; it is where you left the New Testament; it is where you left the churches of Christ, and it is where you can find them when you come back. On this ground and teaching, and only on this, can scriptural unity be had now; on these basic principles of the New Testament Christian unity may always be had.[40]

He concluded his speech with the statement that these departures must be opposed; indeed to oppose such introduction of departures would be "to comply with the command of God to keep his temple and service pure." [41] He would have no "misguided zeal for unity that blinds us to the only way which leads to God and unity." [42]

W. L. Totty, who heard the speech, was quoted in the pamphlet as stating concerning the effect of the speech on its hearers, "He told them in no uncertain terms what had caused the division and what it would take to bring about unity—that if they expected a compromise they were mistaken." [43] B. C. Goodpasture stated that Boles had presented "the only safe and acceptable grounds of unity," and "It will likely be a long time before we see a clearer or more courageous presentation of the issues involved." [44]

Reports of the meeting were soon appearing in the *Gospel Advocate*. J. N. Armstrong thought the meeting was a good thing and encouraged its major thrust,[45] but the general reaction was one of futility at worst and concern at best. Thomas H. Burton saw such meetings as of value for "them" but of no value for churches of Christ.[46] Other reports similar to Burton's view appeared from F. B. Srygley,[47] W. E. Brightwell,[48] and Cled E. Wallace.[49] As the year closed E. C. Koltenbah, who had formerly been in the Christian Church, analyzed the proposals of Witty and Murch and observed that the movement refused to renounce the causes of the division and sought to shift the blame for division from those who introduced and used the objectionable practices to those who opposed them.[50]

Reports concerning the unity efforts continued through the years immediately following. Unity meetings continued to be conducted, but they were attended by only a few men among churches of Christ. John Allen Hudson declined to attend such a meeting in 1941.[51] H. Leo Boles contended that the Christian Church would not renounce the causes of the division and consequently asked, "Why negotiate further with them?" [52] L. L. Brigance saw such meetings as fraught with the danger that Claude Witty would not apply and follow his proposals on unity when the ones with whom he disagreed were premillennialists rather than advocates of instrumental music.[53] H. Leo Boles regarded the unity movement as a fiasco[54] and later offered proof that Murch would not give up the instrument.[55] Boles then replied to Murch's arguments in favor of the instrument.[56] It was apparent by the end of the year 1941 that nothing was to come of the movement by Witty and Murch. After the death of Witty,[57] others were to make similar efforts, but to no avail. For all intents and purposes the attempts to bring about unity between the two groups had come to a close.

The churches of Christ in Tennessee were aware of their identity throughout the period studied. At the time of the census reports in 1906 there was a listing of preachers and churches already in preparation, and the national census effort only served to make apparent what was already known in the state, i.e., that churches of Christ were essentially a different religious body from their religious neighbors in general and the Christian Churches in particular. The five fold series of Hardeman Tabernacle Sermons over the years 1922-1941 put into words various emphases of the churches of Christ in the state. The wide acceptance of Hardeman as a preacher, debater, and educator; the indications of endorsement and expressions of intention that the sermons be regarded as representative of positions held by the group; the thorough support of the leading paper in the state; and the wide acclaim, use, and approval of the volumes underscore the fact that these sermons were indeed expressions of what was believed by the group. These served as expressions of identity as well. The three major attempts to bring about unity between and among estranged brethren made it clear that the churches of Christ knew what they believed and were not willing to surrender these beliefs for the effecting of unity however greatly this was desired. These three major events served to make clear to those within and without the fact that churches of Christ were conscious of their identity, would gladly defend cherished beliefs, and would not sacrifice these beliefs for any reason.

REFERENCES

[1] P. W. Stonestreet, "Nashville Unity Meeting," *Gospel Advocate* 83 (June 26, 1941):614.

[2] M. C. Kurfees, *Instrumental Music in Worship on the Greek Verb Psallo: Philologically and Historically Examined Together With A Full Discussion of Kindred Matters Relating to Music in Christian Worship* (Nashville: Gospel Advocate Company, 1911, Reprint 1950).

[3] Ibid., pp. 250-65.

[4] Ibid., p. 262.

[5] Herman A. Norton, *Tennessee Christians* (Nashville: Reed and Company, 1971), p. 235.

[6] O. E. Payne, *Instrumental Music Is Scriptural* (Cincinnati: The Standard Publishing Company, 1920), p. 52.

[7] F. B. Srygley, "That Commission on Unity, Again," *Gospel Advocate* 64 (June 1, 1922):516-17.

[8] F. B. Srygley, "Will There be a Discussion on the Music Question?" *Gospel Advocate* 64 (June 15, 1922):564.

[9] F. B. Srygley, "Liberty in Christ," *Gospel Advocate* 64 (August 3, 1922):726.

[10] F. B. Srygley, "The Debate is Over," *Gospel Advocate* 64 (August 10, 1922):749.

[11] H. Leo Boles, "Walker-Hall Discussion," *Gospel Advocate* 64 (November 2, 1922):1036-37.

[12] M. C. Kurfees, "The Christian Standard and Honorable Controversy," *Gospel Advocate* 64 (November 2, 1922):1044-45.

[13] F. B. Srygley, "Will the Committees Meet?" *Gospel Advocate* 64 (November 9, 1922):1060-61.

[14] James Marvin Powell and Mary Nelle Hardeman Powers, *N. B. H. A Biography of Nicholas Brodie Hardeman*, with an Introduction by B. C. Goodpasture (Nashville: Gospel Advocate Company, 1964), pp. 184-97.

[15] John T. Hinds, "Union vs. Unity," *Gospel Advocate* 79 (January 14, 1937):29.

[16] James DeForest Murch, *Christians Only* (Cincinnati: Standard Publishing Company, 1962), pp. 263-72.

[17] Ibid., pp. 272-74.

[18] F. B. Srygley, "Two Portentous Meetings," *Gospel Advocate* 79 (April 29, 1937):389-97.

[19] F. B. Srygley, "That Kicking Mule," *Gospel Advocate* 79 (May 6, 1937):413.

[20] D. H. Hadwin, "Can We Reform Them?" *Gospel Advocate* 79 (May 13, 1937):445.

[21] Cled E. Wallace, "On With the Battle!" *Gospel Advocate* 79 (June 17, 1937):562.

[22] Claude F. Witty, "Brethren, You Are Mistaken," *Gospel Advocate* 79 (December 2, 1937):1142.

[23] F. B. Srygley, "Christian Action," *Gospel Advocate* 80 (January 6, 1938):4-5.

[24] Claude F. Witty, "Can We Walk the Wire?" *Gospel Advocate* 80 (February 17, 1938):158-60.

[25] W. E. Brightwell, "He That is Not for Me," *Gospel Advocate* 80 (February 17, 1938):148-49.

[26] H. Leo Boles, "Uniting With A Denomination," *Gospel Advocate* 80 (February 24, 1938), 172-73.

[27] G. C. Brewer, "The Conference on Unity," *Gospel Advocate* 81 (March 3, 1939):198-99.

[28] G. C. Brewer, "Looking Toward Unity," *Gospel Advocate* 81 (March 17, 1939):252-53.

[29] John W. Kurfees, "Letter to Claude F. Witty," *Gospel Advocate* 80 (May 5, 1938):416.

[30] H. Leo Boles, *The Way of Unity Between "Christian Church" and Churches of Christ* (Nashville: Gospel Advocate Company, n.d.).

[31] J. E. Choate, *I'll Stand on the Rock: A Biography of H. Leo Boles* (Nashville: Gospel Advocate Company, 1965), p. 184.

[32] Boles, ibid., p. 1.

[33] Ibid., p. 5.

[34] Ibid., pp. 4-7.

[35] Ibid., 7-10.

[36] Ibid., pp. 10-11.

[37] Ibid., p. 12.

[38] Ibid., p. 13.

[39] Ibid., p. 22.

[40] Ibid.

[41] Ibid., p. 21.

[42] Ibid., p. 22.

[43] Ibid., p. 23.

[44] Ibid.

[45] J. N. Armstrong, "A Great Meeting," *Gospel Advocate* 80 (May 12, 1938):440.

[46] Thomas H. Burton, "Unity Good for 'Them'," *Gospel Advocate* 80 (June 2, 1938):516.

[47] F. B. Srygley, "The Detroit Unity Meeting," *Gospel Advocate* 80 (June 9, 1938):524.

[48] W. E. Brightwell, "Good for What?" *Gospel Advocate* 80 (June 9, 1938):539.

[49] Cled E. Wallace, "Tremendously Interesting," *Gospel Advocate* 80 (August 11, 1938):742.

[50] E. C. Koltenbah, "That 'Five-Point' Program," *Gospel Advocate* 80 (December 1, 1938):1124-25.

[51] John Allen Hudson, "Unity Meeting Declined," *Gospel Advocate* 83 (April 3, 1941):326.

[52] H. Leo Boles, "A Forgotten Unity Proposal," *Gospel Advocate* 83 (January 30, 1941):100-01.

[53] L. L. Brigance, "Liberalism in the Churches of Christ," *Gospel Advocate* 83 (July 24, 1941):708-09.

[54] H. Leo Boles, "The Unity Fiasco," *Gospel Advocate* 83 (April 10, 1941):340.

[55] H. Leo Boles, "The Murch-Witty Unity Plan," *Gospel Advocate* 83 (August 7, 1941):749, 764.

[56] H. Leo Boles, "Answer to Murch's Arguments," *Gospel Advocate* 83 (November 27, 1941):1133, 1140.

[57] Anonymous, "Claude F. Witty," *Gospel Advocate* 83 (July 3, 1941):632.

CHAPTER TEN

THE INSTRUMENTAL MUSIC CONTROVERSY

The division in the Restoration Movement in the latter 1890s resulted, in two similar but estranged groups of which the churches of Christ in Tennessee have been selected for major concern in this study. Previous chapters have indicated that during the period of study the churches of Christ were aware of and preserved their identity. The next two chapters will be concerned with the doctrinal stabilization of the group.

Churches of Christ in Tennessee were faced with the need to preserve their identity, and to do so by means of defense and clarification as well as by the proclamation of their belief and their refusal to enter into unity movements as has already been discussed. In order to do this, doctrinal stabilization was a necessity. Consequently, the group made an effort to strengthen its unique positions, defend these emphases against attack and erosion, and provide a coherent expression of principles which supplied unity and system for the positions held. The first major area of doctrinal stabilization was concerned with instrumental music. This subject was frequently discussed in the period and may be considered as crucial to the identity and advancement of churches of Christ. The course of the controversy is the subject of this chapter.

Earlier chapters have made it apparent that instrumental music was one of the two major issues in the division. Following the division, this subject continued to be a source of major contention. Herman Norton traced a series of losses in the influence of the missionary society efforts in the state[1] and the literature of the group after the early 1920s indicated little concern for the missionary society question except as a secondary issue and as a means of giving perspective to the division. The instrumental music question, on the other hand, was to be a live issue throughout the period. Its involvement in the unity movements over the years has already been sketched, but the centrality of this issue cannot be ignored. Here the group known as churches of Christ had a central issue and doctrinal stabilization and defense on the issue were deemed absolutely necessary.

Developments Prior to 1900

The previous treatment of the issue of music in worship has indicated the centrality of this theme to division in 1897 and following. In the process of these years various articles as well as a few more extended treatments appeared in different publications. The references to articles in the *Millennial Harbinger, Christian Standard, Apostolic Times, Lard's Quarterly,* the *Gospel Advocate* and other periodicals indicated the extensive concern over this issue from the Civil War to the turn of the century. Many of these writings were gleaned by M. C. Kurfees in an extensive chapter in his work on instrumental music in 1911. In 1932 John T. Lewis, in response to a resurgence of the controversy in Tennessee, traced much of the same ground in a discussion precipitated by M. D. Clubb, secretary of the Tennessee Christian Missionary Society.[2] John Allen Hudson included three lengthy articles in his 1947 compilation of articles on *The Pioneers on Worship*.[3] These quotations were generally along the same lines with the objective being to enforce the point that those who opposed the use of the instrument in worship were occupying the same ground, as to principle and practice, as had been occupied by the original workers in the movement. A corollary was drawn that the instrument in worship was an innovation which disregarded the history of the movement and frustrated the plea which had sustained the movement from earlier days.

Two extensive doctrinal treatises discussed in some detail the use of the instrument in worship. In 1868 Robert Milligan, of Kentucky University, published his work, *An Exposition and Defense of the Scheme of Redemption as it is Taught in the Holy Scriptures.* In this work he discussed the subject of praise and included comments on instrumental music.[4] This work, termed by Garrison and DeGroot as coming "as near as any book by a Disciple to being a complete systematic theology," [5] claimed that the psalm of Ephesians 5:19 and Colossians 3:16 "has no reference whatever to instrumental music," and indicated that the author was constrained to think that "instrumental music should not be used in churches." [6] He found such use unwarranted in the New Testament, out of harmony with the tenor and spirit of the Christian institution, conducive to formalism, divisive, and at variance with the law of love.[7] Later in the century Carroll Kendrick published his work *Live Religious Issues of the Day* in which he discussed, among other topics, "Scriptural Church Work." [8] In this work he argued that there was not the "slightest authority for it in the New Testament" and consequently it does not belong to New Testament worship.[9] He indicated that he had investigated the matter and was "unsufferably opposed" to its use. He also felt that he could not worship with a congregation which was using it and that where it was introduced those who felt as he did must "form a new church, and bear all that must come upon them in the faithful performance of their duties." He was happy that there were in his day "many such faithful little bands of disciples bearing reproach, for the name of Christ." [10]

These several publications, books as well as articles, made it clear that the issue was more and more a matter of concern and one which was beginning to dominate the thinking of men in the movement.

The Calhoun-Kurfees Exchanges in 1900

According to Edward Coffman the first oral debate on instrumental music between members of the restorationists involved Clark Braden, for, and Joe S. Warlick, against, in a discussion in Dallas, Texas in 1898.[11] This initial debate was to be followed by many others over the years.

In 1900 Hall L. Calhoun and M. C. Kurfees conducted a series of exchanges of articles on the propriety of instrumental music in church services. These were later published in a pamphlet.[12] Calhoun contended that in spite of the fact that Jews and "sectarian bodies" used the instrument in worship, the "Disciples" did not so use it. This was because they did not "intend" to use the instrument "in worship" but rather used it "as a mere matter of convenience to ourselves." He argued concerning instruments that people today have "no direction given for their use as worship," but felt they could be used as a matter of convenience.[13] Kurfees, in response, argued that this principle of defense proved too much since it would have allowed the Jews in the day of Jesus to defend washing hands by saying they did not "intend" to worship God thereby. He also contended that the reasoning involved rebellion against God since the one kind of music God "explicitly commanded" in the New Testament, vocal music, implies that the other kind, instrumental, is "implicitly forbidden." [14] Calhoun responded that the only real issue was whether the instrument was used in worship and appealed to Kurfees to show whether the lights in the meeting house and the flowers on the pulpit came within the scope of worship or were matters of convenience. If matters of convenience, the scriptures against use in worship would not apply; if they were in the worship, they constituted additions as did the use of the instrument.[15] Kurfees responded that the "intention" canon proved too much and would have allowed Jeroboam to defend his false worship (1 Kings 12:32).[16] Kurfees answered that he did not object to the instrument being present, as with flowers, but objected when use was made of the instrument in worship and claimed the lights did not have the same relation to worship as did the use of the instrument.[17] Kurfees then stated that the real issue was: "Is instrumental music in connection with the singing in the church a part of the worship?" He argued it was and that the use of an unauthorized element made the worship vain.[18]

The exchange terminated abruptly when Calhoun failed to send further replies. The discussion, more an exchange of articles and letters than a public debate, was significant in several respects. First, it presented spokesmen of two different views concerning instrumental music and in the foremat of a controverted exchange. Second, Calhoun conceded worship by means of instruments not to be in truth and not sought or accepted by God.[19] Third, Calhoun pitched the exchange on the plane of definition of worship and consequently of "conveniences" or of aids to the service of God, and did not contend that the use "in" or "in connection with" worship was taught of God. Fourth, Kurfees made it clear, from his standpoint, that the instrument was used "in" worship, that it was used without authority, and that the position of Calhoun entailed the opening of "flood gates for all manner of unscriptural practices in the worship of God." [20] The interesting point was that Calhoun avoided the task of affirming that the use of the instrument "in" or "in connection with" the worship is authorized in the New Testament. The significance of this rather precise way of referring to the point at issue was to become more apparent and significant in later discussions.

The Stark-Warlick Debate, 1903

This debate was both oral and written and was conducted in Henderson, Tennessee, where a major division had occurred earlier in the year. In January 1903 E. A. Elam had preached in a meeting at Henderson. Because of the unwillingness of the leadership of the Christian Church, he was not allowed to use their building but he was allowed to use the meetinghouse of the nearby Baptist Church. The meeting resulted in about seventy five of the people who had formerly attended the Christian Church moving out and beginning to meet separately. Elam told of this development in an article which indicated, among other things, that "every young preacher in the school," Georgie Robertson Christian College, was included in the number who left.[21] In late February the Christian Church held a "Bible Institute" in which a defense of the society and the instrument in worship was made. N. B. Hardeman and several students attended the sessions and challenged for a debate on the issues, but they were refused.[22] By November 1903 a debate had been arranged between J. Carroll Stark of McMinnville, Tennessee, representing the Christian Church, and Joe S. Warlick of Texas who represented the church of Christ.[23] According to Warlick, the day sessions (November 4-6, 1903) began in the building of the Christian Church, but after the first day the use of the building was denied.[24] The place where the rest of the oral discussion occurred is not known.

Stark affirmed the proposition "The word of God authorizes the use of instruments of music for praise in the church of Jesus Christ." The basic argument of Stark was threefold. First, he offered eight arguments from Old Testament passages.[25] The thrust of the arguments was that instruments were used "in the praise of God through all dispensations, and God has never objected to it." [26] Consequently, he reasoned, God accepts in the Christian Age what he accepted in praise in former ages. He buttressed this position with the argument that there is no law against such use of the instrument in praise and there is consequently no sin.[27] Second, Stark contended that worship is the "reveration," exultation, adoration of the heart for some object of highest esteem, and must not be confused with an "act of worship" such as singing a song or thanksgiving. Thus, worship, the emotion in the soul, may produce singing, shouting, praising, leaping, dancing, hand clapping, or thanksgiving, and such expressions are not to be suppressed by man made rules. Some could play the organ or the piano as an expression of worship and this

90

playing would so touch others that they would experience a similar response of heart in worship.[28] His point was to try to avoid having to place "worship," "praising" and "playing" in the same category of authorized activities as would be singing in the service of God. Third, a major argument was made on the meaning of the Greek word *psallo* in Ephesians 5:19 and parallel passages in the New Testament.[29] Here Stark presented an argument which was to recur again and again in debates on the same subject. Stark made his case by appealing to the Old Testament word *Zamar* which he contended entailed the use of an instrument and meant "to sing with instrumental accompaniement." He then claimed that *psallo* in the LXX and in the New Testament meant the same thing.[30] He claimed the support of various lexicographers and commentators on the meaning of *psallo* as gained from letters from two college professors.[31] His conclusion was presented in several ways, all indicating that *psallo* entailed the use of the instrument in praise. Stark had argued that the use of the instrument was authorized in the praise of God and as the debate closed felt confident of victory for himself and also stated that he had kept Warlick from doing any great harm.[32]

Warlick offset the force of Stark's case by a rebuttal to each of the three major arguments and a series of counter arguments and objections. Warlick commended Stark for being willing to affirm his practice and noted that other men were unwilling to do the same.[33] In response to the argument from the Old Testament Warlick contended that this position overlooked the difference between the law and the gospel and the respective dispensations in which each applied.[34] Also, he claimed, this argument assumed that God authorized the use of instruments in praise after they had been invented by David.[35] He then argued that even if he granted that the use of the instrument in Old Testament times was authorized, Stark was still guilty of confusing the law with the gospel.[36] He also claimed that the Old Testament argument proved too much because to be consistent one should also accept animal sacrifices, incense, infant membership, polygamy, and the building of an ark since all were taught in the Old Testament.[37] In response to the second argument, that worship and singing, playing the instrument, praying, etc., are not the same, Warlick replied that it was obvious to all that when one prays to God he worships and that when one sings praises he worships God and the attempt to make such distinctions as Stark tried to do was "worse than nonsense."[38] Later he argued that in relation to God worship is service and service is worship and to take part in the service when saints meet for worship is to take part in the worship. He then referred to the dictionary which showed worship, as a verb, means "to perform acts of worship; to perform religious service."[39] He concluded that Stark was making a distinction without a difference. In response to the argument on *psallo* Warlick noted first that the letters introduced by Stark contained omissions and misrepresentations of the authorities cited as upholding the meaning claimed by Stark.[40] Further, he cited the fact that such lexicographers as Thayer, Robinson, Green, and Bagster "all agree that the New Testament meaning of the word is to sing, and that without an instrument." [41] Warlick then introduced dictionaries and commentaries and translations which led him to the view that all standard works "are a unit in cutting out the instrumental music idea as the New Testament meaning of psallo . . ." [42] After citing references from "some of our purest, wisest, and best scholars," he referred to certain "amusing self-contradictions" of Stark in his treatment of psallo.[43] Stark had argued that the instrument is resident in the word *psallo* itself, but he also had argued that the New Testament did not tell how to praise God and one must go to the Old Testament to find how to praise him.[44] Later Stark denied he believed the New Testament commanded the use of musical instruments in worship.[45] Warlick charged that Stark was involved in a contradiction unless he conceded that the instrument did not inhere in *psallo* so that the command to "psallize" did not require one "to use the instrument in praise or worship to God." [46] Stark felt the force of the charge and sought to regain his ground,[47] but Warlick continued to press the charge of contradiction.[48] These three areas of major affirmation and negation occupied the two disputants most of the debate and set the stage for much of the subsequent debates, particularly the struggle over the meaning of *psallo*.

In the three days of the discussion and in the written exchange the major points of tension were fairly well isolated. Later debates were to trace out the details, but the essence of later disputes can readily be found in this initial exchange. It was obvious that a point of major significance lay in the statement and definition of the proposition. Stark did not want to argue that the instrument was used in the worship, but contended that it would be used as an expression of worship. Warlick insisted the use of the instrument was in the worship and as such was an innovation which profaned the worship. This nicety of statement of the issue was to be of major concern in later discussions. A second feature was the use of three major sources of support by Stark. He appealed to Old Testament passages, passages in Revelation, and the Greek word *psallo*. Warlick responded to these three areas, but in later discussions these general areas of support were to be fought over again and again. A third feature of significance was the fact that now a single issue, the propriety or impropriety of the use of the instrument, had been isolated, accepted in large measure as illustrative if not definitive of respective faith and practice, and had been strongly contested in public debate by respected representatives. This latter feature meant and was to mean more and more that the issue of the use or the non-use of the instrument "in" or "in connection with" the worship would hold such significance for both groups that it could not be accepted or rejected by the respective groups without, as they viewed it, yielding more than they were in conscience able to do. Thus the issue had assumed not only its intrinsic significance as a point for legitimate debate on linguistic and historical grounds, but it had come to represent in a most significant way the point of conflict between what had become and were becoming more and more irreconcilable positions. The significance of the issue of instrumental music in worship for churches of Christ in the state had become such that they felt if they were able to sustain their argument on this issue they were also able to sustain their whole position as a unique religious body. The reason for this lay in the fact that the hermeneutical principles which were inherent in the approach to and the application of the Bible to issues of belief and practice were in essence the same as those which were inherent in the instrumental music controversy. To defend their position as to music in worship had become for them a do or die defense of the rationale on which their whole movement was built. To overthrow this position was, in principle, to overthrow the whole movement. Accordingly, to stabilize the entire movement, in principle, it became necessary to defend the position taken in regard to the instrument "in" or "in connection with" the worship.

The Otey-Briney Debate, 1908

Although this debate was conducted in Louisville, Kentucky it was of importance for the churches of Christ in Tennessee and was attended by such men as M. C. Kurfees who were engaged in the discussion in various ways. The debate grew out of a series of problems involving the Sand Creek, Illinois church, remembered as the scene of the Sand Creek Address and Declaration discussed previously. Cecil Willis, the biographer of W. W. Otey,[49] gave the background in detail. In 1906 and 1907 Otey had preached in meetings at Sand Creek. He pressed J. Fred Jones, who upheld the instrument and the society, for a debate on the issues. At first the discussion was to be at Sand Creek and the printed agreement so stated. At the request of Briney the discussion was held in Louisville and Otey was invited to uphold the position of four churches of Christ in the city.[50] After much negotiation, the discussion was held September 14-18, 1908 at the Trinity Methodist Church. Each speaker had one hour for each speech.

It was clear that the wording of the proposition was of major interest. Briney would not agree to sign an affirmative proposition on the issue of music. Willis noted that although more experienced debating brethren later criticized Otey for affirming a negative, "Otey could not get Briney to affirm his practice on instrumental music," and that Otey said it was either affirm a negative "or let the debate fail to materialize."[51] As agreed to by both men, the proposition was "The use of instrumental music in connection with the songs sung by the church on the Lord's day, when assembled for edification and communion, is opposed to New Testament teaching and sinful."[52]

In the discussion little new material was presented which had not appeared in the *Stark-Warlick Debate*. Otey upheld his case on the basis of four arguments: first, the use of instrumental music in worship was a doctrine of men, sinful, and rendered the worship vain; [53] second, such usage violated the New Testament doctrine of expediency; [65] third, the use of the instrument violated the New Testament doctrine of liberty, [55] and fourth, the use of the instrument was without faith. [56] Briney sought to offset the force of these negative arguments as not applicable to the issue. He stated of Otey's speech, "he fails to connect it with his proposition . . ." [57] Briney at first argued he was not obliged by the proposition to prove anything, [58] but Otey presented his case in such a way that the necessity was soon on Briney to make an affirmative as well as negative case. He stated that he would take an advance step and "say that the New Testament in words authorizes the use of instrumental music in connection with the singing that the New Testament approves . . ." [59] In his defense he introduced Old Testament passages, [60] the word psalm, [61] the book of Revelation, [62] and spent much time on *psallo,* to which he referred again and again. [63] To this latter argument Otey replied by quoting authorities from different religious groups to the point that instrumental music does not inhere in *psallo* and thereby showed that other words must be present to justify such a conclusion. [64]

The issue of the society was equally hard fought but it did not have the intensity of concern as the first issue and was not widely discussed. The debate ended with neither man yielding a single disputed point. The debate was reviewed by such men as R. H. Boll[65] in the *Gospel Advocate* and D. F. Draper[66] in the *Firm Foundation.* J. C. McQuiddy reviewed the debate in the *Gospel Advocate* and took occasion to discuss what he regarded as the central issue at stake. He summed up his attitude, and that of his brethren in the state by telling of a recent conversation with a person who upheld use of the organ. Concerning the whole incident he wrote:

> I then showed him that the discussion was not over an organ or sprinkling a few drops of water on a proper subject, but over a principle—who should erect the standard of worship, God or Man? Have we the right to depart from the principle of walking by faith in order to introduce into the worship things on which the Bible is silent? When a man espouses the principle of introducing the organ and society into the worship, which are not authorized by the word of God, he has accepted a principle which, followed to its legitimate conclusion will admit every innovation upon the New Testament worship which is not forbidden by a "Thus saith the Lord." [67]

Again it was apparent that the issue of instrumental music had taken on much more than its linguistic or polemic significance. It was believed by McQuiddy, and those whom he represented, that the principle enshrined in the discussion and, in reality, lying at the heart of the issue, was of major significance. Here the movement persisted in an effort of stabilization.

Kurfees on Instrumental Music, 1911

In 1906-1907 M. C. Kurfees, of Louisville, Kentucky, conducted a class for young preachers in which a study was made of the use of the instrument in worship. Out of this study emerged the book which, even by its opponents, was acclaimed as the best work on the subject from the point of view of churches of Christ. Kurfees addressed himself primarily to the Greek word *psallo,* noting that some in the controversy had "alleged" that the term "involves the use of an instrumental accompaniment" and that such usage "rests upon divine authority." [68] He regarded the argument as such that nothing "contains a more deceptive and misleading fallacy than that which lurks in the argument based on this modern claim concerning the term *psallo . . .*" [69]

Kurfees argued his basic case along several lines. He argued that the Greek language, as well as English, had undergone changes during its history so that old words were modified or changed in meaning.[70] To be specific, he contended that *psallo* had undergone change and modification with the consequent that in order to understand the meaning of the word one must ascertain when the word was being used, that is, at what period in the history of the word it was being studied and what its meaning was at that period.[71] In a chapter on definition the definitions of *psallo* in seventeen lexicons were cited. The point was made that some of the lexicons were for the Greek language in general, termed classical lexicons, and some were confined to New Testament usage. This fact made it necessary for one to exercise "wise discrimination in the use of lexicons." [72] Of particular significance in the lexicons was the oft recurring phrase "In the New Testament" followed by definition and verses. By focusing on Thayer's definition, "in the New Testament *to sing a hymn, to celebrate the praises of God in song,"* Kurfees called attention to what he argued was a "boundary line between what he gives as the classical meanings of *psallo,* on the one hand, and its New Testament meaning on the other . . ." [73] He added to this use of Thayer the words of E. A. Sophocles, whose lexicon covered the period B.C. 146 to A.D. 1100, to the effect that *psallo* meant, "to chant, sing religious hymns." Other lexicons were quoted to the same effect with the "boundary line" expression "in the New Testament" being stressed. The results of his series of arguments were: First, he stated that the word "at some time" in its history had meant "to make instrumental music." [74] Second, he reasoned that by a process of change the word *psallo* "had entirely lost all of these [classical] meanings before the beginning of the New Testament period," and in the New Testament period "it not only meant to sing, but that is the only sense in which it was used, all other meanings having entirely disappeared." [75] This conclusion was repeated several times in the book,[76] and may be regarded as the crucial point of the book. Third, Kurfees quoted from encyclopedists, historians, and commentators to the effect that in the early centuries of the Christian era vocal music was employed and it was not until after the sixth century that the use of instrumental music became accepted in worship and then only against opposition.[77]

Kurfees felt that he had set forth the relevant facts and had proved his case that in the New Testament the word *psallo* meant to sing and did not mean to play a musical instrument. He charged those who asserted the latter with begging the question "by assuming that the use of the instrument *inheres* in the word." [78] He argued that the word had one radical idea, "to touch," which "runs through all its varied uses and applications," [79] but the particular object touched or struck does not inhere in the word. This radical idea is the "key to the meaning in every instance whether the word be used literally or metaphorically." [80] To establish the presence of an instrument in *psallo* in the New Testament, one must look to the context or some other source and there is no other indication in the New Testament which justifies this inclusion of instrumental music. [81] He concluded,

> . . . the word itself does not indicate the object touched, or the instrument used. It may be the hair or beard, it may be a carpenter's line, it may be a bowstring, it may be an instrument of music, or, metaphorically, it may be the human heart. [82]

Kurfees had to offset certain objections to his position. He noted that Liddell and Scott, John Parkhurst, and Edward Robinson had "ventured to say that *psallo*, in the New Testament, means to make instrumental music . . ." [83] In response he observed that these were "the very same lexicographers who have ventured to say that *baptizo* means 'to pour'." [84] Also, the point was made that Liddell and Scott, in a second edition has "expunged" the definition of *Baptizo*, "to pour," because it was "inadmissible," and this fact was seen as an admission of bias on the part of the writers. Of the whole matter Kurfees stated, "All this only shows that great learning in the languages . . . does not always overcome theological bias." [85] In the rest of the book he offered a chapter on the use of *psallo* in the LXX, [86] argued that the entrance of Peter and John into the Jewish Temple did not prove the use of instrumental music in worship,[87] replied to an argument from passages in Revelation,[88] and denied that Ambrose of Milan or Clement of Alexandria had used language concerning *psallo* which proved the instrument should be used in worship.[89]

This work was recognized by J. B. Briney, who had debated W. W. Otey as noted before, as "the most elaborate and plausible argument . . . that has ever been published in opposition to instrumental music in worship, and it may be regarded as the final word on that side of the question." [90] Briney's review of the book, reviews by other men, and the immediate acceptance of its basic position by many among churches of Christ gave evidence of the fact that Kurfees had argued his case well and, with modifications of greater or lesser importance, his work was to become the most widely accepted statement of the case against instrumental music in worship.

The book was of major significance in that it clearly faced the issue of *psallo* in the context of the controversies of the day and argued a very strong case. It served to provide an elaborate argument, a ready reference source for quotations by "authorities," and gave valuable information for use in strategy and argument on a crucial issue. The book was, therefore, a positive contribution to the stabilization of the movement in the state.

Responses to Kurfees, 1914 and 1919

The work by Kurfees was such that it could not be allowed, by those who favored the use of the instrument in worship, to go without response. Two major responses were offered by J. B. Briney and O. E. Payne. Both men were involved in the background of the Boswell-Hardeman discussion to be noted later, and some attention must be given to their work to supply the relevant context for the encounter in 1923. Briney set forth his reply in 1914 and the copy of M. C. Kurfees, with handwritten notes in the margin, has been preserved. The details of the response by Briney were too lengthy for inclusion, but his conclusions were of significance. Basically he examined each chapter of Kurfees, seeking for an omitted detail, a new interpretation to a line of argument, or charging that the conclusion drawn by Kurfees did not follow. Again and again Briney noted that the lexicons did not "exclude the use of an instrument in New Testament times." [91] On page 61 Kurfees wrote concerning Briney's statement, "I deny that it excludes instrumental accompaniment," as follows: "It does *just as* the definition of baptizo excludes 'pour' and 'sprinkle'—*precisely the same way.*" [92] When Briney stated his position he was very careful to avoid saying certain things about *psallo* which were to become significant in Payne's work and in the debate between Hardeman and Boswell. The clearest statement of his position appeared in a comment on *psallo* in Romans 15:9 in which he wrote, "It is an undeniable fact that *psallo*, . . . if it did not necessarily imply the use of instrumental accompaniment, at least permitted it . . . and Paul sanctions the use of an instrument in doing the singing indicated by psallo." [93] Elsewhere he stated that the word did "permit the use of accompaniment," [94] that 'psallo simply permitted, but did not command the use of the harp, leaving it optional . . .," [95] that the "word allowed its use in every case," [96] that "the word carried with it the idea of accompaniment as permissible," [97] that "no lexicographer says that the use of an instrument inheres in the word," [98] and defended the use of the instrument as an "aid" [99] on the grounds of "expediency," [100] but not on the ground that such was enjoined by *psallo*.

In view of its significance in later developments it is to be noted that Briney, in a significant quote,[101] stated that *psallo* "indicated" singing, did not "necessarily imply the use of instrumental accompaniement," but "at least permitted it." He had, by this statement, given ground to Kurfees that *psallo* meant "singing," and had avoided having to contend that *psallo* could not be obeyed without the use of the instrument. His words show how careful he was to avoid stating or implying that the use of the instrument was necessary to obey the requirement of *psallo*. This precision of statement protected him from such problems as a later reviewer of Kurfees was to face. The one instance in which he departed from his permissible or aid argument appeared in his statement,

> Thus it appears that an organ may be lifted from the plane of a mere help in worship to the position of a means of worship—an instrument by which a heart that is full of devotion may exhibit its adoration and manifest its sentiments of worship as did David with his harp.[102]

In 1920 O. E. Payne published a second reply to Kurfees.[103] He paid respect to Kurfees' work as "being the ablest work on that side" and stated that he intended to "demonstrate" that Kurfees had failed to prove his major contention.[104] This book followed the same basic pattern Briney had employed, but it added many more quotations from Greek authors and several more lexicons.

Payne's work was characterized by a boldness of statement of alleged conclusions which made his work the most extreme statement of the case for *psallo* ever published. Several quotations make it clear that his conclusions were more extreme than either Stark or Briney had been willing to declare. He stated that "instrumental music unavoidably inheres in psallo" and "therefore to employ it is mandatory." [105] Again he claimed that to refrain from the use of the instrument was "to refrain from our duty" and "stifle our conscience." [106] Later he declared that "the one and only musical meaning" of the term was "to play an instrument," [107] and followed with the words that there was "no hint that the word, even remotely or occasionally, indicated vocalization." [108] He further stated that there was in the word "no meaning of merely 'sing' music." [109] He alleged that the term "always indicated an instrument" [110] and that "instrumentation inheres in the word." [111] Consequently, he concluded, to define *psallo* "to sing (without accompaniment) is an arbitrary, impossible definition of the word." [112] He regarded his work as so complete that it set forth more information on the subject than was "ever beheld by any translator or body of translators." [113] His grand conclusion came when he stated "if we forego musical instruments, we cannot conform to the divine injunction to *psallo*." [114] Thus he concluded that the "right, not to say the duty, of Christians to employ instrumental music in worship" should remain "undisturbed," the controversy should cease, and never again should there lodge "in an intelligent mind conscientious scruples against such music in worship . . ." [115]

The bold statements of Payne soon became the source of considerable controversy and prepared the way for the debate between Ira Boswell and N. B. Hardeman. Although M. C. Kurfees offered a reply to the book in a series of *Gospel Advocate* articles which were later incorporated into a book,[116] he was most unhappy with the personal indignity heaped on him by Payne in such statements as the assertion that Kurfees was one who "knowingly misrepresents" [117] statements of writers quoted.

The significance of Payne's statements in the controversy then raging was made clear by Kurfees in his review. He charged that Payne had at last reached the inevitable conclusion to which the argument on *psallo,* begun many years before, had ultimately led.[118] Thus, he argued that, accepting Payne's conclusion, one must as surely have the instrument in worship to obey *psallo* as he must have immersion to obey *baptizo,* because if the instrument "inheres" in *psallo* one cannot *"psallo"* without the instrument.[119] Consequently "mere singing is disobeying God in precisely the same way that men disobey God when they attempt to obey the command to baptize by merely sprinkling water on a person." [120] Logically, he reasoned, the acceptance of Payne's conclusion—that instrumental music in worship is "mandatory"—would end the possibility of arguing that it is "merely an aid" or only used "in connection with" the singing in worship. The logical implications of the conclusions of Payne in relation to argumentative strategy quickly become apparent to defenders of the instrument and their opponents as well. The attempt to force or block the acceptance of the logical implications of the Payne position led to the Hardeman-Boswell debate and supplied a significant aspect of the actual debate itself.

Hardeman-Boswell Discussion, 1923

The immediate background of the Hardeman-Boswell debate was sketched by F. B. Srygley in a series of articles incorporated into the debate book. These articles and several more in the 1922 and 1923 *Gospel Advocate* show how closely the debate and the preceding events were related.

In May 1922 F. B. Srygley replied to a letter from John B. Cowden of the Commission on Unity which was an arm of the Tennessee Missionary Society activities. In the letter Cowden requested the return of a copy of O. E. Payne's book on music which he claimed to have sent to Srygley about a year before. Srygley replied that he had not seen the book which had been sent, but he promised to send a copy of Kurfees' reply to Payne if the Commission would send a copy to all recipients of Payne's work.[121] Cowden soon replied that the commission would accept and distribute the book. Srygley then replied that he felt a good way to get even more light on the subject would be to have a full-fledged debate on the issue provided the Commission would affirm its practice.[122] Cowden responded that the Commission would discuss the matter in a convention and that he personally was willing to have the debate. Srygley noted that the Payne book would be a matter of concern since not only the Commission but also leading men, such as J. B. Briney, had endorsed the conclusions of Payne.[123]

In July 1922 the announcement was made that the challenge for a debate was accepted and the Commission requested that the same issue be discussed at other places in the state if such were the wish of either party.[124] Later in the month Cowden began to seek a release from defending Payne's book, but Srygley noted that Cowden, J. B. Briney, and others had endorsed the position of Payne and the sponsors of the book would not be allowed to retreat from the position set forth therein.[125] Later in the year Srygley observed that the difficulties being faced in defending Payne's book might make the proposed debate impossible.[126]

By the end of the year it was clear that a debate of some type would be conducted shortly, but the issue of defending the use of the instrument in worship and the precise wording of the proposition would be difficulties to overcome.[127] The negotiations continued with efforts on both sides being made to secure the best position on propositions.[128] Against such a background it was only to be expected that those in favor of the instrument would include the phrase "in worship," so the proposition read, "Instrumental music in church worship is scriptural." Ira A. Boswell was to affirm and N. B. Hardeman was to deny.[129] At last the discussion was to take place as an anonymous writer noted on the first day of the discussion and it was to continue five days (May 31–June 4, 1923).[130]

The Discussion

Boswell stated his position in these words, "To sing with or without instrumental music is scriptural," [131] and proceeded to his argument. He cited quotations from an assortment of lexicographers, contemporary writers, scholars, translations, commentaries, and Bible usage to sustain his view. This first speech set the basic tone for the affirmative case. In his reply Hardeman noted that the point in dispute had not been clarified. Boswell, he claimed, had not shown how the instrument was connected with the worship and observed the proposition focused on three expressions, i.e., instrumental music in worship, instrumental music is, not was or will be, and instrumental music is scriptural.[132] In his first speech Hardeman presented several questions which were designed to elicit from Boswell a statement as to whether he agreed with Payne, Cowden, and Briney to the effect that Payne's book had demonstrated that the instrument was necessary to "conform to the divine injunction to 'psallein.' " [133] Also in his first speech Hardeman indicated his position on the controverted *psallo* passages by stating,

> Both the question tonight, and the only one for consideration, is: What, under the New Testament, is the instrument that accompanies the singing? The apostle Paul, in his peerless announcement, settled that once for all. He says we are to sing unto the Lord and "psallo" with the heart—not with the fingers, not with the plectron, but with the heart; and, therefore, the heart is the instrument that accompanies the singing.[134]

Hardeman noted that the lexicons by Thayer and Bagster inserted the key phrase "in the New Testament" in their definitions and thus set the time span of their definition. He then observed that they defined the word as meaning to sing[135] and closed with the point that the leading English versions rendered *psallo* by the term to "sing." [136]

100

Boswell claimed the issue turned largely on the word in dispute,[137] but did not see fit to answer the questions at first. Hardeman noted that Boswell was in the position of arguing, on one hand, that the use of the instrument was in the word *psallo,* and, on the other, arguing that it was not really necessary to use the instrument to obey the word.[138] Hardeman offered to narrow the issue to *"psallo"* and observed that he believed the instrument was the heart and that Boswell contended the instrument was "a mechanical device made by man's hand." [139]

Boswell did not see fit to answer the questions by Hardeman in an extensive way. He stated that it was irrelevant what Payne, Briney, or Cowden had written or said,[140] denied saying that the instrument inheres in *"psallo,"*[141] and denied quoting anything Payne had said.[142] Later he admitted he had quoted from Payne, but denied the need to defend Payne.[143] He stated, "I never have stood for Payne," [144] but then stated that Payne had written "one of the greatest books ever written on the subject." [145] Hardeman noted that Boswell read from Payne but would not endorse his position.[146] He then noted the background of the debate as discussed previously[147] and claimed that the Commission on Unity should repudiate the book or defend it as representative of their position.[148]

There were other points of dispute in the debate, but the major thrust of Hardeman was to force Boswell to either accept or reject the position set forth by Payne and, according to Hardeman, logically attributable to the Commission on Unity and thereby to Boswell. Boswell, on the other hand, carefully refused to accept either horn of the dilemma and argued the basic position of permissibility rather than authorization. Other issues were peripheral to this main concern. It was apparent that Hardeman was constantly concerned to have the position of Payne defended or rejected and Boswell sought to avoid this issue in any depth.

The debate closed with neither man or group conceding defeat, but it was significant that the Commission on Unity, which had previously indicated a desire to repeat the discussion all across the state, lost interest in any further debates. F. B. Srygley observed that John B. Cowden of the Commission on Unity had wanted a repetition of the debate in negotiations prior to the discussion, but noted there was a change afterwards. He stated, "As I now understand the matter, their churches do not want the discussion anywhere since we had the one in Nashville." [149] He concluded by stating that if the churches in the state which used the instrument in worship would not defend such use, "we will continue to show it needs defense." [150]

Later Developments

Subsequent years were to see three major efforts along this same line of argument, but they were largely repetitious of the preceding discussions. In 1927 a written discussion was published on the question: "Is Instrumental Music in Christian Worship Scriptural?" [151] The disputants were M. D. Clubb, Secretary of the Tennessee Christian Missionary Society, in the affirmative, and H. Leo Boles, President of David Lipscomb College, in the negative. Little new material was presented in the exchanges. In 1932 John T. Lewis published a series of quotations and arguments on the twin subjects of instrumental music and the missionary society.[152] This book, written in response to statements by M. D. Clubb, noted above, was an attempt to document the point that the use of the instrument and the society was at variance with principles and statements by early leaders in the movement. Much of the ground covered in earlier chapters was noted briefly. In 1948 G. C. Brewer, a regular writer for the *Gospel Advocate,* published a series of responses to specific arguments on the use of instrumental music in worship.[153] In this work much the same ground was covered as had been worked by Warlick, Kurfees, and Hardeman. An interesting sidelight is Brewer's reference to negotiations with Payne pursuant to a debate. According to Brewer, Payne receded from his published statements and argued instead that *psallo* permitted but did not necessitate the use of the instrument in worship.[154] In later years James D. Bales stated he had seen and copied the letter, dated November 28, 1922, in which Payne had made the statements attributed to him.[155]

The issue of instrumental music was of utmost importance in the division in the late 1890s and subsequent defenders of the position of churches of Christ would not be unconcerned about its importance. The line of defense by analysis and response from Warlick to Otey, Kurfees, Hardeman, Lewis, and Brewer and others made it clear that these men felt it essential to respond to every argument advanced in favor of the practice. The basic case was that the New Testament authorized singing but that playing instruments of music in worship could not be defended as authorized in New Testament worship. The argument in defense of the practice was, in the later years, largely a battle for and against the meaning of a single word, *psallo,* in the New Testament. It was felt by such men as Warlick, Kurfees, and others that to defend the point in dispute was, in principle, to defend an approach to and application of the New Testament in such a way as to undergird and sustain the whole movement. Of the success of the effort in response to the argument on *psallo,* J. W. Roberts, a close student of the entire period and controversy, stated concerning the argument by Payne,

> . . . But the real test of Payne's work came in a debate between N. B. Hardeman and Ira A. Boswell at Nashville, Tenn., in May, 1922 [1923, W. W.] . . . If I am any judge, the Nashville debate justified Kurfees' position and disproved the Payne contention. For many years it practically laid that contention to rest . . . Hardeman showed that when the verb is used intransitively as it is frequently in the Old Testament and late Greek it means to sing or is used figuratively of singing under the figure of *psallo* as making melody (on the strings of the heart). This last is the New Testament situation. With these arguments he carried the day.[156]

The effort was made, therefore, to defend the specific point and in so doing defend an approach to and application of New Testament teaching so as to stabilize a movement. This approach may also be illustrated in the treatment of the next issue.

REFERENCES

[1] Herman A. Norton, *Tennessee Christians* (Nashville: Reed and Company, 1971), pp. 227-77.

[2] John T. Lewis, *The Voice of the Pioneers on Instrumental Music and Societies* (Nashville: Gospel Advocate Company, 1932), pp. 107-84.

[3] John Allen Hudson, ed., *The Pioneers on Worship* (Kansas City: The Old Path Book Club, 1947), pp. 143-62.

[4] Robert Milligan, *An Exposition and Defense of the Scheme of Redemption as it is Revealed and Taught in the Holy Scriptures* (St. Louis: Christian Board of Publication, 1868).

[5] Winfred Ernest Garrison and Alfred T. DeGroot, *The Disciples of Christ: A History* (St. Louis: Christian Board of Publication, 1948), p. 538.

[6] Milligan, ibid., pp. 381, 387.

[7] Ibid., pp. 386-87.

[8] Carroll Kendrick, *Live Religious Issues of the Day* (Nashville: Gospel Advocate Publishing Company, 1890), pp. 465-509.

[9] Ibid., p. 466.

[10] Ibid., pp. 507-08.

[11] Edward Coffman, "The Division in the Restoration Movement" (M. A. Thesis, Vanderbilt University, 1930), p. 251.

[12] Hall L. Calhoun and M. C. Kurfees, *Instrumental Music in Worship. A Discussion between H. L. Calhoun and M. C. Kurfees* (Nashville: Gospel Advocate Publishing Company, 1901).

[13] Ibid., pp. 8-9.

[14] Ibid., pp. 16, 17, 18.

[15] Ibid., pp. 27-28.

[16] Ibid., p. 33.

[17] Ibid., p. 35.

[18] Ibid., p. 36.

[19] Ibid., p. 21.

[20] Ibid., p. 30.

[21] E. A. Elam, "A Meeting at Henderson, Tenn.," *Gospel Advocate* 45 (February 5, 1903):81, 82.

[22] E. A. Elam, "No Title," *Gospel Advocate* 45 (April 9, 1903):225.

[23] J. Carroll Stark and Joe S. Warlick, *A Debate Between J. Carroll Stark and Joe S. Warlick* (Nashville: Gospel Advocate Company, 1903), p. 183.

[24] Ibid., pp. 183-84.

[25] Ibid., pp. 18-19, 40,42,43,44,69,73,74 respectively. (The verses cited were: Amos 6:1-6; Genesis 4:21; 1 Samuel 10:5,6; 2 Kings 3:10-17; 2 Chronicles 5:11-14; 2 Chronicles 29:25; 1 Chronicles 15:16,28; and Psalm 149.)

[26] Ibid., p. 40.

[27] Ibid., p. 12.

[28] Ibid., pp. 103-05; 40-41.

[29] Ibid., pp. 105-14.

[30] Ibid., p. 106.

[31] Ibid., pp. 107-13.

[32] Ibid., p. 180.

[33] Ibid., pp. 25,50,84.

[34] Ibid., pp. 26-29, 62-63, 87-88.

[35] Ibid., pp. 30,53,60,61.

[36] Ibid., p. 62.

[37] Ibid., pp. 30,80,121.

[38] Ibid., p. 32.

[39] Ibid., p. 134.

[40] Ibid., p. 123, 125.

[41] Ibid., p. 124.

[42] Ibid., pp. 126-27.

[43] Ibid., pp. 127-31.

[44] Ibid., p. 133.
[45] Ibid., p. 138.
[46] Ibid., pp. 153-54.
[47] Ibid., pp. 169-73.
[48] Ibid., pp. 185-86.
[49] Cecil Willis, *W. W. Otey: Contender for the Faith* (Akron, Ohio: Privately Published, 1964), pp. 194-214.
[50] W. W. Otey and J. B. Briney, *Otey-Briney Debate* (Cincinnati: F. L. Rowe, 1908), p. 20.
[51] Willis, ibid., p. 197.
[52] Otey and Briney, ibid., p. 9.
[53] Ibid., p. 24.
[54] Ibid., p. 26.
[55] Ibid., p. 73.
[56] Ibid., p. 92.
[57] Ibid., p. 42.
[58] Ibid., p. 32.
[59] Ibid., p. 45.
[60] Ibid., pp. 42-45.
[61] Ibid., p. 46.
[62] Ibid., pp. 47-48.
[63] Ibid., pp. 63,80,115,116,158.
[64] Ibid., pp. 67, 86-88, 104, 124-26.
[65] R. H. Boll, "The Briney-Otey Debate," *Gospel Advocate* 50 (October 8, 1908):642.
[66] D. F. Draper, "Otey-Briney Debate," *Firm Foundation* 25 (September 14, 1909):6.
[67] J. C. McQuiddy, "Otey-Briney Debate," *Gospel Advocate* 51 (June 10, 1909):712-13.
[68] M. C. Kurfees, *Instrumental Music in the Worship on the Greek Verb Psallo Philologically and Historically Examined together with a full Discussion of Kindred Matters Relating to Music in Christian Worship* (Nashville: Gospel Advocate Company, 1908), p. 4.
[69] Ibid., p. 5.
[70] Ibid., pp. 7, 18-44.
[71] Ibid., pp. 7,22,24.
[72] Ibid., p. 17.
[73] Ibid., p. 52.
[74] Ibid., p. 15.
[75] Ibid., pp. 44-45.
[76] Ibid., p. 49, 56, 97.
[77] Ibid., pp. 143-97.
[78] Ibid., p. 64.
[79] Ibid., p. 69.
[80] Ibid., p. 65.
[81] Ibid.
[82] Ibid.
[83] Ibid., p. 68.
[84] Ibid.
[85] Ibid., p. 69.
[86] Ibid., pp. 85-97.
[87] Ibid., pp. 98-107.
[88] Ibid., pp. 108-17.
[89] Ibid., pp. 118-34.
[90] J. B. Briney, *Instrumental Music in Christian Worship* (Cincinnati: The Standard Publishing Company, 1914), p. 46.
[91] Ibid.
[92] Ibid., p. 61.
[93] Ibid., p. 73.
[94] Ibid., p. 46.
[95] Ibid., p. 51.
[96] Ibid., p. 46.
[97] Ibid., p. 57.
[98] Ibid., p. 60.
[99] Ibid., pp. 67-70.
[100] Ibid., p. 119.
[101] Ibid., p. 73.
[102] Ibid., p. 214.

[103] O. E. Payne, *Instrumental Music is Scriptural* (Cincinnati: The Standard Publishing Company, 1920).

[104] Ibid., p. 10.

[105] Ibid., p. 52.

[106] Ibid., p. 56.

[107] Ibid., p. 61.

[108] Ibid., p. 62.

[109] Ibid., p. 64.

[110] Ibid., p. 66.

[111] Ibid., p. 64.

[112] Ibid., p. 79.

[113] Ibid., p. 101.

[114] Ibid., p. 172.

[115] Ibid., p. 320.

[116] M. C. Kurfees, *Review of O. E. Payne's Book on "Psallo"* (Nashville: Gospel Advocate Company, 1922).

[117] Payne, ibid., p. 201.

[118] Kurfees, ibid., p. 8.

[119] Ibid., p. 8.

[120] Ibid., p. 9.

[121] F. B. Srygley, "The Commission on Unity," *Gospel Advocate* 64 (May 18, 1922):461.

[122] F. B. Srygley, "That Commission on Unity, Again," *Gospel Advocate* 64 (June 1, 1922):516-17.

[123] F. B. Srygley, "Will there be a Discussion on the Music Question?" *Gospel Advocate* 64 (June 15, 1922):564.

[124] F. B. Srygley, "Good News from Ovoca," *Gospel Advocate* 64 (July 13, 1922):661.

[125] F. B. Srygley, "Will their Courage Fail?" *Gospel Advocate* 64 (July 20, 1922):686-88.

[126] F. B. Srygley, "Liberty in Christ," *Gospel Advocate* 64 (August 3, 1922):726.

[127] F. B. Srygley, "More About A Debate," *Gospel Advocate* 64 (December 21, 1922):1214-15.

[128] F. B. Srygley, "The Debate," *Gospel Advocate* 65 (March 15, 1923):250-51.

[129] Ira A. Boswell and N. B. Hardeman, *Boswell-Hardeman Discussion on Instrumental Music in the Worship* (Nashville: Gospel Advocate Company, 1923), p. 24.

[130] Anonymous, "Our Messages," *Gospel Advocate* 65 (May 31, 1923):533.

[131] Boswell and Hardeman, ibid., p. 29.

[132] Ibid., pp. 37-38.

[133] Ibid., p. 39.

[134] Ibid., p. 43.

[135] Ibid., p. 44.

[136] Ibid., p. 45.

[137] Ibid., p. 53.

[138] Ibid., p. 56.

[139] Ibid., p. 60.

[140] Ibid., p. 52, 74.

[141] Ibid., p. 89.

[142] Ibid., p. 171.

[143] Ibid., pp. 195-96.

[144] Ibid., p. 213.

[145] Ibid., p. 217.

[146] Ibid., pp. 118, 160-61.

[147] Ibid., p. 184.

[148] Ibid.

[149] F. B. Srygley, "Will There be Another Discussion?" *Gospel Advocate* 65 (September 20, 1923):908.

[150] Ibid.

[151] M. D. Clubb and H. Leo Boles, *Discussion—Is Instrumental Music in Christian Worship Scriptural?* (Nashville: Gospel Advocate Company, 1927).

[152] Lewis, ibid.

[153] G. C. Brewer, *A Medley on the Music Question* (Nashville: Gospel Advocate Company, 1948).

[154] Ibid., pp. 42-43, 70.

[155] James D. Bales, *Instrumental Music and New Testament Worship* (Searcy, Arkansas: James D. Bales, 1973), p. 86.

[156] J. W. Roberts, "Answers to Today's Arguments on Instrumental Music," *Adorning the Doctrine,* Twelfth Annual Lectureship Lubbock Christian College (Lubbock, Texas: L.C.C., 1969), pp. 155-56.

CHAPTER ELEVEN

PREMILLENNIALISM

In the period of this study the churches of Christ faced a second severe doctrinal issue in the lengthy discussion of premillennialism from, roughly, the early days of World War I to World War II. Several crucial concerns were to be faced in these thirty or so years of controversy. These concerns included the clarification of principles of interpretation to be employed in ascertaining Bible teaching, the validity of conclusions reached by the hermeneutical procedures, and the vexing problem of fellowship in view of a specific doctrinal dispute in the presence of considerable agreement otherwise. The tracing of these significant efforts in stabilizing the group can only be done in summary, but the controversy placed in focus many vital aspects of the movement never faced beforehand. Here was a case in point in which the stability of the movement could be tested and the process by which the issue was ferreted out and resolved, such as it was, provides something of a paradigm of the group at work with a difficult internal problem.

The Beginning of the Problem

In 1909 E. A. Elam, long time editor of the front page of the *Gospel Advocate,* decided that he wanted to write along other lines although he wanted to and did continue on the staff of the paper. In his place R. H. Boll of Louisville, Kentucky, was added to the staff. At the same time M. C. Kurfees, also of Louisville but much more widely known, became a member of the staff. Various issues of the paper carried commendations of both Boll and Kurfees as exemplifying the qualities of character and soundness to be possessed by men who wrote for the paper. In 1937 G. C. Brewer wrote that the *Gospel Advocate* at the time (1915-1925) was "at its best" and that the writing of R. H. Boll, along with M. C. Kurfees and A. B. Lipscomb, deserved "a place among the classics." [1]

By October 1909 R. H. Boll was busy studying and writing about the need to interpret the prophecies of the Bible. He argued that the failure to study these Bible truths opened people to the false systems of Jehovah's Witnesses, Mormons, and Adventists of various types. In January 1910 Boll wrote concerning the need to study the second coming of Christ. He stated his lack of patience with the post millennial view which he claimed was held by most members of the church of Christ. Also, after mentioning the millennium and criticizing some objections which were often raised against discussing the millennium, he set forth his intention to continue the study as he saw fit. [2] In April 1910 he wrote that one should interpret Revelation literally rather than figuratively or symbolically unless there were "sufficient reason" for the latter approach. [3]

Here and there through the years Boll gave various indications of his continued interest and study, with emerging conclusions, along the lines of premillennialism. Later years were to confirm this tendency and in 1915 it was to become explicit, rather than implicit, that R. H. Boll was a full fledged premillennialist.

In 1915 R. H. Boll began a series of articles on the theme, "Short Talks on Revelation." By March 11 he indicated that the promise to the church at Philadelphia, "I come quickly," was possible for people living in his day and concluded that Christ might come quickly to those then living.[4] In the same issue F. B. Srygley, frequently a participant in controversies, told that for the first time among his brethren he had read that some believed that the kingdom had not been established, that Christ was not on the throne of David, that the kingdom of David was yet future, that the church is in existence but that the kingdom and the church are different. Srygley quoted H. L. Olmstead who had published an article on this subject and proceeded to reply to the material quoted. He concluded, ". . . I am bound to dissent from Brother Olmstead's idea of a future kingdom of Christ to be set up . . ."[5] After this initial exchange a series of articles began to appear. These articles led to differences and subsequent difficulties which were not resolved during the period of this study and have not been resolved to the present.

The Battle Joined

In April H. L. Olmstead responded to the article by Srygley[6] and Srygley replied.[7] In the next issue of the paper F. W. Smith took the privilege to criticize, "in a friendly and brotherly way," Robert H. Boll and H. L. Olmstead, "who are using their precious time and splendid intellects in speculative theories concerning unfulfilled prophecies."[8] On May 6, 1915 several very important articles were printed. H. L. Olmstead stated his position in great detail, taking pains to deny Christ is on David's throne and to connect Revelation 20:4 with the kingdom he believed was yet to come.[9] R. H. Boll offered a response to F. W. Smith, a response contending for the need to study and interpret all parts of the Bible whether prophecy or history, Acts or Revelation.[10] E. G. Sewell wrote an article affirming the kingdom of Christ has been set up and is not future.[11] An article from David Lipscomb urged the thought that the time of the second coming of Christ is not known and warned that there was a danger that one may become unduly absorbed in the study of the second coming and be led away from everyday work of obedience.[12] Finally, the publishers of the paper stated that they had asked F. W. Smith to write a friendly criticism of "Brother Boll's recent teachings along the line of prophetic interpretation" and "to point out in a brotherly way what we consider to be the wise and safe course in regard to unrevealed things."[13]

Soon R. H. Boll was responding to the publishers of the *Gospel Advocate* and the words of Smith. Boll expressed general agreement with Lipscomb's article, with exceptions noted, and stated that he was only concerned about what had been revealed. He indicated that he was not averse to an exchange with Smith but proposed to have more precise propositions. In closing, he challenged Smith to a discussion of the points of difference and proposed that the details be worked out by private correspondence.[14] The publishers indicated they did not think Boll regarded his views on unfulfilled prophecy as essential to salvation and asked if, in view of this, he would cease to agitate them.[15] Soon Boll, after responding to Smith and explaining his anticipation of the forthcoming debate, stated, "And this, until the debate I called for is arranged, closes my notice of what Brother Smith has to say concerning my work."[16]

Articles on both sides of the discussion continued to be presented until in the June 10, 1915 issue matters came to a head. Boll insisted that he regarded his views on the subject as essential to the full presentation of God's word and reaffirmed his readiness to debate the issues.[17] The publishers responded to Boll's alleged agreement with David Lipscomb and claimed that the attempt was evasive and, in reality, a distortion of David Lipscomb's article and teaching. They claimed that Boll had been treated fairly and stated,

He has been interceded with in private interview and by private correspondence, and was assured that if he would agree to hold his hurtful and divisive theories as private property that not one word of criticism would be printed in reference to them; but, like the self-willed Pharisees, he 'would not.'[18]

They stated that they regarded Boll as "obsessed with the belief that God has especially called him to be a kind of reformer who shall resurrect the Futurist system of interpretation and inoculate the churches with it." In view of this, they further declared,

Having thus afforded him abundant opportunity to set himself right, we herewith close the discussion, so far as the Gospel Advocate is concerned . . . If Brother Boll writes us something along practical lines, as he is fully capable of doing, and wherein his real power lies, we will be rejoiced to give it prominence as heretofore; but if he elects to continue a useless discussion over mere opinion and a wholesale condemnation of his brethren, we will be obliged to accord his articles the treatment which such a spirit deserves.[19]

In spite of this obvious divergence of views, R. H. Boll was listed as one of the editors in each weekly issue of the paper until July 22, 1915. During the interim an article opposing premillennialism appeared from M. C. Kurfees[20] and J. C. McQuiddy gave a series of six articles summarizing and responding to the position.[21] During the interim also it was revealed that R. H. Boll had accepted a position on the staff of another paper, *The Christian Leader*.[22]

These developments made it clear that a serious problem was present between a highly respected writer on the leading paper in the state and the rest of the writers and the publishers. Strongly worded statements of defense and opposition had appeared, private and public notice of desire for and intention to participate in a debate had been given, and the publishers had closed the columns of the paper to Boll's further presentation of his views although he was retained as an editor for a time. It was clear that an intense escalation had occurred from the opening articles early in March until the early fall of 1915. The next phase of the developing controversy was to presage a break which could not be avoided. Attention will be given to this phase shortly but at the close of the summer it was clear that unyielding resistance would be given to the public promulgation of R. H. Boll's views. It was also clear at that point that an agreement by Boll to hold such views as private opinions and without promulgation would have brought the public opposition to an end. The two positions were poised and the future would await a move from one side or another.

The Broken Fellowship

Three events indicated that the fellowship previously enjoyed was breaking and could not be restored. These events involved developments in New Orleans, on the pages of the *Advocate* in 1915 and in Louisville in 1918. These may be noted in summary.

In May 1915 F. B. Srygley told of previous efforts to raise money to assist the work in New Orleans and of the development that Stanford Chambers, of the church at Seventh and Camp, was preaching the same doctrine as had been proclaimed by R. H. Boll. After quoting an article clipped from a New Orleans paper which showed this development, Srygley observed,

> It is a pity that property which was paid for at a sacrifice of good brethren, in order that the people might hear the plain, simple gospel, should be perverted by speculating on how the European War might bring the Jews back to Jerusalem and the literal tabernacle be built again.[23]

On June 17 Stanford Chambers replied[24] and Srygley responded that Chambers had "pressed these speculations to the division of the congregation in New Orleans, and a number have been so harassed by his continual pressing these things that they have quietly withdrawn from the congregation and are meeting in a hall." Also, he noted that Chambers and the remaining congregation had withdrawn from those who left. He continued by quoting letters from W. E. Thompson, formerly of Memphis, Tennessee, who had observed the trouble in the church for a year and from Dr. D. L. Watson who had served as an elder of the church but had been removed by Chambers and others.[25] It was clear, therefore, that the promulgation of the views of Chambers, in essence the same as those of Boll, was causing problems in New Orleans.

The second episode involved the restoration and subsequent removal of Boll as an editor of the *Gospel Advocate*. On November 4, 1915 the publisher stated their "genuine pleasure" to announce that "all differences between Brother Boll and the editors and publishers have been

110

amicably and satisfactorily adjusted" and their "equal pleasure to have him resume his work on the paper . . ." [26] Boll stated that he had "arrived at an amicable understanding" with his former associates and would resume his work "with all personal differences eliminated and with feeling of the most cordial friendship toward all." He stated that he was free to write as he believed he ought to write and restricted only as all other writers were, and indicated his judgment as to matters of recent "disturbance" had not been dictated by any man.[27] Boll's name reappeared as an editor and he began writing his weekly, front page article, but not on the issues earlier in dispute. Shortly after the resumption of the work of Boll a series of commendations of the resolution of the problem appeared. Of significance in light of subsequent developments was the commendation of Campbell A. Taylor of Louisville, Kentucky. Taylor wrote that the resolution of problems would "assist in preserving unity" among the churches, remove the charge of unfair treatment of Boll, and offset the establishment of two groups over this teaching. He also stated his view that Boll's return to the *Advocate* would mean that churches would no longer be disturbed "by this kind of writing and teaching." [28]

These commendations and assurances were, however, to be short lived. On December 9, 1915 the publishers of the *Gospel Advocate* commented at length on the terms of the agreement with Boll and subsequent developments. They indicated that a fuller statement was "imperatively necessary in order that all parties may appear in the proper light." They felt that the doctrinal differences were "vital and fundamental" and stated an agreement along other lines than they were to indicate would not have been acceptable. Consequently they declared, "Hence we now state the fact that there was a positive understanding and agreement between Brother Boll and us that he would stop teaching the things that had been and were disturbing the churches." [29] They indicated that the agreement had not been published because Boll had objected to such publication in view of the fact that other writers were not bound as he felt he was being in this instance. Subsequent developments had shown the mistake of not publishing the whole matter of the agreement and of not indicating that Boll had admitted, in the conference, that he had not been mistreated or misrepresented as to his doctrinal stance. The resumption of Boll's work on the paper was agreed to only after "the verbal agreement had been repeatedly made." [30] The developments since the resumption of Boll's work had been such that the publishers now stated their conclusion,

. . . Our love for Brother Boll has led us to be long suffering and to remain silent in the face of false representations against us in the hope of saving him from his erroneous and grossly carnal teaching. But now, since he has broken faith with us, that hope is gone, and because we love the truth more than we do any man, and have never wavered in our determination not to use our abilities and means in any way that will encourage error, no matter by whom taught, we have written Brother Boll that we will drop his name from our editorial staff.

We make these statements and take this action with profound regret and sorrow, but with a conscience "void of offense toward God and man." [31]

This "verbal agreement" was to be a point of great controversy in the next few years. In 1919 four participants in a discussion about the agreement made with R. H. Boll gave a summary of another session with Boll. The publishers had claimed agreement, others had denied such, and, "This disagreement has been the source of alienation and strife and consequent evil, which is always to be deplored." [32] A prior meeting between the four men and Boll had resulted in a signed statement by Boll. The statement was,

The Point of Misunderstanding

I understand that the word "agreement" is used by Webster in two distinct senses:

1. A concurrence of judgment, coinciding of view, harmony of thought.
2. A compact, covenant, promise, contract.

There was an agreement in the former sense; for without dictation from men, and as free under God and because my judgement approved, I was of the same mind with the other brethren that it was best not to press the doctrines in question. But there was no agreement in the second sense of Webster's definition.

[Signed] R. H. Boll[33]

Unfortunately, the agreement and fervent desire of many were not to result in unity. Further alienation was to be observed in the years after the 1915 agreement, but the significant point for this phase of the study was that the *Gospel Advocate* writers had continued their effort to stabilize the work in Tennessee and elsewhere. In this effort they had not hesitated to oppose and to separate themselves from the doctrine being taught by R. H. Boll. The fellowship known between them and Boll for years was now broken; subsequent years were to see this breaking of fellowship reaching into other areas of the nation.

The third indication of broken fellowship occurred in Louisville and concerned several men of considerable influence and stature. In June 1918 R. O. Rubel, Sr. and C. A. Taylor published an article telling of problems they had experienced in the Highland church in Louisville. A. B. Lipscomb added his comments following an on the site investigation.[34] M. C. Kurfees commented on the incident at length.[35] E. L. Jorgenson, a participant in the episode, contributed a long article[36] to which Rubel and Taylor responded.[37] M. C. Kurfees penned a summary article on the whole episode and its background,[38] E. A. Elam published some correspondence between himself and R. H. Boll and commented on the episode,[39] and the publishers of the *Gospel Advocate* challenged Jorgenson to let both sides be heard in the paper with which he was affiliated as well as in the *Gospel Advocate*.[40] In later years this episode was to be referred to again and again. It received special attention in a 1936 edition of *The Gospel Guardian*,[41] was mentioned in the unpublished autobiography of C. A. Taylor in 1958,[42] and was featured in an article by E. L. Jorgenson in 1961.[43] These articles and the sustained references show the importance the participants and subsequent writers attached to the episode. The story may be told briefly from these records.

The Highland church was established in the 1890s by members from Campbell Street and other churches in Louisville. R. O. Rubel and C. A. Taylor had served as leaders in the work for several years. Isaac Haskins and A. B. Lipscomb had served as regular preachers. In 1913 E. L. Jorgenson came as the preacher, his services being reconsidered each year in a business session. R. H. Boll, E. L. Jorgenson and Don Carlos Janes, of the Highland church, were good friends. The discussions among them resulted in agreement concerning their views on the second coming of Christ and related topics. In 1914 Jorgenson preached several sermons on these topics and encountered some difficulties. In 1915 Stanford Chambers, of New Orleans, was invited to conduct a meeting for the Highland church but, upon indication of opposition, was asked not to come. In the same year resistance was raised to Jorgenson's work as preacher by a strong group in the Highland church, but the majority desired him to stay. In 1916 a paper, *The Word and Work,* was brought from New Orleans to Louisville and Boll became the editor with Jorgenson as the associate editor. This paper began to push the views of Boll with vigor. In 1916 seventeen members at Highland objected to the recall of Jorgenson as preacher and voted publicly to accept his resignation which was tendered each year to be accepted or for Jorgenson to be recalled, but the majority wanted him to stay. In 1917 twenty three members voted against his recall on doctrinal and personal grounds. This group included all the charter members of the church, all the trustees, and nine of the oldest members in point of years of attendance.

In this context of disagreement and friction the episode in 1918 ran its course. In March a letter was sent to several members concerning their continued membership in the Highland church. In a business meeting in April twenty members sought to protest the implications of this letter but were not allowed a hearing. On May 16, 1918 instead of the usual mid-week service a business meeting was conducted. A report was presented to the effect that C. A. Taylor and R. O. Rubel would not make an apology for their previous course of action. Don Carlos Janes made the motion the two men should be withdrawn from as being "factionists." The move was seconded. Rubel and Taylor asked for a postponement to prepare a defense but this was denied. The motion to withdraw carried and the church withdrew from Rubel and Taylor. When the report spread, much displeasure against the action of withdrawal was expressed by members at Highland who asked that their names be removed from the church roll. By June 20, 1918 Rubel and Taylor stated that some thirty five or forty of the former Highland members had moved from

Highland to another meeting place. This group and others became the present Bardstown Road church in Louisville.

A. B. Lipscomb, a former preacher at Highland, made a trip to Louisville to discuss the matter with both groups. He stated his conclusion in these words concerning the charge of factionalism by Rubel and Taylor,

> I therefore asked the pertinent question: "Of what did their factious conduct consist?" During two sessions of several hours each this question was pressed, with no satisfactory answer. They were repeatedly called upon to name or specify a single thing done by these brethren that makes them unworthy of Christian fellowship, but they failed to specify any such thing. I was more than ever convinced that the chief offense committed by these two brethren in the eyes of those who had withdrawn from them had been their conscientious and steadfast objection to certain speculative teachings on unfulfilled prophecies as featured by Brother Jorgenson. After hearing his testimony and noting the willingness of Taylor and Rubel to settle any little personal differences where the question of doctrine was not involved, it was plain to me that the withdrawal action had been wholly unjust and unscriptural and that justice demanded it should be rescinded.[44]

From this point the controversy over Rubel and Taylor began. It was to become a part of the larger controversy which was building up at the same time and was not to be resolved better than was the larger problem.

Efforts were made to resolve the Highland problem over the years. In 1923 a lengthy correspondence between Taylor and the Highland church failed to bring resolution.[45] In 1932 a further series of letters was unsuccessful in resolving the problem.[46] In 1938 a participant in the 1918 meeting, who had voted against Taylor and Rubel, stated his subsequent realization of error some nine years after the incident. He wrote to F. B. Srygley stating that he had asked forgiveness of Taylor and Rubel and had received it.[47] E. L. Jorgenson, reflecting on the 1918 incident, stated the question had often crossed his mind whether the Scriptures had been correctly applied in the final act of withdrawal and wondered if the action should not have been individual rather than congregational. He also alluded to a note to Taylor dated October 29, 1959, in which he had stated, "I know that some have suffered much, since 1918—perhaps I most of all. You know I thought—we all thought—we were in God's will; but if we had those years to go through again, I would certainly try to find a better way, and at any personal cost." [48]

These three incidents—The New Orleans problem, the return and departure of Boll to and from the *Advocate* staff, and the Highland church problem—focused attention on the fact that the differences between the upholders and opponents of premillennialism were real and deep. It was also clear that those who upheld these doctrines were determined to proclaim them in spite of opposition and would be willing to see division come as a result if such were necessary. The opponents of these doctrines had counseled that such views as were held by Boll, Jorgenson, and others should be held as personal property "for the sake of peace and cooperation . . . that we might continue uninterruptedly our work

. . . on the common ground on which we had worked in harmony . . ." [49] This proposal had not been accepted and E. A. Elam charged that division had come as a result in such different places as Beamsville, Ontario, Winchester, Kentucky, the Flat Rock church in Nashville, as well as the Highland church in Louisville and other places.[50] It was evident that a fellowship was on the verge of being broken and in some places was already broken in 1918. Later years would see the shock waves from these incidents increasing with the result that fellowship was no longer enjoyed, to any significant extent, between the two differing groups in the period studied.

The Boll-Boles Debate, 1927

The preceding discussion has shown that the budding premillennial controversy would not be quickly resolved. Over the years several developments showed the drift of the brotherhood. The paper edited by R. H. Boll, *The Word and Work,* as well as the *Gospel Advocate* continued to run articles on the various points of concern. In 1918 the editor of the *Gospel Advocate* stated concerning Boll, "In view of R. H. Boll's past conduct, for which he has made no amends, the Gospel Advocate prints nothing that will give him recognition in its columns . . ." [51] In 1921 F. W. Smith, who had been a leading opponent of Boll since 1915, published a small booklet in review of the "Kingdom Theory" in dispute.[52] In 1923 M. C. Kurfees told of his request to R. H. Boll when the controversy was beginning that his views be held as private property and not be pressed. Instead Boll had refused and difficulties had multiplied. Kurfees summarized his view as to the course to be followed in these words,

> Hence, when men thus persist in teaching and spreading divisive opinions—things which God does not require, and from teaching which they could properly refrain—there is but one proper thing to do, and that is to oppose them with all our might with the word of God. Let them be faithfully pointed out and marked as false teachers and schismatics.[53]

It was becoming clear that the pressing of the views of Boll would continue to create problems and that strong opposition was present. Boll had written two books of major importance, *The Kingdom of God*[54] and *The Revelation,*[55] but these books were not widely known in Tennessee or throughout the brotherhood and the claim was often made that Boll was being misunderstood or misrepresented. R. L. Whiteside and C. R. Nichol tried to explain Boll's teaching and refute it in a small book in 1925.[56] The need of further clarification was obvious to G. C. Brewer who suggested a debate to clear up the uncertainty as to what was really being believed and taught. His words left no doubt as to his desire for clarity on the matters in dispute. He stated,

> Let Brother Nichol or Brother Whiteside or Brother Nelson or somebody who is interested, agree upon propositions with Brother Boll and discuss them to a finish . . . and let the rest of us keep out of the fight . . .
> Until this is done there are those who are going to continue to say that Boll's opponents misunderstand him or misrepresent him. Let him have

equal space and a fair chance with and (sic.) opponent and then we will all see where we agree and where we differ.

Frankly, I do not believe the issues are worth discussing . . . but they are being discussed, then why not treat them as we do other issues—fight them out with their strongest opponent.[57]

By 1927 there had developed such a tense situation over these problems that, along the line of Brewer's suggestion to "treat them as we do other issues," there was arranged a debate between R. H. Boll of Louisville and H. Leo Boles of Nashville on five key propositions. Boll was well known and so was Boles. Consequently, debate articles were exchanged in the *Gospel Advocate* from May 29-November 3, 1927. These were incorporated into a book[58] from which the following references have been taken. The major themes may be isolated for study.

Restoration of Israel

In the first proposition Boll sought to prove that "Israel (fleshly descendants of Abraham through Jacob) shall be nationally restored." [59] This he argued from Old Testament passages which he claimed showed that "some day all of God's predicted plans and intentions concerning them shall be realized." [60] He added to this certain New Testament arguments, particularly Romans 11:11-15, and quotations from Alexander Campbell and other early preachers.[61]

Boles responded with the point that if the proposition of Boll were true, "We ought to find a plain and simple passage of Scripture which so teaches; we are not to find an obscure Scripture and give to that obscure Scripture a 'private interpretation' to support this proposition." [62] The Old Testament passages were claimed by Boles to have reference to events no later than the Babylonian Exile or to have no relevance to the proposition.[63] He then claimed that Boll faced certain problems in his national return view consequent on the lack of Jewish national conversion. The Bible teaching was that people must be converted individually, not nationally, and that once converted they could be Christians and have no need to return to Palestine for any spiritual blessing.[64] Boles noted that the quotations from earlier preachers were not in full agreement with the position of Boll.[65] A major point of concern was developed in Boles' second negative when he claimed that "No one can know the exact meaning of unfulfilled prophecy or how it will be fulfilled." Consequently, "No man can ever be sure that his interpretation of an unfulfilled prophecy is absolutely correct." [66] This meant, according to Boles, that Boll could never prove his proposition since inspiration would be necessary to know when "a correct interpretation of unfulfilled prophecy has been given . . ." [67] He supported this by citing the differences among the earlier preachers introduced by Boll.[68]

As the exchange ended it was clear that the two positions were being fiercely argued but that little hope of reconciliation or agreement was possible.

The Kingdom of God

H. Leo Boles sought to prove that the event signified in the smiting and destruction of the beast in Daniel 2:35,44 began to take place on Pentecost in Acts 2.[69] He analyzed the passages in Daniel, showed their basic components, and cited New Testament passages which, he stated, showed the components had been fulfilled and so, "our proposition is established." [70]

In response Boll declared there was agreement on much of Boles' presentation,[71] but argued that the "establishment and distinct manifestation of the kingdom in sovereign power by the little stone (which itself is the kingdom of God, as Brother Boles says) has never yet taken place." [72] The issue about unfulfilled prophecy being correctly interpreted came up again,[73] and Boles, in response, offered to pause in the discussion until Boll proved "The Scriptures teach that man, unaided by inspiration, can understand how and when unfulfilled prophecy will be fulfilled." [74] Boles claimed that if Boll could not prove this he ought to admit that his affirmations in the debate could not be proved.[75] Boles further noted that the concessions of agreement by Boll involved him in a dilemma, to either admit that the kingdom in Daniel 2 and Acts 2 were the same (and surrender his negative) or agree that God set up two kingdoms during the Roman Empire.[76] To deny this dilemma, Boll would have to argue that the empires from Babylon to Rome, agreed to be indicated in the imagery of Daniel 2, would be re-established.[77]

The discussion revolved around these points for the rest of the exchange. Again the fundamental differences were becoming apparent and the constant pressure of Boles in forcing the implicit positions of Boll out into the open was having its effect.

The Reign of Christ

In this proposition Boll sought to prove that "after his coming Christ will with his saints reign over all the earth." [78] In his affirmation he contended that Satan now prevents the full reign of Christ,[79] quoted passages in Revelation 2:26-27, 3:21, 2 Timothy 2:12, etc. to argue that saints will reign with Christ, and used passages in Revelation 2, 13, 19-20, and Daniel 7 to show that this reign was to be "after" the second coming of Christ.[80]

Boles responded that the interpretation of unfulfilled prophecy issue was crucial and claimed that as long as there was uncertainty in the process of interpretation there would be uncertainty in the conclusion reached.[81] He invited Boll to "give us his credentials that he is an infallible interpreter of unfulfilled prophecy."[82] Boles also claimed that the Bible teaches Christ reigns now and will until all things have been subjected to him at which time the kingdom will be given to God,[83] and that the apostles and saints are today reigning with Christ.[84] In view of the fact that Revelation is largely made up of "figures, symbols, and allegories," Boles challenged Boll to interpret such contents of the book by citing various items in Revelation 13-20 for a specific statement of meaning.[85]

It was now clear that heretofore unrealized positions were imbedded in the general argument of Boll and that Boles was ever alert to force these out into the open. Also, it was clear that the two views as to the reign of Christ could not be reconciled.

Christ on David's Throne

The fourth proposition was in a real sense the opposite position from the third. Boles affirmed that Christ is now reigning on David's throne.[86] He argued that the issue was clear between his view and Boll's and sought to prove his case from Old Testament and New Testament passages. This meant, Boles wrote, that Christ now has all authority and power that the Bible tells he is to have and then concluded that the future claims of Boll were of no relevance.[87]

In response Boll argued that the expression "throne of David" was not fully and clearly defined and thus the issue could not be joined.[88] He charged that the verses introduced were not relevant to the real issue.[89] The argument was made that Christ will reveive the throne of David in a sphere "where he has not been actually exercising it" and that Christ is not now exercising this authority.[90]

A controverted item was introduced when Boles stated that the throne of David was the type of the throne of Christ and that "Christ is now on the throne which was typified by David's literal throne." [91] Boll claimed this meant the prophecies were "not to be taken at what they really say, but figuratively, at what Brother Boles says they typify." [92] He observed that Boles earlier had objected to "private interpretations" and that this approach seemed to be such on the part of Boles.[93] Boles did not respond to this point in detail since it was introduced and discussed in the last respective sections of each man.

Christ's Coming Premillennial and Imminent[94]

The final proposition, affirmed by Boll, was regarded by him as "the main and central teaching" with the preceding being "incidental and subordinate." [95] He argued that there will be "a period of world-wide blessing and universal acknowledgement of God and Christ, and that this period is yet future." [96] Various New Testament passages were cited which Boll claimed to support his view and the argument was made that the "millennium" would occur after the second coming of Christ.[97] This coming of Christ was "always liable to occur" and thus "imminent" but his view did not entail "immediacy" or "date setting." [98] Thus the second coming is always liable to occur and must always be "looked for." [99]

Boles, as had been true with Boll before, spent much time in analysis of the proposition. The key terms "premillennial" and "imminent" had not been shown to be necessarily interdependent and Boles denied that the Scriptures teach a millennium as interpreted by the "theory" of Boll.[100] He discussed the need to spell out the contents of the view of the "millennium" and asked to have Boll's view compared to or contrasted with the general views held by others in the premillennial school of thought.[101] The arguments in support of the proposition were examined and the "assumption" of each was ferreted out and denied. Boles contended that each assumption concealed an unwelcome position, e.g. one meant the church, the kingdom of God, is a failure; another that Christ's first advent was a failure, and the work of the Holy Spirit is discredited.[102] He also contended that if the second coming of Christ is imminent, the things Boll had argued were to be accomplished prior to the coming of Christ, i.e., the return of Rome, the conversion and return of the Jews, etc. are also imminent and thus liable to happen at any moment.[103]

Boll refused to admit that Boles[104] had properly interpreted certain earlier words of himself gleaned from his writings in *Word and Work* from 1916 to 1926[105] and stated that such statements tended to put him in a bad light before the brotherhood.[106] He thanked the editors of the *Gospel Advocate* for the provision of space and the courtesies extended. He also indicated his desire that the questions in dispute might be viewed in a fuller, clearer light and left the readers to weigh and judge for themselves.[107]

Boles closed his work by indicating there was much agreement between the disputants, "enough to fellowship each other as brethren in the Lord," [108] but continued to deny the essential details of Boll's case. He stated that the reader should decide as to whether quotations from earlier writings of Boll meant what he (Boles) said they meant as to the views expressed and summarized what the affirmative had failed to prove.[109] He plead that brethren might continue to study the questions in dispute until "all are at a unit on them, until there be 'one faith' as there is but 'one Lord' and one God and Father of all." [110]

The statements by H. Leo Boles concerning continued fellowship with those who espoused the views of R. H. Boll became a focal point of concern in the next few years. Various writers of the premillennial persuasion had used the statement to claim that fellowship should continue in spite of differences. To this claim Boles replied in an article entitled, "The Issue Now—And Then." In this 1935 article Boles made the following statements:

> At the time this discussion was had the situation had not become so acute as it has now become. R. H. Boll and others who believed as he did were preaching for churches in meetings and in station work for churches which were not in sympathy with those speculative theories. The situation has grown so intense since this discussion that Brother Boll and others who are in sympathy with his theories cannot preach for churches that are opposed to those views; neither can one who opposes the theories propagated by

Brother Boll and his sympathizers preach for churches in sympathy with Brother Boll. . . . Obviously the cause of this condition is the pressing of these theories. The issues involve more and are more far-reaching than was at first realized. The propagators of this speculation have gone to further extremes than it was ever dreamed they would go.

. . . At that time those who held to these speculative theories claimed that Christians could do all the work the Lord requires of them to do without knowing or believing in the speculative theories which were being discussed; he conceded that Christians could worship God acceptably without believing the propositions which he affirmed or without denying the propositions which he denied. Evidently, some of those who now hold to these theories have changed as they are contending now that a belief in these theories is essential to Christian growth and development, and even essential to salvation.

. . . But the leaders of this movement, including Brother Boll himself, evidently believe that they are important enough to justify pressing them upon churches even to the dividing asunder the body of Christ, for in the face of widespread disruption in the church, they have not relented, but rather intensified their efforts to extend their theories. To some these theories take position in the plan of salvation and the development of the Christian life with equal rank of faith, repentance and baptism. . . .

At the time the discussion was held on "Unfulfilled Prophecy" it was thought that the discussion would help maintain peace in the brotherhood and harmony with the people of God. Brother Boll himself said, "Might we not hope that this discussion may itself be a means to help brethren everywhere to study, weigh, and discuss these teachings without allowing them to disturb their harmony and love and Christian fellowship?" (Unfulfilled Prophecy, Page 33). Brother Boll was urged at that time to express himself fully, clearly, accurately, and specifically on every point; he was urged to keep nothing back; he had ample time and opportunity to express himself clearly on every point and make himself clear as to what he believed and taught on these speculative theories. The discussion was fraternal; each regarded the other as a brother in the Lord searching for the truth; each expressed confidence in the other as a brother in the Lord and enjoyed fellowship with each other in Christ. Conditions have changed in the brotherhood generally since this discussion, due to the extremes to which the leaders of this movement have gone. They have gone beyond the boundary not only of truth, but of reason and brotherly love. They have exalted these theories to a level with the word of God. They have gone out from the faithful brethren in the Lord. Some of them have gone to the extreme of fellowshipping the denominations and affiliating with denominational preachers who blaspheme the church of our Lord. It is not fair to the present situation to quote me in 1927 from the book, "Unfulfilled Prophecy", which expressed the attitude then and apply these quotations to the extremities to which these brethren who have so far departed from the faith, have gone in exalting their theories.

The language used in that book could perhaps be applied to some of these brethren now, who do not press these theories to the division of the church and who are not aligned with the contingency doing so, but it cannot apply to those who are wedded like Ephraim of old to their idols and who have suffered division to come rather than recede from their theories. A discussion of these questions now, must, as a matter of fact, be held in light of the issue now—not then. Later developments reveal the character of the movement even from incipiency and justifies the attitude of such men as F. W. Smith and M. C. Kurfees, who were criticized for their attitude on the issue.[111]

In this way Boles stated his awareness of a change in his thinking and an explanation of his words in the debate. The following pages will note some of the changes which were taking place, but it seems appropriate to provide this important article by H. Leo Boles.

Evaluation of Debate

The primary concern of this effort has not been to evaluate the discussion in terms of truth or falsity of Bible teaching, though the writer upholds the positions defended by H. Leo Boles. Rather, the discussion may be evaluated from the standpoint of stabilization of the churches in the state. Several characteristics of the exchange may be noted from this viewpoint.

First, it was significant that the leading paper among churches of Christ in the state and one of the leading preachers in the state were involved. One of the stated desires of the debate was that of removing prejudice, antagonism, and misconceptions concerning the issues so as to bring about a better understanding between brethren and thereby to heal sores and breaches which may have occurred in any place.[112] This contributed to the strengthening of the cause in the state.

Second, it was indicated that difficulties were present and had been present for some time over these issues. This "tense situation" in the brotherhood at large called for attention from the beginning of the discussion[113] and was to recur from time to time. Boles did not want the differences to destroy fellowship[114] and Boll did not, but both recognized that problems were abroad over the matters discussed.

Third, the debate achieved the result of clarifying exactly what was believed by the leading spokesman of the new views about the second coming of Christ and related matters. This clear presentation, in a widely circulated weekly paper and subsequent book, let all readers know exactly what was believed by Boll and his associates and the charge of misstatement or misrepresentation could not properly be made subsequently.

Fourth, Boles pressed into the open certain assumptions and implications which previously had not been apparent to all. The preachers and members in the state who read the various exchanges could soon see the patterns of thought in the two men and the positions advocated. Boll did not make his implications apparent until pressed, but tried to defend them when brought out. Again, understanding and insight were the result.

Fifth, the articles, when gathered into the subsequent book, provided a type of handbook for extracting and refining the arguments pro and con. Subsequent discussions were to modify, expand, and eliminate one argument or another, but the basic positions were set forth vigorously and lines of attack and response were roughly set for others to use as they would and could.

In summary, the Boles-Boll debate served to inform members in the state concerning the issues at variance, implications of each, arguments for and against, and the lines along which analysis and evaluation could proceed. In this way the debate was a major contribution to the doctrinal stabilization of the churches of Christ in the state.

The Neal-Wallace Debate, 1933

The presentation of the opposing positions in the Boll-Boles debate served to crystallize brotherhood thought as well as the respective views concerning the second coming of Christ and related issues. It did not serve to remove the controversy which had been engendered by the writings of Boll and others some twelve or so years before. Rather, the debate could be viewed as providing an array of arguments to be hammered and shaped in succeeding encounters, and there were succeeding encounters.

The details of these subsequent discussions would be far afield from the concern of this study, but one of considerable importance may be noticed. On January 2 to January 6, 1933 Charles M. Neal, preacher for the Main Street church of Christ in Winchester, Kentucky, and Foy E. Wallace, Jr., editor of the *Gospel Advocate,* Nashville, Tennessee, conducted a debate in Winchester, Kentucky on the proposition: "The Bible clearly teaches that after the second coming of Christ and before the final resurrection and judgement, there will be an age or dispensation of one thousand years during which Christ will reign on earth." [115]

The details of the debate need not be pursued in depth. It was made clear that division over the issue was present in the Winchester church, that brethren met in different places in alienation,[116] and that Neal regarded his position as necessary to be upheld to defend the faith of the gospel.[117] Wallace quoted the correspondence which led to the debate to show that Neal had issued the challenge which resulted in the debate.[118] Because of certain conditions required of the disputants after the debate began,[119] to which Wallace objected strenuously,[120] the fourth, and fifth nights of debate were conducted in the local courthouse.[121] In the fourth night Neal challenged Wallace to repeat the debate in Nashville,[122] and the challenge was accepted by Wallace "If the brethren in Nashville invite the discussion . . ." [123] Also, R. H. Boll expressed willingness to debate in Louisville.[124] The proposed debates in Louisville and Nashville did not materialize, but the disputants in Winchester, Kentucky later conducted a similar debate in Chattanooga, Tennessee which was incorporated into the book in the Winchester debate.[125]

This debate showed clearly that the advocates of the views previously set forth by R. H. Boll felt that they had more solidly constructed their case, at least in specific details, and were more aggressive in their presentation. Also, it was significant that the upholders of premillennial views were taking the lead in challenging for debates. The effort was now being made to place opponents of premillennialism on the defensive and not to take a place of relative passivity in teaching on the disputed themes. It was clear, by the mid thirties, therefore, that the views originally advocated by R. H. Boll had solidified into a cherished system of thought with articulate, aggressive defenders who sought to promote their view not only by writing and preaching but also by the polemics so popular in that day. It was also true that there were no indications by writers on the *Gospel Advocate* staff that they were desirous of yielding their opposition. The two positions were now solidly established and could be capably argued. The remaining question was whether they could remain in fellowship.

The Issue of Fellowship

A development of major significance was concerned with the fellowship between the two differing groups, and on it different views were to emerge among those who were united as to their opposition to premillennialism. The earliest view concluded that the position of Boll, if held as an opinion and not preached or taught publicly, would be no barrier to fellowship. One notes this recurring theme through the years. In 1923 J. C. McQuiddy reflected this view when he told that he had urged a number of young preachers in 1914 to hold their views on premillennialism as "private property and not to propagate them to the disturbance of the churches." He had warned that the disturbance of the churches would necessitate opposition. He had continued to urge the same view, but to no avail.[126] Later in that same year, M. C. Kurfees stated the same view as McQuiddy when he wrote that the having or holding of opinions on premillennialism or other matters was not wrong when held privately, but to teach and practice them where strife and division resulted was wrong and must be opposed.[127]

H. Leo Boles, at the conclusion of his debate with R. H. Boll in 1927, while deploring the disturbance of churches,[128] wanted to avoid having these subjects made into "a test of fellowship," [239] and claimed that if these issues were confined to "the proper field," "Brethren should not be disturbed over these questions; churches should not be divided over them." [130] R. H. Boll stated as much as to his views on fellowship in reference to these subjects.[131] Boles began his closing article by stating, "Brother Boll and I hold many things in common—enough to fellowship each other as brethren in the Lord." [132] In 1927 then, the view was present that the teaching of Boll was not essential to the faith and could be regarded as a private conclusion, without being pressed upon others, and the fellowship could be preserved in firm but brotherly disagreement. Attention has been called, earlier, to a change in thought by Boles, and the reader is urged to note this change as it relates to the present discussion.

The next few years, however, saw a gradual change come over the minds of brethren who opposed the views of Boll. This shift in evaluation of significance grew out of the failure to resolve the disagreement, the persistent effort of the premillennialists to urge, with some success, their case, and the awareness that the plea to hold the disputed view as private property without proclamation was not working. This awareness became evident in the debate noted before in 1933. Foy E. Wallace, Jr., in view of division in the Winchester church over the premillennial issues, plead that these "theories" cease to be taught "and we will have unity." He clarified by stating, "We do not tell you to quit *believing* them. We only ask you to quit *pushing* them on us." He proposed that unity between the two divided churches of Christ in the city could be restored if Neal would stand and declare he would hold "these theories as private opinion and cease teaching them as cardinal doctrine . . ." [133] He repeated this several times,[134] but Neal countered with a request for apologies and retractions by Wallace which, if met, would open the way to talk about the path to unity.[135] He denied his views were theories and speculations but were a part of the faith[136] and wondered if anything else had caused division in the body of Christ other than "prophetic teaching." [137]

One may conclude from this debate, therefore, that by the 1933 discussion a hardening of the position of the premillennialists was present. The advocates of the views set forth by Boll refused to accept the designation of their position as a theory or speculative, but insisted that it was in fact the correct exposition of relevant Bible teaching. They were unwilling to accept responsibility for misunderstandings or division and were willing rather to challenge for debates and defend their cause. A turning point had been reached and the level of resistance as well as defense was to be escalated more intensely than before.

The summary of arguments in the followup debate in Chattanooga (June 6 to 9, 1933) indicated a hardening of resistance to the premillennial case as well. Neal plead that there was no desire or reason for separation and that there was no reason why differences on prophecy should raise a barrier to fellowship.[138] Wallace stated that there could be no compromise on the issues and pointed out that Neal had refused to accept the offer of restored fellowship in Winchester, Kentucky as well as later by failing to "withdraw the wedge of division which had been driven." [139] He went on to discuss what he termed "The menace of Premillennialism." [140] The consequences of the doctrine were said to be "vitiating to the gospel of Christ." He closed by stating his conviction in these words,

Once informed of the essence of these theories with their lurking errors, I do not believe the churches of Christ, composed in the main of people opposed to religious speculation, will tolerate such travesty on the study of

God's word, nor countenance the men among us who indulge in it.[141]

By the mid 1930s it was apparent that the earlier solution of regarding premillennialism as an opinion, restraining the teaching on the controversial topics, and continuing fellowship between the two differing groups among churches of Christ did not provide acceptable terms of fellowship for the majority of churches of Christ in the state. By the late 1930s it was increasingly clear that fellowship between those in favor of and those opposed to premillennialism could no longer be maintained to any meaningful extent. In July 1938 Batsell Baxter summarized the situation in an article on "Trouble in the Family." [142] He traced the history in much the fashion noted above and observed that those holding the premillennial view had become a faction, were destroying unity in the brotherhood, and had hindered mission work. In September R. L. Whiteside reflected on his increased concern about premillennialism. He indicated that he had at first thought little about the subject but the more he studied the problem the more vigorously he opposed it.[143] In October F. B. Srygley again spoke out against the views of Boll, claiming that Boll was minimizing the problem of fellowship and comparing the introduction of premillennialism to the introduction of the instrument years before. He concluded that "The truth should be preached and error exposed." [144] From October 16 to 31, 1938, N. B. Hardeman conducted his fourth series of sermons at the Ryman Auditorium in Nashville, Tennessee. He spoke pointedly against premillennialism and indicated there should be no compromise with it. He also said that it was in principle a duplicate of the music and society disturbance.[145] He agreed one could hold the view as an opinion if one would keep it to himself and advised all others to do the same, but he stated the pushing of the doctrine, as had been done in places in Kentucky, Texas and elsewhere, would result in continued opposition and division.[146] F. B. Srygley summed up the effect of the Hardeman meeting in stating that Hardeman, in a quest for unity, had called the brethren to be faithful to the gospel and oppose false teaching, particularly premillennialism, without compromise.[147]

Over the years until the close of the period studied there was a frequent restating of the view that the premillennial advocates did not keep their position to themselves, but rather taught it at every opportunity. In 1941 H. Leo Boles provided a summary article as to the beliefs of the premillennialists[148] and pointed out their fallacies as he saw them.[149] B. C. Brewer wrote several articles along the same line.[150] In 1945 Foy E. Wallace, Jr. presented a series of sermons in the Music Hall in Dallas, Texas, January 21-28, "Exposing Modern Millennial Theories." [151] After a study of such major themes as the nature of prophecy, the church age, the throne of David, and the second coming of Christ, he summed up "The Consequences of Premillennialism." [152] The point was made that no one could believe the gospel and the theories of premillennialism.[153] The line had now run out, the premillennial position could not be reconciled with the truth of the gospel and only open division could obtain between those who upheld and those who opposed such teaching.

There were some who claimed they opposed premillennialism but objected to the exposure of it as harsh and unkind, and there were some such as John Nelson Armstrong, who compared the issue to the meat and herb problem in Romans 14, urged all to allow everyone to decide the issue for himself, felt no issue of fellowship was involved, and objected to what was termed the persecution of R. H. Boll and others concerning these matters.[154] This approach opened a new problem within the ranks of the opponents of premillennialism, but its effect was less widespread and acceptable to the majority of the brethren in the state than was the approach of Boles, Hardeman, Wallace and others. As the years passed the latter position more and more prevailed so that the general stance of churches of Christ in Tennessee has been in opposition to premillennialism.

The premillennial issue arose in the leading paper among churches of Christ in Tennessee, was explored and debated by leading men in the state, and was resolved, by what was in effect a severing of fellowship, along lines articulated by leading Tennessee writers and preachers. It had become clear, after several years of discussion and debate, that the advocates of premillennialism would not desist and the leading writers and preachers of the state, with very few exceptions, called for and received a virtual breaking of fellowship over the issues raised. The premillennial cause gained only a slight following among the churches of Christ in Tennessee during the period studied. The preachers and papers had stabilized the churches to resist and exclude this teaching.

The churches of Christ in Tennessee, in the period studied, confronted doctrinal problems of serious import. Two of these were of greatest significance, namely, instrumental music in worship and premillennialism. The last two chapters have traced the general course of stabilization by which the inroads of these doctrinal issues were resisted. Several general lines of such stabilization have been shown to exist. These included a clear identification of the exact point or points in dispute, a period of exchange of views as various spokesmen probed the components and content of the problem, a representative book or two on various issues which focused attention on the most urgent areas of disagreement, and ultimately debates between representative men who tested the arguments for the respective positions. After the debates there was a time for further reflection and discussion. There was a genuine desire on the part of all the interested persons to avoid a rupture of fellowship if at all possible. This interest in and effort to preserve fellowship was maintained for several years in each of the controversies. When it ultimately became apparent that mutually exclusive positions had emerged and that the advocates of the positions in dispute would not relent but would push their beliefs and practices to the disturbance of the peace of the churches, there was a ringing cry to sever the fellowship which had obtained and to defend the faith which was cherished and the unity of the churches which embodied such faith.

Gradually the problems rose, were clearly defined, argued and observed for effect on the churches. When the private views of men, however staunchly their friendships had previously been enjoyed, hindered the peace of the churches there was an all out plea to resist and the churches would respond in accordance with this appeal. The pattern of emergence, analysis, debate, observation of effect, and appeal to sever fellowship to preserve what was believed and maintain unity in the churches manifested the program to confront controversial issues and stabilize the churches. The relative loss of strength by those who advocated the use of the instrument in worship and upheld premillennialism as an essential to the faith, in comparison with those who opposed both of these views, indicates the effectiveness of stabilization of the churches in the state.

REFERENCES

[1] G. C. Brewer, "I Sat Where They Sat," *Gospel Advocate* 79 (December 16, 1937):1179.

[2] R. H. Boll, "A Grievous Mistake," *Gospel Advocate* 52 (January 20, 1910):65-67.

[3] R. H. Boll, "The Profitable Study of 'Revelation'," *Gospel Advocate* 52 (April 7, 1910):417-18.

[4] R. H. Boll, "Short Talks on Revelation: Sardis and Philadelphia," *Gospel Advocate* 57 (March 11, 1915):226.

[5] F. B. Srygley, "Is Christ on the Throne of David?" *Gospel Advocate* 57 (March 11, 1915):228.

[6] H. L. Olmstead, "David's Kingdom, No. I," *Gospel Advocate* 57 (April 8, 1915):330-31.

[7] F. B. Srygley, "Brother Srygley's Reply," *Gospel Advocate* 57 (April 8, 1915):331-32.

[8] F. W. Smith, "Interpreters of Divine Prophecy," *Gospel Advocate* 57 (April 15, 1915):357.

[9] H. L. Olmstead, "David's Kingdom, No. 3," *Gospel Advocate* 57 (May 6, 1915):435-36.

[10] R. H. Boll, "Reply to F. W. Smith," *Gospel Advocate* 57 (May 6, 1915):438.

[11] E. G. Sewell, "Has the Kingdom of Christ been set up or is it still in the Future?" *Gospel Advocate* 57 (May 6, 1915):443.

[12] David Lipscomb, "The Second Coming of Christ and Prophetic Study," *Gospel Advocate* 57 (May 6, 1915):444.

[13] Publishers of Gospel Advocate, "No Title," *Gospel Advocate* 57 (May 6, 1915):444.

[14] R. H. Boll, "On Things Revealed and Unrevealed," *Gospel Advocate* 57 (May 20, 1915):481-82.

[15] Publishers of the Gospel Advocate, "Publishers' Statement," *Gospel Advocate* 57 (May 20, 81915):482.

[16] R. H. Boll, "My Second Reply to Brother Smith," *Gospel Advocate* 57 (June 3, 1915):538.

[17] R. H. Boll, "Answer to the Publishers' Question," *Gospel Advocate* 57 (June 10, 1915):561-62.

[18] Publishers of Gospel Advocate, "Reply.—What Are Essentials?" *Gospel Advocate* 57 (June 10, 1915):564.

[19] Ibid.

[20] M. C. Kurfees, "The Gospel Advocate And the Issues in the Current Controversy," *Gospel Advocate* 57 (August 12, 1915):798-99.

[21] J. C. McQuiddy, "Premillennialism, No. 1," *Gospel Advocate* 57 (September 2, 1915):879-80. Note: The last in the series appeared November 14, 1915, pp. 1008-09.

[22] M. C. Kurfees, "There Are No Restrictions," *Gospel Advocate* 57 (September 2, 1915):878-79.

[23] F. B. Srygley, "Another Speculation Heard From," *Gospel Advocate* 57 (May 20, 1915):483.

[24] Stanford Chambers, "Reply to Brother Srygley's Charge, *Gospel Advocate* 57 (June 17, 1915):586-87.

[25] F. B. Srgyley, "Brother Srygley's Reply," *Gospel Advocate* 57 (June 17, 1915):587-89.

[26] Publishers Gospel Advocate, "Brother Boll Back on the Gospel Advocate," *Gospel Advocate* 57 (November 4, 1915):1110.

[27] R. H. Boll, "Brother Boll's Statement," *Gospel Advocate* 57 (November 4, 1915):1110.

[28] Anonymous, "Pleased With the Adjustment," *Gospel Advocate* 57 (November 25, 1915):1184.

[29] Publishers of Gospel Advocate, "The Agreement Made With Brother Boll," *Gospel Advocate* 57 (December 3, 1915):1240.

[30] Ibid., p. 1241.

[31] Ibid.

[32] J. C. McQuiddy, A. B. Lipscomb, F. W. Smith, and M. C. Kurfees, "The Agreement Brother Boll Made," *Gospel Advocate* 61 (October 2, 1919):695.

[33] Ibid.

[34] A. B. Lipscomb, "Fruits of Speculative Teaching in Louisville," *Gospel Advocate* 60 (June 20, 1918):588-89.

[35] M. C. Kurfees, "The Sad Case in the Highlands and the Duty of the Hour," *Gospel Advocate* 60 (June 27, 1918):610-12.

[36] E. L. Jorgenson, "The Advocates' Challenge and the Highland Church," *Gospel Advocate* 60 (October 10, 1918):963-67.

[37] R. O. Rubel and C. A. Taylor, "Another Statement from R. O. Rubel and C. A. Taylor," *Gospel Advocate* 60 (October 10, 1918):967-68.

[38] M. C. Kurfees, "E. L. Jorgenson's Reply With the Facts Submitted in Reply," *Gospel Advocate* 60 (October 10, 1918):969-74.

[39] E. A. Elam, "What Respect was Shown for the church in the Highland Trouble?" *Gospel Advocate* 60 (October 10, 1918):974-76.

[40] Publishers Gospel Advocate, "Our Challenge and Brother Jorgenson's Failure to Meet it," *Gospel Advocate* 60 (October 10, 1918):976-77.

[41] T. Q. Martin, "The Highland Church Action," *The Gospel Guardian* 2 (January 1936):13-17.

[42] C. A. Taylor, Autobiography of C. A. Taylor (handwritten copy, 1958), pp. 7-13.

[43] E. L. Jorgenson, "Fear and Fellowship," *The Word and Work* 55 (June 1961):134-37.

[44] A. B. Lipscomb, ibid., p. 589.

[45] See Letter from C. A. Taylor to L. M. Jackson, April 26, 1923; Letter from C. A. Taylor to R. C. Bagby, Sr., December 8, 1923; and Letter from Highland church of Christ to C. A. Taylor, December 7, 1923.

[46] Letter from Highland church of Christ to C. A. Taylor, May 12, 1932; Letter from C. A. Taylor to Highland church of Christ, May 26, 1932; Letter from R. O. Rubel to Highland church of Christ, June 16, 1932.

[47] Letter from H. L. Hickman to F. B. Srygley, February 26, 1938. See, F. B. Srygley, "An Acknowledgement," *Gospel Advocate* 80 (March 17, 1938):244.

[48] E. L. Jorgenson, ibid., pp. 136-37.

[49] M. C. Kurfees, "E. L. Jorgenson's Charge with the Facts in Reply," *Gospel Advocate* 60 (October 10, 1918):970.

[50] E. A. Elam, "What Respect was Shown for the Church in the Highland Trouble?" *Gospel Advocate* 60 (October 10, 1918):974.

[51] Editor, "Editor's Note," *Gospel Advocate* 60 (June 27, 1918):603.

[52] F. W. Smith, *A Review of R. H. Boll's Kingdom Theory* (Nashville: McQuiddy Printing Company, 1921).

[53] M. C. Kurfees, "A Most Vital and Radical Distinction," *Gospel Advocate* 65 (October 25, 1923):1036.

[54] R. H. Boll, *The Kingdom of God* (Louisville: The Word and Work, n.d.).

[55] R. H. Boll, *The Revelation* (Louisville: The Word and Work, n.d.).

[56] R. L. Whiteside and C. R. Nichol, *Christ and His Kingdom: A Review of R. H. Boll* (Clifton, Texas: Mrs. C. R. Nichol, Publisher, n.d.).

[57] G. C. Brewer, "Random Remarks," *Firm Foundation* 42 (July 7, 1925):3.

[58] H. Leo Boles and R. H. Boll, *Unfulfilled Prophecy* (Nashville: Gospel Advocate Company, 1928).

[59] Ibid., p. 7.

[60] Ibid., p. 12.

[61] Ibid., pp. 16-20.

[62] Ibid., pp. 23-24.

[63] Ibid., pp. 26-28.

[64] Ibid., pp. 24, 31.

[65] Ibid., pp. 73-74.

[66] Ibid., pp. 44-45.

[67] Ibid., pp. 66-67.

[68] Ibid., p. 81.

[69] Ibid., p. 83.

[70] Ibid., pp. 83-93.

[71] Ibid., p. 97.

[72] Ibid., p. 98.

[73] Ibid., p. 94.

[74] Ibid., p. 105.

[75] Ibid.
[76] Ibid., p. 107.
[77] Ibid., p. 109.
[78] Ibid., p. 147.
[79] Ibid., pp. 148-49.
[80] Ibid., pp. 150-54.
[81] Ibid., pp. 155-56.
[82] Ibid., p. 156.
[83] Ibid., p. 160.
[84] Ibid., p. 161.
[85] Ibid., pp. 163-65.
[86] Ibid., p. 221.
[87] Ibid., p. 231.
[88] Ibid., p. 235.
[89] Ibid., p. 237.
[90] Ibid., p. 243.
[91] Ibid., p. 290.
[92] Ibid., p. 301.
[93] Ibid.
[94] Ibid., p. 314.
[95] Ibid.
[96] Ibid., p. 315
[97] Ibid., p. 320.
[98] Ibid., p. 321.
[99] Ibid., p. 329.
[100] Ibid., pp. 330-31,333.
[101] Ibid., pp. 332, 335.
[102] Ibid., pp. 334-37.
[103] Ibid., pp. 339-40.
[104] Ibid., pp. 363.
[105] Ibid., pp. 386-90.
[106] Ibid., p. 390.
[107] Ibid., pp. 393-94.
[108] Ibid., p. 395.
[109] Ibid., pp. 402-10.
[110] Ibid., p. 412.
[111] H. Leo Boles, "The Issue Now—And Then," *The Gospel Guardian* 1 (October 1935):5.
[112] Boles and Boll, ibid., pp. 393-412.
[113] Ibid., p. 42.
[114] Ibid., p. 395.
[115] Charles M. Neal and Foy E. Wallace, Jr., *Neal-Wallace Discussion on the Thousand Years Reign of Christ* (Nashville: Gospel Advocate Company, 1933), p. 9.
[116] Ibid., pp. 20, 96-98, 108-09, 134-37, 184-86, 194-97.
[117] Ibid., pp. 10, 30, 39-41, 48, 51-52, 78, etc.
[118] Ibid., pp. 130-33.
[119] Ibid., pp. 118-19.
[120] Ibid., pp. 130-35.
[121] Ibid., pp. 175, 233.
[122] Ibid., p. 205.
[123] Ibid., p. 232.
[124] Ibid., p. 150.
[125] Ibid., pp. 291-350.
[126] J. C. McQuiddy, "Christian Unity," *Gospel Advocate* 65 (January 18, 1923):58.
[127] M. C. Kurfees, "Teaching Publicly Speculative Opinions," *Gospel Advocate* 65 (November 8, 1923):1084.
[128] Boles and Boll, ibid., pp. 42, 65.
[129] Ibid., p. 43.
[130] Ibid., p. 65.
[131] Ibid., pp. 33, 53-54.
[132] Ibid., p. 395.
[133] Neal and Wallace, ibid., pp. 194-95.
[134] Ibid., pp. 216-17.
[135] Ibid., pp. 237-38.

129

[136] Ibid., p. 10.

[137] Ibid., p. 263.

[138] Ibid., p. 339.

[139] Ibid., p. 341.

[140] Ibid., pp. 346-50.

[141] Ibid., p. 349.

[142] Batsell Baxter, "Trouble in the Family," *Gospel Advocate* 80 (July 14, 1938):643.

[143] R. L. Whiteside, "The Kingdom Question," *Gospel Advocate* 80 (September 8, 1938):833, 841.

[144] F. B. Srygley, "What Is It All About?" *Gospel Advocate* 80 (October 27, 1938):1004-05.

[145] N. B. Hardeman, *Hardeman Tabernacle Sermons*, IV (Nashville: Gospel Advocate Company, 1938), pp. 82.

[146] Ibid., pp. 82-83, 143.

[147] F. B. Srygley, "The Hardeman Meeting," *Gospel Advocate* 80 (November 3, 1938):1028.

[148] H. Leo Boles, "Premillennialism," *Gospel Advocate* 83 (April 17, 1941):365.

[149] H. Leo Boles, "Fallacies of Premillennialists," *Gospel Advocate* 83 (April 24, 1941):389.

[150] G. C. Brewer, "The Second Coming of Christ," *Gospel Advocate* 83 (May 22, 1941):482-83, 495, and G. C. Brewer "Ludicrous and Fallacious Assumptions Restudied," *Gospel Advocate* 83 (July 31, 1941):726-27.

[151] Foy E. Wallace, Jr., *God's Prophetic Word* (Lufkin, Texas: The Roy E. Cogdill Publishing Company, 1946).

[152] Ibid., pp. 283-318.

[153] Ibid., pp. 287, 318.

[154] L. C. Sears, *For Freedom: The Biography of John Nelson Armstrong* (Austin, Texas: Sweet Publishing Company, 1969), pp. 275-99.

CHAPTER TWELVE

NUMERICAL STRENGTH

The history of churches of Christ in Tennessee from 1906 to 1950 has shown their recovery from division by the achievement of the clarification of their identity and doctrinal stabilization. In view of such awareness of identity and stabilization growth was possible for them if the efforts of many people, known and unknown, could be effectively united. The present chapter will discuss one area of continued progress by the group in the state and later chapters will consider other expressions and means of their growth.

Any attempt to establish more than a general estimate of the numerical strength of churches of Christ on a state or national level immediately confronts a series of problems. For one thing, the fear by many that such recording of figures might be sinful, as per David and the numbering of Israel, has not encouraged statistical accuracy. Alexander Hall noted this in 1848,[1] and the concern was shared by David Lipscomb in 1881.[2] Again, there was stubborn resistance to any national or state coordinating agency in view of problems with and over the missionary society. Also, the various men who tried to gather statistics had to rely upon religious journal articles, word of mouth, and mailings to inform churches and individuals of the desire, plan, and procedure of such endeavors. These factors, along with the limitations of such means, the independence of individuals and churches, and the indifference of many to such attempts meant that the statistics obtained were at best of limited accuracy. Leslie G. Thomas, who collected the 1936 reports, lamented the effects of such factors when he explained the relatively limited participation of individuals and churches and observed that the obvious decreases in statements of membership and churches did not reflect the true figures.[3] One must accordingly take note that statistics about churches of Christ from national or individual sources do not, in the nature of the case, produce more than tentative and partial conclusions.

Subject to these limitations and being aware of the incompleteness produced thereby, one is able to obtain broad patterns of growth which, while tentative, are of value in reflecting the fact that significant progress was being made in Tennessee by churches of Christ. A broad comparison over the years makes this observation apparent. Hall reported 141 churches with 9,664 members, in 1848.[4] In 1885 the *Yearbook* reported 363 churches with 15,545 members and observed that many churches had not supplied the requested information.[5] In 1895 the report showed 512 churches with 45,125 members.[6] In 1900 the report showed 540 churches with 47,111 members.[7] In 1907, David Lipscomb stated he had a list of some 800 churches in the state with many of the counties not being reported when the article was written. He estimated some 900 churches of Christ were in existence at that time.[8]

Several details of the 1906 census reports by way of background and significance have already been given, and need not be repeated. One can gain a general picture of growth by comparative study of the reports in 1906, 1916, and 1926 respectively.[9] For reasons previously noted and observations forthcoming it was apparent that the 1936 report was unreliable. The reports showed for 1906: 631 churches with 41,411 members, for 1916: 995 churches with 63,521 members, for 1926: 978 churches with 72,015 members. The 1936 report showed a significant drop in both areas with only 564 churches and 49,379 members being indicated. The results may be tabulated as follows:

Year	Churches	Members
1848	141	9,664
1885	363	15,545
1895	512	45,125
1900	540	47,111
1906	631	41,411
1907	900	X
1916	995	63,521
1926	978	72,015
1936	564	49,379

Two lines of evidence combine with previous remarks to show that the 1936 figures were inaccurate for the state of Tennessee and for the nation as a whole. First, the figures in 1936 do not agree with other data. A comparative table shows the national figures as follows:

Year	Churches	Members	% of Change Churches	Members
1906	2,649	159,658	X	X
1916	5,570	317,937	110.3	99.1
1926	6,226	433,714	11.8	36.4
1936	3,815	309,551	—38.7	—28.6

In evaluating this national statistic, one notes an interesting series of tables by W. E. Brightwell, news editor of the *Gospel Advocate,* for a period ending in 1938.[10] He had collected statistics from the "News and Reports" columns of the *Gospel Advocate* from mid 1933 to 1938. Calculating from reports of total additions (baptisms and corrections of erring members) in 1932 and 1933, giving the figures he had kept of baptisms from 1934-1937, and projecting his figures as of September 1938, he gave the following statistics. A related figure is shown of the baptisms for June and July in respective years from 1934-1938 as Brightwell had earlier given them.[11]

Years	Baptisms per year	Baptisms in June & July
1932	18,906	X
1933	17,546	X
1934	16,687	2,360
1935	16,072	2,468
1936	12,269	1,815
1937	12,797	2,285
1938	18-20,000	2,503

When one observes, as did J. L. Hines,[12] that these figures only indicated the reports from a single paper and many preachers and churches would make reports in other papers than the *Gospel Advocate,* it is apparent that the figures in the 1936 report cannot be reconciled with the increase of 56,825 known for the period 1934-1937 and the additional total of 54,452 for 1932, 1933, and 1938 calculated by Brightwell from known figures. Allowing for deaths and losses by attrition or other means, a 28.6% decrease in membership and 38.7% decrease in churches cannot be regarded as accurate in view of the record in just one religious paper of the period, to say nothing of reports in other papers. Rather one should recognize that indifference if not opposition to the gathering of statistics more likely accounted for the decrease in the 1936 report.

The continued growth of the churches of Christ in America was shown later in the period when W. E. Brightwell gave the number of baptisms reported in the 1947 *Gospel Advocate* as 15,260.[13] Also in 1948 M. Norvell Young, after a period of research which began in 1946,[14] gave his estimate of membership of the churches. He noted the obvious inaccuracy of the 1936 census reports and projected his own estimate after receiving government reports from his earlier work. He estimated 6,318 church buildings, 682,172 members, and 429,072 Sunday school students.[15] He concluded that churches of Christ had been growing rapidly over the years. One would not be justified in postulating a specific percentage of these figures being claimed by churches in Tennessee, but it is readily apparent that progress rather than decline was being enjoyed by the churches of Christ in the state as well as in the nation.

A second line of statistical study for the churches of Christ in Tennessee was presented by John P. Fogarty and Olan Hicks in 1947.[16] In their work Fogarty and Hicks listed the names, addresses, names of persons contacted, and other information for churches of Christ in America and foreign lands. This procedure gave the work an authenticity not previously enjoyed and entitled the figures to as near an authoritative status as is possible. They were conscious of the problem of omission and duplication, but claimed their list of churches was "perhaps the most thoroughgoing one to be printed to date." [17] They listed for Tennessee 1515 churches of Christ but did not give an indication of membership. Allowing for duplication in the actual count, some 1500 or more churches of Christ were present in the state by 1950. Also, if one applies the lowest average membership in the churches reported in the census figures (57 for 1916) and the highest (81 for 1936) to the rule of thumb figure of 1500 churches, the membership in the state was roughly 85,000 to 121,500 by 1950. The 1926 figure of 72,015 and the indications of progress as given by Brightwell leads one to conclude the total membership was nearer the latter figure than the former. Accordingly, the present study concludes the membership of churches of Christ in Tennessee by 1950 was between 100,000 and 125,000 in some 1500 churches. If so, the number of members from 1906 to 1950 had approximately doubled and the number of churches had increased from about 900 to some 1500. In the nature of the case these figures are only estimates and approximations, but they do indicate a continued growth of the churches of Christ in the state in the period studied.

REFERENCES

[1] Alexander Hall, *The Christian Register* (Loydsville, Ohio: The Compiler, 1848), pp. 1-3.

[2] David Lipscomb, "Those Statistics," *Gospel Advocate* 23 (February 24, 1881):114.

[3] Leslie G. Thomas, "The 1936 Census Report," *Gospel Advocate,* 83 (June 12, 1941):570.

[4] Hall, ibid., pp. 36-39.

[5] *Yearbook of the Disciples of Christ* (Cincinnati: General Christian Missionary Convention, 1885), pp. 88-94.

[6] G. A. Hoffman, *Yearbook of the Disciples of Christ* (St. Louis: Christian Publishing Company, 1895), p. 47.

[7] Benjamin L. Smith and C. C. Smith, eds., *Yearbook of Churches of Christ (Disciples of Christ)* (Cincinnati: American Christian Missionary, 1900), p. 43.

[8] David Lipscomb, "The 'Church of Christ' and the 'Disciples of Christ,' " *Gospel Advocate* 49 (July 18, 1907):457.

[9] U.S., Department of Commerce, *Census of Religious Bodies, 1936,* Churches of Christ Statistics, History, Doctrine and Organization, Bulletin 46 (1940):1-7.

[10] W. E. Brightwell, "The Sum Total," *Gospel Advocate* 80 (September 1, 1938):828.

[11] W. E. Brightwell, "The Sum Total," *Gospel Advocate* 80 (August 11, 1938):751.

[12] J. L. Hines, "Let There Be No Cessation," *Gospel Advocate* 80 (September 1, 1938):820.

[13] W. E. Brightwell, "15,260 Additions Reported," *Gospel Advocate* 90 (January 15, 1948):69.

[14] M. Norvel Young, "The 1946 Religious Census," *Gospel Advocate* 88 (November 21, 1946):1109.

[15] M. Norvel Young, "A Report on the Census and an Estimate," *Gospel Advocate* 90 (April 29, 1948):430-31.

[16] John P. Forgarty and Olan Hicks, *1946-1947 Yearbook of Churches of Christ* (Abilene, Texas: Hicks Publishing Company, 1947), pp. 108-33.

[17] Ibid., p. vi.

CHAPTER THIRTEEN

PATTERN OF GROWTH

The preceding chapter has indicated some general estimates of the growth of churches of Christ in Tennessee in the period studied. A survey of the literature over the years indicates the pattern of this growth. Other parts of this chapter will present converging material which is pertinent to methodology, but several insights can be gleaned from the articles and news reports of active workers.

Autonomy of the Church

It was apparent that the autonomy of the local church was preserved and any attempt to tie or appear to tie the churches together in associations or societies was most vigorously resisted. An example in 1910 illustrates this concern. In the January 13, 1910 *Gospel Advocate* there was an announcement of a requested meeting in Henderson of preachers, elders, and all interested Christians to gather information about the condition of the work in West Tennessee, determine places of greatest need and secure a plan or means of organization to more effectively evangelize the area. The meeting was set for January 25-28, 1910.[1] The next week David Lipscomb expressed doubt about the wisdom of such a meeting, commended the work of John R. Williams who received support directly from churches, and cautioned that no good could come from such activities.[2] After some discussion, an article appeared stating that the difficulties had been removed and that the Henderson church was sending a man into the field. The article exhorted that those who wanted to assist might "fellowship the work by sending contributions to the evangelist in the field." [3] The controversies and difficulties were too recent and intense to allow even the hint of any structure such as had been opposed for so long; consequently the proposal was dropped and another approach was followed.

The method of supporting missionaries at home and abroad ran a tight course between opposition to missionary society activities and non-cooperative efforts. The precise details of such a steerage were to engender serious controversies shortly after the period of this study, but to the churches of the period there was a way to make the passage. The local church alone was the unit of work and others who desired to assist could do so but always with rugged independence and complete local autonomy. The arrangements of who, where, how long, and how much support were left solely in the hands of the local church which made an agreement with a preacher or preachers and sustained the work, either on their own or with support from interested churches and individuals on a purely voluntary basis. In this way the pattern of evangelism may be traced throughout the period. As early as 1906 the practice was in wide use. Several churches in Nashville reported sending different preachers throughout the state for a summer of preaching in tents with the result of some 500 baptisms.[4] Later a report was given of two men who had established some twenty eight churches over the years of their ministry.[5] An article admonished brethren to prepare for a gosplel meeting by prayer, good advertising, attention to singing and related efforts.[6] Various churches in Henderson County had kept a man in many tent meetings as was reported for the summer of 1906,[7] and a student at Nashville Bible School told of his success in tent meetings as well.[8] Over the years one notes the use of various adaptations such as a camp meeting by N. B. Hardeman at Pittsburgh Landing, Tennessee,[9] the various Ryman Auditorium meetings by Hardeman as previously noticed, a cooperative effort such as that by sixteen churches in Graves County,[10] and a simultaneous meeting among the churches in Nashville with 330 baptized.[11]

The success of the efforts in evangelism may be traced in the weekly reports of baptisms in the *Gospel Advocate* and the record of churches established through the years. For example, a weekly count of baptisms reported in the paper for the entire nation gave a total of 6423 baptisms in 1909, ranging from a high of 354 in one week to a low of 10 in the first week of the year. The report of W. E. Brightwell indicates the same frequency of baptisms as reported in the 1938 statistic. One finds the same reporting of numerous baptisms through the years. The paper also carried numerous reports of the building of meetinghouses through the years. Often a meeting at some point would result in an appeal for money to assist in building a meetinghouse. In passing one notes the interesting fact that of 135 churches in the state who presented information for inclusion in the list of churches compiled by Baxter and Young,[12] 34 indicated they began before 1900, 69 stated they originated between 1900 and 1950, 29 stated they began after 1950, and 3 did not tell of their beginning. Whatever the statewide validity, it was obvious that a large number of churches began during the period of study. A further interesting figure results from comparing Norton's statement that Nashville had 30 churches of Christ in 1924 [13] with Brightwell's claim of 54 churches of Christ in the same city in 1937.[14]

The *Gospel Advocate* offered its services to encourage mission work and equip preachers. E. A. Elam told that special numbers of the paper were designed to serve as "a kind of reference on the subject that would be worthy of preservation." [15] These special numbers show the direction of effort by leading writers over the years. Fred Dennis offered a series of suggestions concerning the growth of the church by advertising, bulletin boards, newspaper ads, etc.[16] As radio became more popular, the *Gospel Advocate* promoted this work. A manual was promoted so preachers could learn about the new media.[17] The Laurel Avenue church in Knoxville began a program in 1938 as a means of evangelizing the difficult sections of East Tennessee.[18] In spite of these efforts, W. E. Brightwell lamented the fact that growth was not as rapid as it should be and plead for greater teaching concerning the responsibility of the church.[19]

From the early years of the period under study churches of Christ in Tennessee were anxious to grow. The primary means was by evangelistic efforts either in a tent in a new area, or a building or hired hall. Interested churches sent preachers across the state and these men preached at out of the way places as well as at large centers of population. Each church was encouraged to win converts. A small band would be reached in a tent meeting, they would decide to establish a church, make an appeal for help and soon a new meetinghouse would be announced and the cycle would begin again. Preachers and editors kept up a constant encouragement of mission work, told of places in need, fostered a spirit of optimism by reports of success, and by special editions of the papers provided material particularly adapted to special needs of the time. As new means of reaching people became available, writers would tell of their efforts and encourage others to do likewise. In this way the numerical growth of the period was made possible.

Congregational Development

The constant growth in the churches of Christ in Tennessee was paralled by a constancy of congregational development. Without a centralized agency to direct or supervise and with a rather individualistic tendency to be noted as to group and personal characteristics, it was remarkable that an approximate unanimity was maintained by the churches in the period studied. With allowance for some diversity, the judgment of Banowsky is generally correct. Banowsky surveyed the historical and doctrinal development of churches of Christ in the period 1918 to 1964 as portrayed in the Abilene Christian College Lectureship Books and concluded, "But churches of Christ, according to one of the clearest conclusions of this study, have undergone no major theological shifts since 1900." [20] As revealed in his discussion of major doctrinal themes, so it was in the sphere of congregational development; a central position was clearly traceable with minor differences occurring as more an exercise of varying opinion than an attempt to overthrow the general pattern of congregational development. Several facets of congregational development may be noted.

Restrictive Clauses

Attention has already been called to the practice of appealing for help in the erection of the buildings as needed by newly established churches. One feature of prominence was the use of restrictive clauses in the deeds to property. Generally these forbade the use of missionary societies and instrumental music in worship and were regarded as legitimate and proper safeguards of the property held by the church. At first David Lipscomb had some problems accepting the idea of a restrictive clause because this seemed to be using human laws to maintain the church,[21] but the loss of buildings to those he termed "innovators" gradually led to a change of heart. He noted with pleasure the ruling of a Texas court that the original faith and practice of a church should be preserved when a group, in the majority or minority, changed its faith.[22] By 1906 he was arguing for the propriety of the restrictive clause as a means to preserve "the cause of right" by "peaceful means."[23] The right of these restrictive clauses was challenged by such men as J. B. Briney who regarded it "a barrier to restoration of unity,"[24] but it was defended by such men as F. B. Srygley[25] and G. K. Wallace[26] as being a merely description of ownership and as setting forth the conditions for transfer of property. R. L. Whiteside, who had defended the restrictive clause for years,[27] regarded the trustees as obliged to see that the property was protected by legal means,[28] although he thought ideally the elders should serve as trustees.[29] The congregations were making it as sure as possible that church property would be protected. The experience of losing buildings in the past was not forgotten.

Church Organization

What is termed church policy or organization among churches of Christ showed a consistency of basic position with some divergence over the years. G. C. Brewer stated the general position in his words concerning the duties of elders,

> We have already seen that all the teaching in the congregation is to be done under the oversight of the elders. We may now add that all other activities of the church are to be directed and supervised by the elders. They do not do all the work, by any means; but they take the oversight and see that what is done by the others is done rightly. . . . They will decide what course the congregation is to pursue in any matter, and their decision will be final.[30]

Brewer added that this rule was to be similar to the rule of the father in a family and, avoiding a spirit of self will, self opinionism, and domination, the elders should consult the members for preferences and general interest. He summed up by saying, "In all cases where no principle of right or wrong is involved, the elders should have due regard for the wishes of the congregation." But he noted that, "If any movement is started in the congregation that is contrary to God's word, the elders must stand firm for God and put down the evil."[31]

The problems concerning the elders were not only concerned with their role, but the proper qualifications and the manner of appointment were frequently disputed questions. The qualifications in I Timothy 3 and Titus 1 were the occasion of frequent discussion. Of particular concern were such questions as the extent to which one should manifest the characteristics of temperance, sober mindedness, being given to hospitality, etc. Also, much discussion was given to the need to be married, how many children the proposed elder was to have, and how many of the children had to be Christians. Contrasting conclusions may be noted in

138

the words of E. G. Sewell and David Lipscomb as reported by M. C. Kurfees. In answering the questions must elders be married, Sewell answered that the Bible indicated the elder should be married and to only one wife. Lipscomb answered, "We believe an unmarried or childless man, if otherwise qualified, may be a bishop or deacon." [32] Brewer[33] and others [34] agreed more with the Lipscomb view, but generally the position of Sewell proved to be more widely accepted. While upholding the principle of highest character for all Christians and especially for prospective elders, Lipscomb and Sewell noted that brethren should not require perfection in those considered for the eldership and should encourage men to accept the work of the elders in spite of their humanity, liability to error, and faults of human weakness.[35] As the period of study was closing, questions about qualifications of elders were still being answered by writers in the *Gospel Advocate,*[36] but the general practice had become one of each church making its own decision with a concurrent acceptance, sometimes reluctant, by neighboring churches and individuals.

The appointment of elders was a constant source of difficulty. B. K. Smith noted this problem in 1869 [37] and it endured through the years. The difficulty turned on whether any appointment were necessary, and if so what it should entail. H. Leo Boles stated the three general positions which had been held at various times by brethren. Remarkably he showed that three members of the Lipscomb family had held these three different views. William Lipscomb had concluded that no appointment was required but rather the older men grew into the eldership; David Lipscomb felt there was to be a growth into the work but concluded that some type of appointment was proper; and Granville Lipscomb had argued that there should be the accompaniment of appointment by prayer, fasting, and laying on of hands.[38] Although the first view was widely held before the turn of the century,[39] the period of this study did not have strong advocates for the view. Instead, the view of David Lipscomb largely prevailed. He argued that the laying on of hands was for the importation of spiritual gifts, was likely possible only for those who were spiritually endowed, had been rejected years before by representative men, and consequently was not to be a part of the appointment of elders.[40] G. C. Brewer felt the laying on of hands was "the New Testament custom," but admitted there was a difference of opinion on the subject and thought it "best to leave the manner of appointing optional with the congregations." [41] In the later years a discussion between H. Leo Boles [42] and John W. Kurfees [43] restated some of the arguments, but the general practice was to appoint men judged by the respective congregations to be qualified without laying on of hands or other elaborate ceremony.

Other matters of polity were discussed over the years. David Lipscomb was not fully decided as to the "position and work" of the deacons.[44] G. C. Brewer recognized the duties of bishops and deacons were different but felt the rank and importance of their respective work often involved the estimation of men. He also believed that the practice of having temporal affairs overseen by the deacons and spiritual affairs overseen by the elders was "generally agreed." [45] Nichols, in response to a query, later argued that the deacons should be under the oversight of the elders and that though they were to be kept informed and encouraged to assist, by the elders, they were not to function as elders.[46] H. Leo Boles contributed a discussion of the meaning, qualification, and work of deacons.[47] He also argued for the perpetuity of elders [48] and B. C. Goodpasture regarded the challenging of the continuation of elders as an example of emphasizing motes and urging a hobby.[49] John D. Cox lamented the use of "leaders" instead of elders, felt that elders were not properly respected and claimed that they were often prevented from serving because of impossible standards.[50] Deaconesses were discussed from time to time but little certainly was present concerning them. H. Leo Boles did not think it clear that deaconesses were equal to deacons as to appointment although he recognized a place of great service by the women of the congregations.[51] Brewer recognized the disputed nature of the question of deaconesses, felt there was no way definitely to settle the issue, but claimed there was some evidence in favor of the idea.[52]

The organization structure of churches of Christ involved the oversight of elders who were men judged by the local churches as possessing the qualifications the Bible set forth. There was some disagreement about the nature and extent of possession of such qualifications requisite to the eldership as well as disagreement as to the way to appoint men as elders. The general practice was to allow the questions to be decided as each church judged best, although members often raised questions of wide interest as shown by various articles in the *Gospel Advocate.* When appointed, elders had the oversight of the church over which they had been appointed. Each church was fully autonomous and had its own elders. Deacons worked under the direction of the elders and the members did the same. To avoid needless friction as well as to secure the best methods of service, the practice was for elders to receive counsel and advice from the brethren before making decisions about the affairs of the church. In this way the elders functioned as overseers of the respective churches.

Preachers

The role of the preacher among churches of Christ in the period studied presents the need for careful discrimination as to the meaning of the terms employed since there was not always present the desired clarity or consistency of usage. This ambiguity of terminology and of the role of the preacher in the congregation needs to be remembered as this section develops. The essence seems fairly stable, but the language in which the essence was sketched constantly posed problems.

Given the outlook of churches of Christ as to the role of the elders in the local churches and the danger of losing such oversight, in principle or practice, when a capable preacher wielded his influence in a particular church one can recognize the concern of various writers over the years. In 1869 Jacob Creath expressed stong opposition to any preacher being over the elders of the church.[53] W. J. Burchard reflected the attitude of his contemporaries in the state when he commented on the announcement that the church in Martin, Tennessee was to have a "pastor" who had been called "to the charge of the church" in 1903. He denied that the title of "pastor" was proper for the preacher and strongly objected to "any one man's having charge of a church," [54] L. L. Brigance charged that the "pastor system" among Disiples of Christ was an outgrowth of liberalism.[55] Through the years, therefore, the opposition to a "pastor system" was intense and abiding.

The need to express clearly what was entailed in the work of the preacher, while opposing the "pastor system," did not generally emerge until the 1920s. Prior to this time the work of preachers had primarily been that of moving from church to church for a meeting and from town to town with a tent to reach as many as possible. By the end of the 1920s and continuing through the period studied churches developed the ability to secure the services of a man for full time work as the preacher.[56] The essential ingredients of such an arrangement had been present before, but the gathering of them all together on a wide scale basis produced a series of exchanges as to the propriety of this development. In these exchanges the need for careful discrimination of meaning became evident.

David Lipscomb observed that although churches should not have a "pastor system" they should still have preaching as regularly and often as possible.[57] E. A. Elam agreed with this position in the same issue of the paper [58] and followed in the next week with a defense of the preacher being paid and being at a particular place for an indefinite period of time.[59] Jesse P. Sewell wrote shortly thereafter commending an article he had read showing that there was no Bible warrant for calling the preacher the pastor and noting there was a difference between the pastor and an evangelist.[60] F. W. Smith commented on the hired preacher by observing that the one who did the preaching could properly be supported in full time work and reasoned that a religious teacher, whether called a preacher or evangelist, could properly remain with the church so long as a needed work was to be done.[61] It was apparent, therefore,, that the possibility of a man doing full time preaching for a particular church was well known by the mid 1920s and the objection to such was in effect more of an objection to abuse than principle.[62]

As the years passed there were frequent expressions of concern that the elders were nearly being reduced to figure heads without real authority and influence. Evangelists had been hired, in some instance, to feed the flock and to take the oversight thereof and this was regarded as "a suspicious similarity to the pastor system." [63] F. L. Paisley wrote two articles analyzing the "pastor system" as to its cause [64] and its cure.[65] L. L.

Brigance stimulated nearly a year of exchanges on the subject by his article on the pastor system in early 1941.[66] These expressions of concern evoked a series of responses by men who had served as preachers for several years and who did not accept the charge of being "pastors' as the articles of several other men had opposed. L. R. Wilson asked for the rule to distinguish between the evangelist all admitted to be proper and the pastor as was being opposed. He asked if it were not possible to be a located preacher and not be a pastor. He denied he was a pastor and called for a "showdown" on the question once the issue had been clarified when those who objected had set forth what they opposed in more specific terms. He set forth the situation involved in his own work, outlining the work of the elders, deacons, and members and concluded by asking, "If this is the 'pastor system,' will you kindly help us to correct our error?" [67] F. L. Paisley, while objecting to the "pastor system," stated that brethren did not object to a man preaching at a given place regularly, twice a week, for any number of years. Indeed, he stated that "almost any preacher of the gospel will contend that such is not unscriptural, *per se.*" He then stated, "It is the growing tendency of the preacher's 'taking charge' of things to which lovers of Bible order object."[68] R. L. Whiteside, who later was to stress the need of clarification as to the meaning of terms in discussion,[69] pointed to the heart of the problem in pleading that preachers in their role as preachers neither seek nor be allowed to oversee the church.[70] B. C. Goodpasture plead that brethren avoid confusing the preacher with a pastor and keep the issue clear.[71]

As the years passed it became obvious that churches of Christ in the state were developing the ability to hire men to preach regularly and in so doing were seeking to increase the effectiveness of their local program of teaching, edification, and evangelism. In spite of some controversy and in the presence of considerable need of clarification as to what was being done and as to what was being opposed, the practice continued. The chuches were careful to maintain the oversight in the hands of elders and preachers were kept busy in the work of teaching nad preaching. Exceptions and abuses came from time to time, but the general attitude was one of acceptance and appreciation of the practice. This practice, combined with others to be noted shortly, was a significant factor in the growth of the churches in the last two or three decades of the period studied.

The Religious Education Program

The religious education program of local churches of Christ constituted a most significant factor in the growth of these churches through the period studied. A recent dissertation by Thomas L. Campbell [72] has surveyed the development of religious education among churches of Christ in general until the time of the death of David Lipscomb (1917) and this study will be accepted as a general background for the following survey of developments. Campbell argued that the religious education contributions of Lipscomb and his paper had played a vital role in the growth of churches of Christ through the years [73] and concluded that the "educational pattern" set forth by Lipscomb and his associates as largely adopted by churches of Christ.[74] Campbell noted that the use of the Sunday School or Bible Classes could be traced as far back as 1834 among the early churches.[75] In 1866 David Lipscomb had encouraged the use of "lesson leaves" adapted to different age groups,[76] and had encouraged a teachers' institute in Nashville in 1878 where such topics as lesson preparation and delivery, administration, and principles of learning were stressed.[77] David Lipscomb did not object to the term Sunday School although such men as E. G. Sewell were a bit hesitant.[78] Tolbert Fanning, David Lipscomb, and others insisted that the Sunday school was to be a part of the work of the church, not an independent entity, and that all phases of the work should be under the elders.[79]

Considerable benefit was derived from the use of the International Lesson Series following the encouragement of their use in 1878. Soon David Lipscomb was writing a weekly commentary on these lessons and later compiled books of comments on the yearly studies. By the 1880s the Gospel Advocate Company was publishing literature for all age groups.[80] These publications continued over the years. The relation of the Gospel Advocate Company with the International Lesson Series was later changed, but by the turn of the century it was apparent that religious education, primarily by means of the Sunday School program, was a vital part of the work of the churches of Christ in the state.

In the 1906 Census the number of scholars in the Sunday School work was reported as 8,719 with only 122 of the 631 churches reporting. In 1926 the census records showed 51,676 scholars with 827 of 933 churches reported for the state. Whatever one makes of the accuracy of the figures in the respective years, by the turn of the century the Sunday School program was an established part of the work of churches of Christ in the state.

The religious education efforts of churches of Christ showed two general characteristics over the years to 1950. There was a constant and increasingly successful defense of their use and there was constant improvement as to quality of instructional materials and methods. The first of these characteristics shows a rather constant pattern of opposition and defense as a sample of articles in the early, middle, and later decades of the period shows. In the early period the pattern was to organize a Sunday School along with the start of a new work. For example, N. B. Hardeman stated that the Henderson church, resulting from a division over instrumental music in worship, had organized a Sunday School February 1, 1903 with eighty six members.[81] E. G. Sewell argued that no specific method of teaching was given in the Bible and, consequently, churches could use the method best adapted to their abilities and judgment. When the elders called the young people and others together and taught them in the various classes with their respective teachers, this was the church at work and was right and proper for the church to do.[82] E. A. Elam reasoned that the work must always be under the oversight of the elders,[83] a position which such men as John R. Williams had often stressed.[84] E. G. Sewell argued that the classes were distinct from the worship service, but not separate from the direction of the elders, and that in view of this women could and should teach the children.[85] He also stated that he saw no legitimate ground for such opposition and felt that those who opposed the work were making laws God had not made.[86]

Writers kept up a steady response to such objections as comparing the Sunday School to the Missionary Societies,[87] claiming the schools were a substitute for the church and home,[88] and claiming the schools were equal to using an organ in worship.[89] The writers also responded to criticisms about literature in classes,[90] lesson helps,[91] and printed lessons.[92] While upholding a proper use of such printed materials, the writers were careful to stress the need to avoid displacing the Bible by the printed materials.[93] The collections of the writings of David Lipscomb [94] alone and those of David Lipscomb and E. G. Sewell [95] showed a strong support for all phases of the Sunday School work in the early years. The thrust of these combined efforts was to continue the work which had long been seen to be effective. Opposition was not to be allowed to hinder this good work.

In the years of World War I and on into the 1920s there were enough articles on the subject to show the same problems were being faced and in much the same way as before. J. C. McQuiddy wrote several articles on the topic in 1918. He argued for the use of classes, lesson helps, and women teachers early in the year.[96] He followed with a longer defense of women teachers,[97] and of classes in general.[98] In reply to questions by D. S. Ligon [99] he argued the same points more forcefully.[100] Such opposition, he concluded, was exaltation of opinion beyond proper bounds.[101] A few years later F. B. Srygley set forth basically the same positions.[102] In 1924 Joe S. Warlick and George Phillips, for and against respectively, engaged in oral and written debates on the question "Is it Scriptural to Have A Sunday School?" [103] The problem had become such that Warlick plead for a careful reading of the book to counteract the influence of "a few inferior preachers" who were urging the use of Sunday Schools as a "cause for division among the brethren." [104] By 1924 it was evident that a real problem was present and, as C. W. Sewell had suggested several years before,[105] a series of debates were concluded to be necessary to avert division if possible or to stabilize brethren if division should come. For several years the problem had been building and the debates were soon to begin as a means of resolving difficulties. These came, but their specific arguments do not constitute an essential point of this study.

In 1937 W. E. Brightwell concluded that the problem over the Sunday School was not a true issue but a fight without a real cause.[106] By 1941

144

Tennessee churches were being warned that a man opposed to Sunday Schools was at work in Humphreys County.[107] In 1944 Brightwell wrote several articles on the theme, "The Teaching Mandate," beginning in January.[108] In the latter part of the same year Guy N. Woods began a series of articles on the topic by discussing women teachers.[109] In February 1948 Roy H. Lanier presented a long series of articles on the whole question.[110]

It was becoming apparent that the writings and debates, as well as the total impact of the times and the needs of various age groups, were being effective when leading preachers who had long opposed the Sunday School began to renounce their opposition. L. W. Hayhurst gave up his opposition and proposed taking the lead in reaching others of the opposition [111] and John F. Lilly told why he had turned from his opposition to this work.[112] There were to be other debates as W. S. Boyett [113] and Clyde O. Moore [114] reported, but the opposition to Sunday Schools was losing its strength if not its determination. By the end of the period studied opposition had all but ceased in Tennessee and the practice of Sunday Schools was accepted by almost all of the churches in the state.

The second characteristic of religious education in the period was improvement of materials and methods. As early as 1878, as previously noted, attention was being given to the practical aspects of Sunday School operation and this continued to be the case. In 1910 several churches in Nashville met together for several Sunday afternoon sessions on improvement of instruction.[115] In 1918 a series of thirty two articles was carried by the *Gospel Advocate* to give instruction on the training of little children.[116] In the same year attention was called to the use of teachers guides, Peloubet's *Notes;* and various quarterlies were made available for better instruction.[117] Until his death in 1929, E. A. Elam wrote the comments on the weekly Bible study lessons. In 1922 the International Council of Religious Education was organized with H. Leo Boles of the *Gospel Advocate* as a member. He served for nineteen years as a representative for the Gospel Advocate Company. After E. A. Elam's death H. Leo Boles became the editor of the notes. He and several others served in this capacity until 1946 when B. C. Goodpasture became the editor of the series.[118]

These years saw many developments of value in the advancement of religious education among churches of Christ in the state. In 1910 the *Gospel Advocate* carried notice of "Bible Lesson Helps" which included an advanced quarterly, intermediate, primary, and "Juvenile" lessons along with "Lesson Leaflets" for the intermediate grade, "Bible Lesson Pictures," and Jewel Bible Lesson cards for small children.[119] These graduated studies, written by such men as F. W. Smith and F. B. Srygley, received commendations over the years.[120] The work of E. A. Elam in editing the Improved Uniform International Series of Bible School Lessons (1922-1929) was deeply concerned with the effectiveness of the work of the schools in general as well as the mastery of the lessons in particular. In the 1926 edition, for instance, Elam included a series of charts on Bible dates, several hints and helps for teachers, explanatory notes, outlines, poems and other helps for the teacher and student.[121] As the years went by the techniques in Bible school work improved in the churches. H. Leo Boles took great interest in this work. His lessons on Bible study were offered by correspondence [122] and he presented articles on church programs,[123] the improvement of Bible study,[124] and Vacation Bible Schools.[125] It was increasingly clear that the value of the Sunday School work was recognized and widely used among churches of Christ in Tennessee as well as other states. It was also clear that the various new insights and techniques for organizing, supervising, and conducting such work had been learned by interested writers of ability and were being shared with churches through quarterly and annual study helps, books, and articles. The progress, in spite of considerable controversy, had been constant.

The religious education program among churches of Christ had achieved stability and was making significant progress in Tennessee by 1950. Subsequent years were to reflect greater growth, but the foundations had been carefully laid by such men as David Lipscomb, E. A. Elam, and H. Leo Boles. Opposition had been faced and largely overcome, materials for teachers and for students had been published by interested and capable brethren, and the churches were eager to utilize effectively these avenues of service and strength.

REFERENCES

[1] J. W. Dunn, et al, "Let Preachers and Elders Take Notice," *Gospel Advocate* 52 (January 13, 1910):59.

[2] David Lipscomb, "A Meeting of Elders and Preachers Called," *Gospel Advocate* 52 (January 20, 1910):81.

[3] J. C. McQuiddy, "The Work Commended," *Gospel Advocate* 52 (April 14, 1910):457.

[4] David Lipscomb, "South Nashville Church of Christ," *Gospel Advocate* 48 (January 25, 1906):57.

[5] Frank Morrow, "The Maury County Tent," *Gospel Advocate* 48 (March 15, 1906):171.

[6] C. E. Holt, "Prepare In Advance," *Gospel Advocate* 48 (October 11, 1906):655.

[7] W. A. Austin, "Mission Work in Tennessee," *Gospel Advocate* 48 (November 29, 1906):762.

[8] T. C. Fox, "My Work For 1906," *Gospel Advocate* 49 (January 31, 1907):79.

[9] A. E. Emmons, "Camp Meeting at Shiloh," *Gospel Advocate* 65 (September 13, 1923):898-99.

[10] J. B. Hardeman, "Hardeman-Wheeler Meeting," *Gospel Advocate* 80 (September 1, 1938):826.

[11] Anonymous, "Nashville Meetings Prove Successful," *Gospel Advocate* 80 (May 12, 1938):444.

[12] Batsell Barrett Baxter and M. Norvel Young, *New Testament Churches of Today*, 2 vols. (Nashville: The Gospel Advocate Company, 1960-68), 2 (1968), pp. 247-300.

[13] Herman Norton, *Tennessee Christians* (Nashville: Reed and Company, 1971), p. 249.

[14] W. E. Brightwell, "The Notion Counter," *Gospel Advocate* 79 (March 11, 1937):235.

[15] E. A. Elam, "The Purpose of Special Numbers," *Gospel Advocate* 61 (August 14, 1919):787-88.

[16] Fred E. Dennis, "Several Things," *Gospel Advocate* 83 (October 23, 1941):1020.

[17] "Advertisement," *Gospel Advocate* 80 (March 10, 1938):238.

[18] Elders, "Knoxville on the Air," *Gospel Advocate* 80 (September 8, 1938):852.

[19] W. E. Brightwell, "Who Should Teach Whom?" *Gospel Advocate* 83 (July 10, 1941):655-63.

[20] William S. Banowsky, *The Mirror of A Movement* (Dallas: Christian Publishing Company, 1965), p. xii.

[21] David Lipscomb, "Our Response," *Gospel Advocate* 34 (July 7, 1892):429.

[22] David Lipscomb, "Conclusions of Law," *Gospel Advocate* 43 (August 29, 1901):553.

[23] David Lipscomb, "The Creed in the Deed," *Gospel Advocate* 48 (January 11, 1906):25.

[24] J. B. Briney, quoted by E. A. Elam, "The Creed in the Deed," *Gospel Advocate* 48 (January 4, 1906):1.

[25] F. B. Srygley, "The Restrictive Clause in the Deed," *Gospel Advocate* 65 (June 28, 1923):623-25.

[26] G. K. Wallace, "Creed in the Deed," *Gospel Advocate* 91 (March 10, 1949):148-49.

[27] R. L. Whiteside, "The Creed in the Deed," *Gospel Advocate* 50 (February 27, 1908):131.

[28] R. L. Whiteside, "Questions from Louisville," *Gospel Advocate* 80 (August 11, 1938):743.

[29] R. L. Whiteside, "Are They Scriptural?" *Gospel Advocate* 80 (August 25, 1938):791.

[30] G. C. Brewer, *The Model Church* (Nashville: *Gospel Advocate,* 1957), pp. 44-45.

[31] Ibid., p. 46.

[32] David Lipscomb and E. G. Sewell, quoted by M. C. Kurfees, *Questions Answered* (Nashville: McQuiddy Printing Company, 1921), p. 204.

[33] Brewer, ibid., p. 32.

[34] Herbert Winkler, *The Eldership* (Nashville: Private Publication, 1950).

[35] Lipscomb and Sewell, quoted by Kurfees, ibid., pp. 197-99.

[36] Gus Nichols, "Questions Answered," *Gospel Advocate* 91 (January 13, 1949):20-21.

[37] B. K. Smith, "Church Organization—Continued," *Gospel Advocate* 11 (April 15, 1869):340-43.

[38] H. Leo Boles, "More About Elders," *Gospel Advocate* 83 (February 20, 1941):173, 181.

[39] W. Y. Singleton, "The Figurative Use of the Term MAN," *Gospel Advocate* 11 (April 15, 1869):376-78.

[40] Lipscomb and Sewell, quoted by Kurfees, ibid., pp. 194-95, 285-87.

[41] Brewer, ibid., p. 76.

[42] H. Leo Boles, "How Elders Are Appointed," *Gospel Advocate* 83 (January 2, 1941):4-5.

[43] John W. Kurfees, "More About Elders," *Gospel Advocate* 83 (February 20, 1941):171.

[44] Lipscomb and Sewell, quoted by Kurfees, ibid., p. 163.

[45] G. C. Brewer, ibid., p. 100.

[46] Gus Nichols, "Questions Answered," *Gospel Advocate* 91 (July 28, 1949):467.

[47] H. Leo Boles, "The Deacons," *Gospel Advocate* 83 (March 27, 1941):292-93.

[48] H. Leo Boles, "Perpetuity of Elders," *Gospel Advocate* 83 (January 16, 1941):53,64.

[49] B. C. Goodpasture, "Motes and Hobbies," *Gospel Advocate* 83 (August 14, 1941):772.

[50] John D. Cox, "Where Are We Heading?" *Gospel Advocate* 91 (June 23, 1949):384,392.

[51] H. Leo Boles, "Deaconesses," *Gospel Advocate* 83 (April 3, 1941):312.

[52] Brewer, ibid., 101.

[53] Jacob Creath, "One Overseer Over A Plurality of Overseers in One, Two or Three Churches," *Gospel Advocate* 11 (April 1, 1869):301-02.

[54] W. J. Burchard, "Employs A Pastor," *Gospel Advocate* 45 (February 26, 1903):139.

[55] L. L. Brigance, "Liberalism," *Gospel Advocate* 83 (February 20, 1941):178.

[56] Banowsky, ibid., pp. 215-18.

[57] David Lipscomb, "No Title," *Gospel Advocate* 43 (June 20, 1901):385.

[58] E. A. Elam, "No Title," *Gospel Advocate* 43 (June 20, 1901):384.

[59] E. A. Elam, "No Title," *Gospel Advocate* 43 (June 27, 1901):400.

[60] Jesse P. Sewell, "The Church, The 'Pastor,' and The Evangelist," *Gospel Advocate* 44 (July 24, 1902):467-68.

[61] F. W. Smith, "The Hired Preacher," *Gospel Advocate* 64 (March 23, 1922):277.

[62] U. G. Wilkinson, "Shall We Criticize?" *Gospel Advocate* 64 (August 3, 1922):728.

[63] Banowsky, ibid., p. 218.

[64] F. L. Paisley, "The 'Pastor System'—Its Cause," *Gospel Advocate* 79 (February 25, 1937):177.

[65] F.L. Paisley, "The 'Pastor System'—Its Cure," *Gospel Advocate* 79 (March 4, 1937):205.

[66] L. L. Brigance, "Evils of the Pastor System," *Gospel Advocate* 83 (March 6, 1941):229.

[67] L. R. Wilson, "Give Us A Moses," *Gospel Advocate* 79 (March 11, 1937):235.

[68] F. L. Paisley, "The 'Pastor System'—Its Cause," *Gospel Advocate* 79 (February 25, 1937):177.

[69] R. L. Whiteside, "A Letter from Clifton Inman," *Gospel Advocate* 83 (August 14, 1941):777.

[70] R. L. Whiteside, "Elders—Confusion—Trouble," *Gospel Advocate* 79 (January 14, 1937):35.

[71] B. C. Goodpasture, "We Should Keep the Issue Clear," *Gospel Advocate* 83 (July 24, 1941):700.

[72] Thomas Lee Campbell, "The Contribution of David Lipscomb and the Gospel Advocate to Religious Education in the Churches of Christ" (DRE dissertation, Southern Baptist Theological Seminary, 1968), pp. 2, 5, 102, 115-16, 123.

[73] Ibid., p. 2.

[74] Ibid., p. 5.

[75] Ibid., p. 102.

[76] Ibid., p. 123.

[77] Ibid., pp. 115-16.

[78] Ibid., pp. 103-04.

[79] Ibid., pp. 116-18.

[80] Ibid., pp. 124-25.

[81] E. A. Elam, "A Letter from Brother Hardeman," *Gospel Advocate* 45 (February 19, 1903):113.

[82] E. G. Sewell, "The Sunday School, or Teaching the Word of God," *Gospel Advocate* 44 (March 6, 1902):152-53.

[83] E. A. Elam, "Elders and the Sunday School," *Gospel Advocate* 48 (January 11, 1906):23.

[84] John R. Williams, "Notes from West Tennessee," *Gospel Advocate* 43 (September 19, 1901):606.

[85] E. G. Sewell, "The Sunday School," *Gospel Advocate* 44 (May 8, 1902):297.

[86] E. G. Sewell, "What is A Sunday School?" *Gospel Advocate* 44 (February 20, 1902):120-21.

[87] E. A. Elam, "The Bible School, Again," *Gospel Advocate* 43 (October 10, 1901):642-43.

[88] David Lipscomb, "How Can the Children be Saved?" *Gospel Advocate* 44 (January 2, 1902):8-9.

[89] J. C. McQuiddy, "The Unvarnished Facts," *Gospel Advocate* 51 (June 24, 1909):770-72.

[90] E. G. Sewell, "The Use of Literature in the 'Sunday School'," *Gospel Advocate* 44 (April 3, 1902):216-17.

[91] E. A. Elam, "Lesson Helps," *Gospel Advocate* 44 (June 12, 1902):369.

[92] E. A. Elam, "Printed Lessons," *Gospel Advocate* 45 (July 23, 1903):465-66.

[93] E. A. Elam, "Lesson Helps," *Gospel Advocate* 44 (June 12, 1902):369.

[94] David Lipscomb, *Queries and Answers*, ed. J. W. Shepherd (Nashville: McQuiddy Printing Company, 1910), pp. 80-81, 93-94, 263-64, 446-54.

[95] Lipscomb and Sewell, quoted by Kurfees, ibid., pp. 654-59, 674-78, 729-36, 738-40.

[96] J. C. McQuiddy, "The Method of Teaching the Truth," *Gospel Advocate* 60 (February 28, 1918):199-200.

[97] J. C. McQuiddy, "No Title," *Gospel Advocate* 60 (May 16, 1918):470.

[98] J. C. McQuiddy, "Teaching the Word of God," *Gospel Advocate* 60 (May 30, 1918):511-12.

[99] D. S. Ligon, "Teaching the Word of God," *Gospel Advocate* 60 (July 11, 1918):652-53.

[100] J. C. McQuiddy, "Is it A Sin to teach the Bible to Classes?" *Gospel Advocate* 60 (July 11, 1918):656-57.

[101] J. C. McQuiddy, "Exalting Opinions," *Gospel Advocate* 60 (August 15, 1918):775-76.

[102] F. B. Srygley, "The Sunday School," *Gospel Advocate* 65 (March 1, 1923):194-95.

[103] Joe S. Warlick and George W. Phillips, *A Debate on the Sunday School Question* (Dallas: Private Publication, 1924).

[104] Ibid., p. 9.

[105] C. W. Sewell, "A Discussion Needed," *Gospel Advocate* 51 (July 29, 1909):952.

[106] W. E. Brightwell, "Dropping the Case," *Gospel Advocate* 79 (January 28, 1937):90-91.

[107] J. E. Green and J. A. Robertson, "Byno Rhodes Opposes Class Teaching, etc.," *Gospel Advocate* 83 (April 3, 1941): 333.

[108] W. E. Brightwell, "The Teaching Mandate," *Gospel Advocate* 86 (January 27, 1944):81-83.

[109] Guy N. Woods, "An Examination of 1 Cor. 14:34-35," *Gospel Advocate* 86 (October 12, 1944):672-73.

[110] Roy H. Lanier, "The Sunday School Question," *Gospel Advocate* 90 (February 26, 1948):201, 205.

[111] Leonard Mullins, "Brother Hayhurst's Plan," *Gospel Advocate* 90 (May 6, 1948):443.

[112] John F. Lilly, "Why I Changed," *Gospel Advocate* 90 (May 27, 1948):509, 517.

[113] W. S. Boyett, "The Woods-Bonneau Debate," *Gospel Advocate* 91 (February 3, 1949):78-79.

[114] Clyde O. Moore, "Mayer-Johnson Debate," *Gospel Advocate.* 91 (September 22, 1949): 606.

[115] J. W. Shepherd, "Miscellany," *Gospel Advocate.* 52 (January 6, 1910): 16 and "Miscellany," *Gospel Advocate.* (January 27, 1910): 112.

[116] Bertha Emlin, "Training Little Children," *Gospel Advocate.* 60 (March 7, 1918): 225.

[117] Anonymous, "Attention Sunday School Teachers," *Gospel Advocate.* 60 (December 5, 1918): 1157.

[118] J. E. Choate, *I'll Stand on the Rock: A Biography of H. Leo Boles* (Nashville: Gospel Advocate Company, 1965), pp. 230-38.

[119] Anonymous, "Bible Lesson Helps," *Gospel Advocate.* (January 6, 1910): 6.

[120] Anonymous, "Commending the Quarterlies," *Gospel Advocate* 64 (January 5, 1922): 15.

[121] E. A. Elam, *Elam's Notes on Bible School Lessons 1926* (Nashville: Gospel Advocate Company, 1925).

[122] Anonymous, "Boles' Bible Lessons by Correspondence," *Gospel Advocate,* 83 (November 27, 1941): 1145.

[123] H. Leo Boles, "Church Programs," *Gospel Advocate.* 86 (July 13, 1944): 456.

[124] H. Leo Boles, "How to Improve Bible Study," *Gospel Advocate,* 86 (July 20, 1944): p. 473.

[125] H. Leo Boles, "Vacation Bible Schools," *Gospel Advocate* 86 (August 10, 1944): 521.

148

CHAPTER FOURTEEN

MISCELLANEOUS EXPRESSIONS OF PROGRESS

In addition to the indications of progress noted previously, there were other indications which deserve brief attention. These may be viewed as contributory to progress as well as indicative of growth taking place.

Mission Work

Attention has been called to the evangelistic work of the local churches and the general principles previously illustrated are pertinent to the present section. In this phase of study attention will be called to what is usually termed home and foreign mission work.

In this study of mission work one must be aware of three major factors which supply background and context for the progress made. First, churches of Christ in the state of Tennessee and elsewhere were fully committed to opposing missionary societies or any other authoritative, quasiauthoritative or potentially authoritative arrangement of churches and/or individuals for the proclamation of the gospel. Second, there was a genuine interest in and promotion of missionary work by the churches in the state and elsewhere. Third, the principles and practices of mission work in the period studied were often searched, discussed, and evaluated in a serious controversy which developed shortly after the close of the period of this study. These three factors, viewed in retrospect, provide an awareness of resistance, progress, and precedent which later writers were to search for their own purposes. The present study has earlier given attention to the first of these areas; the third lies beyond the scope of this effort; and the second constitutes the thrust of this section of study.

There was no question of interest and encouragement for mission work over the period studied. In 1902 David Lipscomb told of an interest in mission work in Armenia and gave an account of the work of supporting the missionary, A. Paul, by a cooperative effort of three churches in Nashville.[1] He later was quoted as using this example to show an interest in mission work and an awareness of the need of cooperation.[2] In 1906 the budget of the Tenth Street church in Nashville showed that one third of its resources went for mission work.[3] M. C. Kurfees told brethren that opposition to the missionary society was not adequate for the service of God.[4] Earlier he plead that churches "wake up" to this responsibility [5] and lamented that not many churches were as interested [6] as they needed to be. J. E. Dunn commended such appeal and endorsed the need to keep such interest alive.[7] With little difficulty one could find an urgent appeal to greater interest in mission work almost every year in the pages of the *Gospel Advocate*. Also, one could easily find reports of missionary efforts in foreign and home fields. For example, a special edition of the paper was given to the need of work in the Northeastern United States [8] and H. Leo Boles expressed encouragement for missionaries and mission work.[9]

The practical aspects of mission work were recognized as entailing the need of cooperation among the churches. Consequently, while opposing missionary society arrangements, the churches worked together in evangelism and other activities. David Lipscomb urged that brethren not go to the extreme of "refusing all co-operation among churches in supporting missionaries" while they opposed missionary societies.[10] He stated he had "repeatedly and continually advocated this cooperation in churches," and cited examples of such cooperation in foreign work in Armenia and home missions around Nashville.[11] He elaborated on the manner of such cooperation in these words,

> Let each church as it is able support a preacher of the gospel. If one is not able to support one within itself, let it or them confer with one or more neighboring churches, and let so many as are needed to support a man do it by regular contributions; but by all means avoid associations that ignore and take the work out of the hands of the churches.[12]

Over the years the practice of cooperating in mission work was essentially as David Lipscomb had described in the quote above. He gave an example of several churches contributing to the purchase of a tent to be used as weather permitted in the summer and told of three churches being established by this effort.[13] M. C. Kurfees advocated such arrangements in a later article.[14] In 1923 H. Leo Boles commended a plan by the church in Harper, Kansas to support the W. N. Short family in Bulawayo, South Africa. A church in Harper, Kansas had secured the cooperation of brethren in Amarillo, Texas who in turn had sent F. B. Shepherd among the churches to inform brethren of the need and secure assistance if possible. The missionary was responsible to the Harper, Kansas elders and those who were interested in assisting were asked to contact the elders in Kansas or in Texas. Boles commended this as "A Scriptural Precedent" and encouraged support wherever possible. He concluded, "In New Testament times the evangelist was amenable to the church or churches sending him out and supporting him without the intervention of a society, agent, or even any other church." [15] In 1944 Boles encouraged mission work in Cuba. He gave some statistics of the growth in Cuba for the five years just passed and also appealed for assistance to the Cuban work in building a meetinghouse. The Central church, in Miami, was leading in the Cuban work and of the cooperation to be expected Boles stated, "All funds should be sent to this address, as Brother Vaughn and the elders of the church at Central will be responsible for the amount raised." [16] These examples indicated the recognition and utilization of cooperative efforts in evangelizing. There was no connection betwen the churches other than interest in a common good, but there was mutual sharing of information and financial resources to spread the message they believed.

Foreign mission work was encouraged and supported but not so extensively before 1950 as afterwards. Early missionaries, such as J. M. McCaleb, who went to Japan in 1892, were followed by others, but the depression in the 1930s and World War II limited financial strength and made foreign mission work most difficult if not impossible. Shortly after the war, foreign mission work began in earnest. In 1947 Olan Hicks, a compiler of church statistics and editor of a Texas paper promoting missionary work by churches of Christ, told of missionary work being done in China, Japan, Britain, France, Africa, Canada, Hawaii, Alaska, Mexico, and Cuba.[17] Churches in Tennessee had a part in this work. Readers of the *Gospel Advocate* were kept informed about the progress of foreign work in such places as South Africa,[18] Germany, [19] Holland,[20] and elsewhere. Of particular interest was the work in Belgium which was supported by the Sparta, Tennessee church [21] and the work in Japan which the Union Avenue church in Memphis was supporting.[22] The various workers were often invited to come to Tennessee churches to explain their work and to be assisted by contributions.[23] Students from various countries were in the colleges in the state to prepare for mission work upon return to their native country.[24] There were frequent reports of home mission efforts such as the Hillsboro work in Kentucky.[25]

In summary, it was clear that churches of Christ in Tennessee were interested and active in missionary work. The local churches were the sole means of such work and the elders and members firmly insisted on the need of such independence being respected. There were various cooperative efforts between and among churches but always with great respect for the autonomy of churches and avoidance of any hint of what was termed "societyism."

Benevolent Work

In benevolent work the churches of Christ in Tennessee maintained a quiet program of good deeds, by churches and individuals, over the years. As will be noted, there was some opposition, but for the most part the opposition was in other places than Tennessee. An article by Homer Hailey in 1948 underscored the attitude toward benevolence one finds reflected throughout the period. He observed that purity of doctrine is greatly to be desired and is to be maintained faithfully, but he also urged brethren and churches to be active in benevolent work lest they be keepers of orthodoxy but not doers of the work.[26]

The care of orphans was a concern of the churches since the early days of the work in Tennessee. Tolbert Fanning approved and commended such work by churches in the early issues of the *Gospel Advocate*.[27] David Lipscomb gave his views in a strongly worded article in 1906. He stated, "Yet I fully believe the great work of caring for orphans and teaching the Bible must be done by churches and Christians in their private and personal walk in life." [28] Through the years report after

151

report was given concerning the Tennessee Orphan Home at Spring Hill, Tennessee. The needs, fortunes, and achievements of the home were presented with regularity. In 1918, for example, J. C. McQuiddy gave a report of contributions from churches and individuals in the state and elsewhere,[29] and a later writer plead for greater assistance to orphans.[30] In the mid-thirties opposition reached such a pitch in the Midwest that debates, such as the Ketcherside-Porter Debate,[31] began to be conducted, but the churches in Tennessee were not seriously troubled by such opposition. J. D. Tant upheld the care of orphans in a 1937 article.[32] Homer Hailey commended the orphan homes for the care of dependent children [33] and G. K. Wallace encouraged churches to assist in the work.[34]

Over the years other benevolent works were reported or suggested in the pages of the *Gospel Advocate.* Of some interest to the churches during World War I was a War Sufferers Fund. A. B. Lipscomb received and forwarded contributions to relief agencies to assist distressed people in such places as Armenia, Syria, Russia, and Palestine.[35] Another area of relief work was the assistance to Allied nations through the Red Cross. J. C. McQuiddy stressed the need and propriety of such work,[36] E. A. Elam asked if churches were going to aid in the work,[37] and the Bethlehem church in Wilson County, Tennessee supplied a hospital bed for France.[38] Other expressions of concern for those in need were the proposal for homes for the aged to be assisted by churches [39] and the establishment of day care centers for children.[40] Churches often responded to disasters of various kinds as the reports about relief work in the 1937 Ohio River Valley flood made clear.[41]

The churches of Christ in Tennessee were aware of and responsive to the needs of people. They cared for their souls and for their physical welfare. Orphans, disaster victims, war sufferers and those who had been rendered unable to care for themselves in various ways were often assisted by the churches and individual members. The local churches were kept informed of needs, activities and progress and the churches in turn responded with money and supplies. They responded to the opportunity to do good unto all men.

Christian Colleges

The theme of Christian education in colleges has often been before churches of Christ. Norvel Young discussed the subject rather thoroughly in a history of the colleges.[42] Earl West surveyed much of the material in the period between the Civil War and the turn of the century.[43] Biographers have discussed colleges indirectly as they treated the lives of such men as N. B. Hardeman at Freed-Hardeman College,[44] H. Leo Boles at David Lipscomb College,[45] and J. N. Armstrong at Harding College.[46] Marion West has presented an extensive study of Burritt College, Spencer, Tennessee, which college went out of existence in 1938.[47] These works supply a broad context for considering the work of college training among churches of Christ in Tennessee.

The present section will be concerned with a brief treatment of matters relating to the two colleges in the state—Freeh-Hardeman College and David Lipscomb College—which continued through the period studied. Burritt College, which rendered great service in training such leaders as H. Leo Boles and pioneering in educational concepts later to be observed in the two colleges studied, may be omitted from consideration.

It was clear from the beginning to the close of the period that there was support for the colleges which brethren operated. David Lipscomb declared his support for "Bible schools, Bible academies, and Bible colleges" in 1877 [48] and wondered how a Christian could teach in or support a school which was not a Bible school. [49] He along with James A. Harding was responsible for the beginning of the Nashville Bible School which opened October 5, 1891. [50]

Before long the school in Nashville was a focal point for controversy as to its scriptural propriety. By 1902 Daniel Sommer began a series of attacks on the schools in Nashville and elsewhere. West observed that Sommer offered such objections to the colleges as the danger of promoting "preacherisms" and thereby "societyism," glorifying men, misappropriating the Lord's money since the schools and not the church received support, and serving as innovations equal to the missionary society. [51] Over the years these and similar objections were to be often discussed in the *Gospel Advocate* and other papers. It is not germane to the present study to note the controversy in depth, but the general trend may be observed by reference to samples of articles from time to time. E. A. Elam argued the schools were individual and not church activities and not parallel to the society. [52] J. N. Armstrong indicated that even with opposition being present in some areas the college where he served continued to be supported by churches and individuals. [53] J. P. Sewell defended the colleges by showing their purpose and usefulness. [54] F. B. Srygley, after drawing a parallel between Sommer's paper and the Bible colleges, [55] indicated his readiness for a debate with Sommer on the Bible college issue. [56] Morrison refers to correspondence between N. B. Hardeman and Daniel Sommer in which Hardeman proposed a debate on the college question in 1930 but Sommer did not accept. [57] In 1933 G. C. Brewer devoted many pages of the *Gospel Advocate* to the defense of the colleges. He later published his articles in a tract. [58] H. Leo Boles argued the colleges and churches were completely separate and that the churches could support this good work if they desired. [59] The position of schools and the right or lack of right of churches to support them continued to be discussed, but the general view of churches in the state was that set forth by N. B. Hardeman. He argued that the college was "a supplement to the home" and even without the teaching of the Bible would merit the support of Christians. He maintained the colleges were not owned or operated by the churches and had no control of churches. He concluded that if a church believed a college to be teaching the truth and furnishing an avenue through which parents might train their children, the church could help the school if it desired to do so.[60] Others were to agree and disagree, but the general position was that churches were free to assist the colleges if they chose and the colleges were not to seek any type of authoritative or coercive action toward the churches.

In 1948 L. Arnold Watson prepared a comparison of the various colleges among the churches of Christ as reported for 1947.[61] His statistics gave a good comparison of the relative strength of these schools in different areas. A summary of these statistics appears below.

	DLC*	FHC	HC	FC	ACC
Enrollment	712	377	727	106	1655
Members of church of					
Christ	618	350	590	103	1490
Ministerial Students	140	168	102	24	265
Ministerial Students					
Preaching each Sunday	86	85	78	4	100
Preparing for Foreign					
Mission Work	20-50	39	5-6	2	25-50
States represented	36	26	32	13	36
Faculty members	37	19	47	14	92

*DLC = David Lipscomb College, FHC = Freed-Hardeman College, HC = Harding College, FC Florida College, ACC = Abilene Christian College (now University).

It was not necessary to treat the history of the two schools in Tennessee in any detail. The works previously noted have supplied the general information. The last decade of the peiod may be noted as the time of greatest achievement in the respective schools. Young traced the achievement of David Lipscomb College in some detail.[62] He noted that an expansion program was begun in 1944. In five years eight buildings had been erected and at the close of 1948, $1,088,000 had been raised in cash while friends of the school had pledged $500,000 to be matched by additional funds. The assets of the college had increased from $584,212 in 1942 to $3,195,000 in October 1948. A ten year program of expansion was adopted in 1948 with a plan proposed to raise an additional million dollars. The third and fourth years of college work were added in 1947 and 1948 respectively, and a graduating class received baccalaureate degrees in 1948. Teacher training programs were approved by the state in 1948 and plans were in process to seek membership in the Southern Association of Colleges. By the close of the period studied David Lipscomb College was a strong and vital part of the educational program of the state of Tennessee as well as the college work among members of churches of Christ.

Freed-Hardeman College enjoyed significant growth in the closing decade of the present study. Young traced the history of this school in some detail.[63] In the 1940-41 session 251 students were enrolled and the

154

college property, valued at $233,728, was free from debt. In 1948 the enrollment was 417. The college had long held membership in the Tennessee Association of Colleges and American Association of Junior Colleges. As early as 1938 the college was planning to seek membership in the Southern Association,[64] but the acceptance did not come until 1956. The college was noted for its emphasis on the training of preachers. Young observed that over the years the college had become "one of the largest training centers for preachers of the Church of Christ." [65] Although the school remained a junior college, there was begun in 1948-1949 a three year course for preachers. Also of importance were the lecture courses which began in 1937. H. Leo Boles, the first lecturer, commended the program.[66] Over the years reports of plans for expansion,[67] the general status,[68] and the prospects for the future appeared in the *Gospel Advocate*. Freed-Hardeman College was making progress in its chosen field of religious education and was enjoying the support and assistance of interested brethren.

Over the years of this study the colleges supported by members of the churches of Christ became vital parts of the success of the churches. Young men and women were trained in the liberal arts and were offered the wholesome influence of a Christian environment and the stabilizing influence of Bible and Bible related study. From these schools preachers, teachers, elders, deacons, song leaders, homemakers, businessmen and others went forth to serve. There was a constant concern for the preservation of their integrity and role by all and frequent opposition by some, but the colleges kept to their role of training and inspiring students. In Tennessee David Lipscomb College and Freed-Hardeman College gradually made their way. They rendered such service as the above to the churches and, along with this, were achieving recognized status as educational institutions of the state or nation. Though the colleges were not owned or operated by the churches, they aided the churches in the state and elsewhere in their progress.

The *Gospel Advocate* And Its Publications

The relation of the *Gospel Advocate* to the growth of the churches of Christ in America and the world is a story yet to be told. The present study has revealed the indispensable nature of the paper as a primary source for the history of the churches of Christ in Tennessee, but in large measure the same was true of its significance in broader affairs of the brotherhood. The present section will set forth a summary of the influence of the paper on the growth of churches of Christ in the period.

It should always be remembered that the *Gospel Advocate* was and is not in any sense of the term a brotherhood publication. It began and has continued as a private publishing effort of interested individuals. It is not organically connected with churches of Christ and does not exercise regulatory authority over the churches. Its influence is and always has been that of moral persuasion and the convincing effect achieved by its writers. The service rendered, to the satisfaction of those who through the years have subscribed to the paper and purchased the various publications presented and recommended, has been the basis of its influence. Two aspects of this effective service may be noted in relation to the growth of the churches.

The weekly publication of the *Gospel Advocate* for the entire period of study supplied several invaluable contributions to the growth of churches. The previous study has documented several controversies and problems which impinged on the churches. In each of these the various men engaged sent articles of explanation, refutation, and counsel on the points of conern. Those who read the paper were able to examine the issue as the exchanges continued week by week. Participants in the discussions could be invited for speaking engagements, questions, and counsel. Often the series of exchanges would be published in tracts, pamphlets, and books for more permanent circulation. By these means preachers, teachers, and elders were kept informed and supplied with reference material on matters of concern.

In 1890 J. H. Garrison predicted the end of the *Gospel Advocate* because of its opposition to missionary societies. F. D. Srygley mused on this prediction and concluded that it was false.[69] Time has proved the accuracy of Srygley's assessment. Indeed the paper has continued and rendered service in many ways. The numerous appeals for help, the reports of good work done, the record of churches established, and the encouragement of growth reported have been noted in the preceding study. Warnings of dangers of a less apparent nature, such as extremism,[70] can be found on the pages of the paper. The answering of hundreds of questions through the years was a vital part of the role of the paper. Also, one could learn of the lives of outstanding men,[71] the start of new papers,[72] the growth of schools, and even a proposed tour to the World's Fair.[73] The news of special events, such as a lectureship conducted by churches, received notice.[74] Occasionally, when a change of view had occurred, one would publish this change in the paper.[75] Of interest also were the special issues of the paper which were devoted to such topics as How to Prepare Sermon (November 17, 1919), A Worthy Woman (March 8, 1923), What Must I Do to Be Saved? (April 26, 1923), The Church (December 23, 1937) and Back to the Bible (November 17, 1938).

In 1910 M. C. Kurfees projected the six key themes he thought should be promoted by writers on the paper through the year. These included: Piety in the home, Orderly conduct among Christians, First Principles of Salvation, Mission Work, Resistance to denominationalism inside and outside the churches and Unity upon he Bible alone.[76] In 1937 W. E. Brightwell surveyed 940 articles in the paper for he preceding year. These were divided into topics and numbers as follows: Edification (233), Doctinal (137), Evangelistic (87), Controversial (95), Premillennialsim (48), and General (340).[77] These two articles summarize the general content

156

and thrust of the paper and a survey of the years would strongly support the view that the paper aimed at and succeeded in stressing these areas of interest. The readers were accordingly taught and stabilized by these articles.

A second area of contribution to the churches was in the frequent presentation of books on vital themes. In addition to books referred to previously, many of which the Gospel Advocate Company published, there was a large host of other books which informed, strengthened, and edified the members of the churches. Among these books were reprints of older works such as the debate between Alexander Campbell and Robert Owen,[78] and the classic work by Brents on the plan of salvation.[79] Preachers especially were benefitted by books of sermons by various writers. Over the years there were specific works which addressed themselves to particular problems. A. N. Trice wrote concerning Roman Catholicism,[80] E. A. Elam compiled a series of essays on evolution,[81] and Charles Roberson and A. N. Trice responded to modernism.[82] Another major effort of the Nashville publishers was the presentation of a series of commentaries on New Testament books. Some of these were prepared by one man, e.g., H. Leo Boles on Luke,[83] but others were compiled from notes and writings of David Lipscomb. In this way C. E. W. Dorris compiled the notes on the Gospel of John [84] and J. W. Shepherd prepared the work on Romans.[85] These works still enjoy a favorable reception by brethren. Not to be omitted were various debates such as the Nichols-Weaver debate on such topics as Holy Spirit baptism and the washing of feet.[86] H. Leo Boles wrote a major work on the Holy Spirit,[87] and J. W. Shepherd was frequently in print with the reprint of his 1912 work on baptism [88] and his work on church history.[89] These books were eagerly used by various members, preachers, teachers and elders. In them respected writers gave their best efforts to clarify and explain difficult subjects. Those who published these works, as well as the authors and users, were aiding the progress of the church.

It was obvious in the period studied that churches of Christ were making progress in Tennessee. Their numerical growth, resulting from a pattern of evangelism and establishment of churches, was parallel to a continued congregational development. This increased capability expressed itself in an improved religious education program as well as in mission work, benevolence, and Christian colleges. In all this period the *Gospel Advocate* continued to enjoy the support of the churches by its writings and counsel.

REFERENCES

[1] David Lipscomb, "Missionary Wrok," *Gospel Advocate* 44 (August 28, 1902):552.

[2] David Lipscomb and E. G. Sewell, quoted by M. C. Kurfees, *Questions Answered* (Nashville: McQuiddy Printing Company, 1921), pp. 145-46.

[3] Anonymous, "Miscellany," *Gospel Advocate* 48 (January 18, 1906):37.

[4] M. C. Kurfees, "False Standards of Mission Work," *Gospel Advocate* 44 (July 17, 1902):450.

[5] M. C. Kurfees, "Let Us Wake Up the Churches," *Gospel Advocate* 44 (June 5, 1902):354.

[6] M. C. Kurfees, "Mission Work—Going and Sending," *Gospel Advocate* 44 (June 19, 1902):386.

[7] J. E. Dunn, "Stirring Up the Churches," *Gospel Advocate* 44 (July 3, 1902):430.

[8] Special Issue, *Gospel Advocate* 86 (March 9, 1944).

[9] H. Leo Boles, "Missionaries and Mission Work," *Gospel Advocate* 86 (September 14, 1944):601.

[10] Lipscomb and Sewell, quoted by Kurfees, ibid., p. 146.

[11] Ibid.

[12] Ibid., pp. 146-47.

[13] David Lipscomb, "Missionary Work," *Gospel Advocate* 44 (Ocotber 16, 1902):664-65.

[14] M. C. Kurfees, "Common Sense and Business in Methods of Mission Work, No. 1," *Gospel Advocate* 60 (September 19, 1918):898-99.

[15] H. Leo Boles, "A Scriptural Precedent," *Gospel Advocate* 65 (February 22, 1923):172-73.

[16] H. Leo Boles, "The Cause of Christ in Cuba," *Gospel Advocate* 86 (June 29, 1944):425.

[17] Olan Hicks, "Open Letter to Editor of 'Look' Magazine," *Christian Chronicle* 5 (November 26, 1947):7.

[18] Reuel Lemmons, "New Testament Christianity to be planted in South Africa," *Gospel Advocate* 91 (July 28, 1949):777.

[19] Otis Gatewood, "Sixth Congregation Begins in Germany," *Gospel Advocate* 91 (October 13, 1949):654.

[20] L. Arnold Watson, "Temple (Texas) Church to fully Support Native Holland Worker," *Gospel Advocate* 91 (April 28, 1949):269.

[21] Billy Norris, "Sparta, Tennessee to Send 2nd Worker to Assist Timmerman in Belgium," *Christian Chronicle* 8 (October 4, 1950):6.

[22] Anonymous, "New Testament Chrisitanity Firmly Established in Japan," *Christian Chronicle* 6 (November 24, 1948):8.

[23] A. R. Holton, "Nashville Chruch Calls Meeting for Work in Germany," *Christian Chronicle* 8 (May 31, 1950):1.

[24] Cathryn Patton, "Three German Youths in U. S. for Bible Training," *Christian Chronicle* 6 (October 27, 1948):5.

[25] B. C. Goodpasture, "Hillsboro Sponsors Meeting In Kentucky," *Gospel Advocate* 83 (October 2, 1941):958.

[26] Homer Hailey, "Keepers of Orthodoxy," *Gospel Advocate* 90 (February 19, 1948):175.

[27] Tolbert Fanning, "Orphan School," *Gospel Advocate* 1 (September 1855):91.

[28] David Lipscomb, "Some Plain Words," *Gospel Advocate* 48 (August 16, 1906):521.

[29] J. C. McQuiddy, "Tennessee Orphan's Home," *Gospel Advocate* 60 (February 14, 1918):153.

[30] Anonymous, "In Behalf of Orphans," *Gospel Advocate* 60 (February 21, 1918):180.

[31] W. Carl Ketcherise and Rue Porter, *The Ketcherside-Porter Debate* (Barnard, Missouri: Rush Printing Company, 1937).

[32] J. D. Tant, "Where Will it End?" *Gospel Advocate* 79 (December 16, 1937):1185.

[33] Homer Hailey, "Dependent Children," *Gospel Advocate* 91 (November 10, 1949):710-11.

[34] G. K. Wallace, "Orphan Homes," *Gospel Advocate* 91 (November 17, 1949):726-27.

[35] Anonymous, "The War Sufferers' Fund," *Gospel Advocate* 48 (January 3, 1918):12.

[36] J. C. McQuiddy, "Relief Work," *Gospel Advocate* 60 (May 6, 1918):462-63.

[37] E. A. Elam, "What Do Churches Intend to do about Contributing through the Red Cross to the Sick and the Wounded?" *Gospel Advocate* 60 (August 8, 1918):757.

[38] E. A. Elam, "The Bethlehem Church, Wilson County, Tenn., Endows a Hospital Bed in France," *Gospel Advocate* 60 (September 12, 1918):876.

[39] S. H. Hall, "Gifts to the Home for the Aged," *Gospel Advocate* 69 (February 3, 1927):100-01.

[40] S. H. Hall, "The Church of Christ Day Home and Clinic," *Gospel Advocate* 69 (February 10, 1927):136-37.

[41] Anonymous, "How to Send Flood Relief," *Gospel Advocate* 79 (January 28, 1937):92.

[42] M. Norvel Young, *A History of Colleges Established and Controlled by Members of the Churches of Christ* (Kansas City, Missouri: The Old Paths Book Club, 1949).

[43] Earl West, *The Search for the Ancient Order,* Vol. 2 (Indianapolis: Religious Book Service, 1950), pp. 113-27; 268-96.

[44] James Marvin Powell and Mary Nelle Hardeman Powers, *N. B. H.: A Biography of Nicholas Brodie Hardeman* (Nashville: Gospel Advocate Company, 1964).

[45] Leo Lipscomb Boles and J. E. Choate, *I'll Stand on the Rock: A Biography of H. Leo Boles* (Nashville: Gospel Advocate Company, 1965).

[46] L. C. Sears, *For Freedom: The Biography of John Nelson Armstrong* (Austin, Texas: Sweet Publishing Company, 1969).

[47] Marion West, "Pioneer of the Cumberlands: A History of Burritt College" (Master's thesis, Tennessee Techological University, 1971).

[48] David Lipscomb, "Bible Colleges," *Gospel Advocate* 19 (August 16, 1877):505.

[49] David Lipscomb, "Teaching the Bible" *Gospel Advocate* 46 (August 11, 1904):505.

[50] West, ibid., pp. 372-76.

[51] Ibid., pp. 385, 393, 395.

[52] E. A. Elam, "No Title," *Gospel Advocate* 43 (August 1, 1901):314-15.

[53] J. N. Armstrong, "Western Bible and Literary College," *Gospel Advocate* 49 (February 14, 1907):106.

[54] Jesse P. Sewell, "Christian Education, No. 1," *Gospel Advocate* 60 (August 1, 1918):724-25.

[55] F. B. Srygley, "The Apostolic Review and Bible Colleges," *Gospel Advocate* 65 (August 16, 1923):790-91.

[56] F. B. Srygley, "Does Brother Sommer Want A Debate?" *Gospel Advocate* 65 (October 4, 1923):958-59.

[57] M. C. Morrison, "Daniel Sommer's Seventy Years of Religious Controversy" (Ph.D. dissertation, Indiana University, 1972), p. 255.

[58] G. C. Brewer, *Congregations and Colleges* (Privately published, n.d.), pp. 3-18.

[59] H. Leo Boles, "Colleges and Church Autonomy," *Gospel Advocate* 79 (February 25, 1937):170.

[60] N. B. Hardeman, "Position of Freed-Hardeman College Regarding 'Bible Schools,' " *Gospel Advocate* 89 (February 13, 1947):132,144.

[61] L. Arnold Watson, "Know Our Christian Schools," *Gospel Advocate* 90 (January 15, 1948):60.

[62] Young, ibid., pp. 96-97.

[63] Ibid., pp. 97-109.

[64] N. B. Hardeman, "Endowment for Freed-Hardeman," *Gospel Advocate* 80 (August 11, 1938):748.

[65] Young, ibid., p. 108.

[66] H. Leo Boles, "Freed-Hardeman Special Course," *Gospel Advocate* 79 (February 11, 1937):133.

[67] N. B. Hardeman, "Expansion Program Launched," *Gospel Advocate* 83 (January 27, 1941):85.

[68] L. L. Brigance, "Freed-Hardeman College Steers Straight Ahead," *Gospel Advocate* 86 (June 29, 1944:426-27.

[69] F. D. Srygley, "From the Papers," *Gospel Advocate* 32 (April 23, 1890):257.

[70] Joe S. Warlick, "Salutory," *Gospel Advocate* 44 (May 15, 1902):312.

[71] H. Leo Boles, "A Scholar and an Author," *Gospel Advocate* 79 (January 14, 1937):26, 39.

[72] Full Page Ad, *Gospel Advocate* 80 (June 9, 1938):544, concerning *The Bible Banner.*

[73] Anonymous, "Gospel Advocate's Trip to World's Fair, July 6-29" *Gospel Advocate* 57 (February 18, 1915):156.

[74] Anonymous, "Ninth Annual Bible Lectureship"' *Gospel Advocate* 91 (January 20, 1949):46.

[75] W. Curtis Porter, "Marshall Conner Renounces Judgement Heresy," *Gospel Advocate* 91 (April 7, 1949):221.

[76] M. C. Kurfees, "Brief Outline for th New Year," *Gospel Advocate* 52 (January 6, 1910):14.

[77] W. E. Brightwell, "The Notion Counter," *Gospel Advocate* 79 (January 7, 1937):20.

[78] Robert Owen and Alexander Campbell, *The Evidences of Christianity* (Nashville: Gospel Advocate Company, 1946).

[79] T. W. Brents, *The Gospel Plan of Salvation* (Nashville: Gospel Advocate Company, 1950).

[80] A. N. Trice, *The Bible Versus Romanism* (Nashville: Gospel Advocate Company, 1928).

[81] E. A. Elam, ed., *The Bible Versus Theories of Evolution* (Nashville: Gospel Advocate Company, 1925).

[82] Charles H. Roberson and A. N. Trice, *The Bible Versus Modernism* (Nashville: Gospel Advocate Company, 1946).

[83] H. Leo Boles, *A Commentary on the Gospel by Luke* (Nashville: Gospel Advocate Company, 1940 [1950]).

[84] David Lipscomb and C. E. W. Dorris, *A Commentary on the Gospel of John* (Nashville: Gospel Advocate Company, 1950).

[85] David Lipscomb and J. W. Shepherd, *A Commentary on the New Testament Epistles,* Vol. 1, Romans (Nashville: Gospel Advocate Company, 1943).

[86] Gus Nichols and C. J. Weaver, *Nichols- Weaver Debate* (Nashville: Gospel Advocate Company, 1944).

[87] H. Leo Boles, *The Holy Spirit: His Personality, Nature, Works* (Nashville: Gospel Advocate Company, 1942).

[88] J. W. Shepherd, *Handbook on Baptism* (Nashville: Gospel Advocate Company, 1912, reprint 1950).

[89] J. W. Shepherd, *The Church, The Falling Away and the Restoration* (Nashville: Gospel Advocate Company, 1948).

159

CONCLUSION

The summary conclusions at the end of various chapters of this work have made an extensive concluding section unnecessary, but a general statement of conclusion seems important.

During the period of this study, 1906-1950, churches of Christ in Tennessee demonstrated their ability to develop into a stable and expanding religious body. For nearly one hundred years before the beginning of this study there were churches in the state composed of members who sought to restore what they understood to be the Christianity of the first century. They sought to return to the teaching of the Bible, restore the church, and by evangelistic effort win others to this desired relationship and work. Their history for the period hass been the subject of this study.

Prior to 1906 it became clear that major differences were present, within the group, over several practices such as the use of missionary societies and the use of instrumental music in worship. Other differences were present, as noted in the study, but these were the leading ones. These differences gradually moved the respective advocates and opponents to a division. Those in favor of the instrument in the worship and the use of missionary societies became known as the Christian churches or Disciples of Christ. Those who opposed the instrument in worship and the missionary society, along with their representative stance as indicated in the chapters on their consciousness of identity, became known as churches of Christ. This division resulted in the necessity of churches of Christ making their way as a unique religious body. There was before them the need to identify themselves, stabilize the churches, and make requisite progress. In the period studied they achieved each of these major objectives.

The identity of churches of Christ was made clear by several major developments. The census reports of 1906 made public what had been apparent for some time, namely that a division of major proportions was present within the ranks of the restorationists. Those who opposed the practices which they regarded as innovations were aware of their identity and were not willing to give up their opposition even for the sake of continued fellowship. Shortly afterwards a series of public meetings with the influential spokesman N. B. Hardeman served to further indicate the unique position of the churches of Christ. Hardeman told of the generally accepted views of the group on such matters as the church, the Bible, the plan of salvation, worship, and related matters. In a series of three attempts to restore unity the identity of the group was further made clear. The group was fully aware of its own religious position, had developed competent spokesmen, and was willing to consider a restoration of fellowship with estranged brethren but only without compromise of cherished views and positions. This identity was capable of being seen in the writings and preaching of representative men of the period and served as a strength of the group.

In order to maintain themselves certain stabilizing efforts were made by the group. These efforts at stabilization can best be understood by considering two doctrinal disputes of major import, instrumental music and premillennialism. Instrumental music in worship had long been a subject of controversy among the churches. The stabilization of the churches on the subject came by means of a series of debates and a rather definitive book in opposition to the practice. The discussions, reviews, and debates resulted in general stabilization by the mid 1920s. Subsequent years saw little advance in basic position, argument, and response on the subject. Premillennialism emerged among churches of Christ shortly before World War I. Its defense by a popular writer on the *Gospel Advocate* staff presented considerable difficulties as to proper practical response. Proponents of the doctrine insisted on introducing and defending these beliefs in the churches and this led to controversy and the general pattern of stabilization was repeated. Books and debates, oral and written, refined the issues and set forth the arguments pro and con. By the mid 1930s it was clear that the advocates of the doctrine would not relent and the cry for severance of fellowship again was heard. By the mid 1940s this cry was accepted, generally, and the fellowship was broken. These two larger controversies showed the pattern of stabilization generally followed, i.e., writings in the various papers, a definitive book or two on the respective positions, a series of debates, a period for consideration and cessation of upholding the offensive doctrine or practice, and when this failed a severing of fraternal ties. Thus were the churches stabilized in the period studied.

The churches of Christ in Tennessee showed continuous growth in vital areas of church life during the period studied. It is not possible to give an exact number of churches and members during the time of this study, but general estimates may be gathered. In 1906 there were some 800 to 900 churches of Christ in the state with 40,000 to 50,000 members. In 1950 there were some 1,400 to 1,500 churches of Christ in the state with some 100,000 to 150,000 members. These increases were traceable to a constant evangelistic program in the state by preachers and members. Tent meetings, private sessions, large camp meetings, and in later years radio preaching were the methods employed with corresponding success. The churches formed were organized with elders and deacons, had preachers working in the evangelistic effort at home and in unreached areas, and had an active membership which tried to advance their cherished beliefs. The religious education program saw continued progress as to both extent and methodology. The missionary work at home and abroad, along with benevolent work, demonstated the desire of the churches to serve the needs of people. The interest in Christian colleges continued through the period with David Lipscomb College and Freed-Hardeman Collge making significant progress by 1950. The *Gospel Advocate* continued to enjoy the support of churches and individuals as it spoke to needs and questions of the day. All these expressions of religious interest, on the part of the group and interested individuals, made it clear that progress was being made in the expression of their allegiance to cherished beliefs.

It was obvious that in the period studied the churches of Christ in Tennessee emerged from a division in 1897-1906 in a viable condition as a unique religious group. In the period from 1906 to 1950 they identified themselves, stabilized their members and churches as to doctrinal positions they embraced, and made significant progress as a religious group in the state. In these activities the brethren were standing for their faith.

SELECTED BIBLIOGRAPHY

Primary Source

Gospel Advocate (Nashville, Tennessee), 1855-1861; 1866-1950, Vols. I-XCII.

Books

Ahlstrom, Sydney E. *A Religious History of the American People.* New Haven: Yale University Press, 1972.

Bales, James D. *Instrumental Music and New Testament Worship.* Searcy, Arkansas: James D. Bales, 1973.

Banowsky, William S. *The Mirror of A Movement.* Dallas: Christian Publishing Company, 1965.

Barzun, Jaques, and Graff, Henry F. *The Modern Researcher.* New York: Harcourt, Brace & World, Inc., 1970.

Baxter, Batsell Barrett, and Young, M. Norvel. *New Testament Churches of Today,* Vol. II. Nashville: The Gospel Advocate Company, 1968.

Boles, H. Leo. *A Commentary on the Gospel by Luke.* Nashville: Gospel Advocate Company, 1940.

———. *The Holy Spirit: His Personality, Nature, Works.* Nashville: Gospel Advocate Company, 1942.

———. *The Way of Unity Between "Christian Church" and Churches of Christ.* Nashville: Gospel Advocate Company, n.d.

———, and Boll, R. H. *Unfulfilled Prophecy.* Nashville: Gospel Advocate Company, 1928.

Boll, R. H. *The Kingdom of God.* Louisville: The Word and Work, n.d.

———. *The Revelation.* Louisville: The Word and Work, n.d.

Boswell, Ira A., and Hardeman, N. B. *Boswell-Hardeman Discussion on Instrumental Music in the Worship.* Nashville: Gospel Advocate Company, 1923.

Brents, T. W. *The Gospel Plan of Salvation.* Nashville: Gospel Advocate Company, 1950.

Brewer, G. C. *A Medley on the Music Question.* Nashville: Gospel Advocate Company, 1948.

———. *Congregations and Colleges.* Privately published, n.d.

———. *The Model Church.* Nashville: Gospel Advocate Company, 1957.

Briney, J. B. Instrumental Music in Christian Worship. Cincinnati: The Standard Publishing Company, 1914.

Brown, John. *Churches of Christ.* Louisville: John P. Norton and Company, 1904.

163

Calhoun, Hall L., and Kurfees, M.C. *Instrumental Music in Worship. A Discussion between H. L. Calhoun and M.C. Kurfees.* Nashville: Gospel Advocate Publishing Company, 1901.

Choate, J. E. *I'll Stand on the Rock: A Biography of H. Leo Boles.* Nashville: Gospel Advocate Company, 1965.

Clubb, M. D., and Boles, H. Leo, *Discussion—Is Instrumental Music in Christian Worship Scriptural?* Nashville: Gospel Advocate Company, 1927.

DeGroot, Alfred Thomas. *The Grounds of Divisions Among the Disciples of Christ.* Chicago: Privately Published, 1940.

Eckstein, Stephen Daniel. *History of Churches of Christ in Texas, 1825-1950.* Austin: Firm Foundation Publishing House, 1963.

Elam, E. A. *Elam's Notes on Bible School Lessons 1926.* Nashville: Gospel Advocate Company, 1925.

————, ed. *The Bible Versus Theories of Evolution.* Nashville: Gospel Advocate Company, 1925.

Fogarty, John P., and Hicks, Olan. *1946-1947 Yearbook of Churches of Christ.* Abilene, Texas: Hicks Publishing Company, 1947.

Garrison, Winfred Ernest. *Religion Follows the Frontier.* New York: Harper and Brothers, 1931.

————, **and DeGroot, Alfred T.** *The Disciples of Christ: A History.* St. Louis: Bethany Press, 1948.

General Christian Missionary Convention. *Yearbook of the Disciples of Christ.* Cincinnati: General Christian Missionary Convention, 1885.

Goodpasture, B. C., ed. *The Sermon Outlines of M. C. Kurfees.* Nashville: Gospel Advocate Company, 1940.

Grant, J. W. *A Sketch of the Reformation in Tennessee.* Unpublished manuscript, the original of which is in the Tennessee State Archives. A copy was prepared by Carroll B. Ellis, 1968.

Hailey, Homer. *Attitudes and Consequences in the Restoration Movement.* Rosemead, California: Citizen Print Shop, Inc., 1952.

Hall, Alexander, *The Christian Register.* Loydsville, Ohio: The Compiler, 1848.

Hardeman, N. B. *Hardeman's Tabernacle Sermons* (5 Vols.). Nashville: Gospel Advocate Company, 1922-1942.

Harrell, David Edwin, Jr. *A Social History of Disciples of Christ,* Vol. I: *Quest for a Christian America: The Disciples of Christ and American Society to 1866.* Nashville: The Disciples of Christ Historical Society, 1966. Vol. II: *The Social Sources of Division in the Disciples of Christ, 1865-1900.* Atlanta and Athens, Georgia: Publishing Systems, Inc., 1974.

Hoffman, G. A. *Yearbook of the Disciples of Christ.* St. Louis: Christian Publishing Company, 1895.

Hudson, John Allen, ed. *The Pioneers on Worship.* Kansas City: The Old Path Book Club, 1947.

164

Kendrick, Carroll. *Live Religious Issues of the Day.* Nashville: Gospel Advocate Company, 1890.

Ketcherside, W. Carl, and Porter, Rue. *The Ketcherside-Porter Debate.* Barnard, Missouri: Rush Printing Company, 1937.

Kurfees, M. C. *Instrumental Music in Worship on the Greek Verb Psallo: Philologically and Historically Examined Together With A Full Discussion of Kindred Matters Relating to Music in Christian Worship.* Nashville: Gospel Advocate Company, 1911, Reprint, 1950.

——, ed. *Questions Answered by* (David) *Lipscomb and* (E. G.) *Sewell.* Nashville: McQuiddy Printing Company, 1921.

——. *Review of O. E. Payne's Book on "Psallo".* Nashville: Gospel Advocate Company, 1922.

Lewis, John T. *The Voice of the Pioneers on Instrumental Music and Societies.* Nashville: Gospel Advocate Company, 1932.

Lipscomb, David, and Dorris, C. E. W. *A Commentary on the Gospel of John.* Nashville: Gospel Advocate Company, 1950.

——, and Shepherd, J. W. *A Commentary on the New Testament Epistles,* Vol. I, Romans, Nashville: Gospel Advocate Company, 1943.

Milligan, Robert. *An Exposition and Defense of the Scheme of Redemption as it is Revealed and Taught in the Holy Scriptures.* St. Louis: Christian Board of Publication, 1868.

Murch, James DeForest. *Christians Only.* Cincinnati: Standard Publishing Company, 1962.

Neal, Charles M., and Wallace, Foy E., Jr. *Neal-Wallace Discussion on the Thousand Years Reign of Christ.* Nashville: Gospel Advocate Company, 1933.

Nichols, Gus, and Weaver, C. J. *Nichols-Weaver Debate.* Nashville: Gospel Advocate Company, 1944.

Norton, Herman A. *Tennessee Christians.* Nashville: Reed and Company, 1971.

Otey, W. W., and Briney, J. B. *Otey-Briney Debate.* Cincinnati: F. L. Rowe, 1908.

Owen, Robert, and Campbell, Alexander. *The Evidences of Christianity.* Nashville: Gospel Advocate Company, 1946.

Payne, O. E. *Instrumental Music is Scriptural.* Cincinnati: The Standard Publishing Company, 1920.

Powell, James Marvin, and Powers, Mary Nelle Hardeman. *N. B. H.: A Biography of Nicholas Brodie Hardeman,* with an Introduction by B. C. Goodpasture. Nashville: Gospel Advocate Company, 1964.

Roberson, Charles H., and Trice, A. N. *The Bible Versus Modernism.* Nashville: Gospel Advocate Company, 1946.

Roberts, J. W. "Answers to Today's Arguments on Instrumental Music," *Adorning the Doctrine,* Twelfth Annual Lectureship Lubbock Christian College. Lubbock, Texas: L.C.C., 1969.

Rogers, James R. *The Cane Ridge Meeting-house* to which is appended the Autobiography of B. W. Stone, Cincinnati: The Standard Publishing Company, 1910.

Sears, L. C. *For Freedom: The Biography of John Nelson Armstrong.* Austin, Texas: Sweet Publishing Company, 1969.

Shepherd, J. W. *Handbook on Baptism.* Nashville: Gospel Advocate Company, 1912, reprint, 1950.

————, ed. *Queries and Answers by David Lipscomb.* Nashville: McQuiddy Printing Company, 1910.

Smith, Benjamin J., and Smith, C. C., eds. *Yearbook of the Churches of Christ (Disciples of Christ).* Cincinnati: American Christian Missionary Society, 1900.

Smith, F. W. *A Review of R. H. Boll's Kingdom Theory.* Nashville: McQuiddy Printing Company, 1921.

Stark, J. Carroll, and Warlick, Joe S. *A Debate Between J. Carroll Stark and Joe S. Warlick.* Nashville: Gospel Advicate Company, 1903.

Taylor, C. A. Autobiography of C. A. Taylor. Handwritten copy, 1958.

Twice, A. N. *The Bible Versus Romanism.* Nashville: Gospel Advocate Company, 1928.

Tucker, William E. *J. H. Garrison and Disciples of Christ.* St. Louis: Bethany Press, 1964.

U. S. Department of Commerce, *Census of Religious Bodies, 1936.* Churches of Christ Statistics, History, Doctrine and Organization, Bulletin 46 (1940), pp. 1-7.

Wallace, Foy E., Jr. *God's Prophetic Word.* Lufkin, Texas: The Roy E. Cogdill Publishing Company, 1946.

Ware, Charles Crossfield, *Barton Warren Stone* St. Louis: The Bethany Press, 1932.

Warlick, Joe S., and Phillips, George W. *A Debate on the Sunday School Question.* Dallas: Private Publication, 1924.

West, Earl Irvin, *The Life and Times of David Lipscomb.* Henderson, Tennessee: Religious Book Service, 1954.

————. *Search for the Ancient Order,* I. Nashville: The Gospel Advocate Company, 1949; II. Indianapolis: Religious Book Service, 1950.

Whiteside, R. L., and Nichol, C. R. *Christ and His Kingdom: A Review of R. H. Boll.* Clifton, Texas: Mrs. C. R. Nichol, n.d.

Willis, Cecil. *W. W. Otey: Contender for the Faith.* Akron, Ohio: Privately Published, 1964.

Winkler, Herbert. *The Eldership.* Nashville: Private Publication, 1950.

Young, M. Norvel. *A History of Colleges Established and Controlled by Members of the Churches of Christ.* Kansas City, Missouri: The Old Paths Book Club, 1949.

Articles

Anonymous. "Do the Unimmersed Commune?" *Lard's Quarterly,* I (September, 1863), 41-53.

Ash, Anthony L. "Old Testament Studies in the Restoration Movement." *Restoration Quarterly,* X (Second Quarter, 1967), 89-98.

Brewer, G. C. "Random Remarks." *Firm Foundation,* XLII (July 7, 1925), 3.

Campbell, Alexander. "The Church in Nashville." *Millennial Harbinger,* II (March, 1831), 121-23.

―――. "Church Organization―No. 1." *Millennial Harbinger,* VI (February, 1849), 90.

―――. "Instrumental Music." *Millennial Harbinger,* Fourth Series, I (October, 1851), 582.

Creath, Jacob. "Conventions―No. IV." *Millennial Harbinger,* Third Series, VII (November, 1850), 615.

Draper, D. F. "Otey-Briney Debate." *Firm Foundation,* XXV (September 14, 1909), 6.

Ellmore, Alfred. "Wheat and Chaff." *Christian Leader,* III (December 17, 1889), 4.

Fanning, Tolbert. "Church Organization." *The Christian Review,* I (February, 1844), 27-28.

Franklin, Benjamin. "Instrumental Music in Churches." *American Christian Review,* III (January 31, 1860), 19.

―――. "No Title." *American Christian Review,* VI (October 6, 1863), 152.

Hayden, A. S. "Instrumental Music." *Millennial Harbinger,* XXXVI (January, 1865), 38-40.

―――. "Expediency and Progress." *Millennial Harbinger,* XXXIX (March, 1868), 135-44.

―――. "Reply to Brother McGarvey." *Millennial Harbinger,* XXXIX (June, 1868), 330.

Henley, T. M., and Richardson, Robert. "Co-operation of Churches." *Millennial Harbinger,* VII (July, 1836), 333-34.

Jorgenson, E. L. "Fear and Fellowship." *The Word and Work,* LV (June, 1961), 134-37.

Lard, Moses E. "Instrumental Music in Churches and Dancing." *Lard's Quarterly,* I (March, 1864), 330-31.

―――. "Can We Divide?" *Lard's Quarterly,* III (April, 1866), 330-36.

Loos, C. S. "Ohio Missionary Meeting." *Millennial Harbinger,* XXXVII (June, 1866), 274-75.

McGarvey, J. W. "Instrumental Music in Churches." *Millennial Harbinger,* Fifth Series, VII (November, 1864), 510.

―――. "Bro. Hayden on Expediency and Progress." *Millennial*

Harbinger, XXXIX (April, 1868), 217.

————. "Beliefs Here and There." *American Christian Review,* XXVIII (March 12, 1885), 82.

Munnell, Thomas. "Untying the Missionary Knot, No. 1." *Millennial Harbinger,* XXXIX (August, 1868), 459-64.

P., W. H. "Answer to A Query of A Young Disciple in St. Louis." *American Christian Review,* VI (November 24, 1863), 185.

Patton, Cathryn. "Three German Youths in U.S. for Bible Training." *Christian Chronicle.* VI (October 27, 1948), 5.

Pendleton, W. K. "Address Delivered at the Eighteenth Anniversary of the American Christian Missionary Society." *Millennial Harbinger,* XXXVII (November, 1866), 494-514.

————. "Remarks." *Millennial Harbinger,* XXXIX (August, 1868), 464-65.

Pinkerton, L. L. "Instrumental Music in Churches." *American Christian Review,* III (February 28, 1860), 34.

Rogers, John "Dancing." *Millennial Harbinger,* Fourth Series, I (August, 1851), 467-68.

Rowe, John F. "The Old and the New Order," *American Christian Review,* XXIII (March 30, 1880), 100.

Smith, Joseph. "Review of Franklin's Article on Instrumental Music." *American Christian Review,* VI (October 6, 1863), 158.

Warren, E. P. "Sand Creek Address and Declaration." *Christian Leader,* III (September 10, 1889), 2.

Warren, W. R. "Concerning Our Statistics." *The American Home Missionary,* XVI (January, 1910), 69-70.

"W", and Henshall, J. B. "Instrumental Music." *Ecclesiastical Reformer,* IV (March 15, 1851), 171.

Theses

Ash, Anthony L. "Attitudes Toward Higher Criticism of the Old Testament Among the Disciples of Christ," Unpublished Ph.D. dissertation, University of Southern California, 1966.

Campbell, Thomas Lee. "The Contribution of David Lipscomb and the Gospel Advocate to Religious Education in the Churches of Christ." Unpublished DRE dissertation, Southern Baptist Theological Seminary, 1968.

Coffman, Edward. "The Division in the Restoration Movement." Unpublished M.A. thesis, Vanderbilt University, 1930.

Humble, Bill J. "The Missionary Society Controversy in the Restoration Movement (1823-1875)." Unpublished Ph.D. dissertation, The State University of Iowa, 1964.

Merritt, Floyd E. "An Institutional Study of the Hardeman Tabernacle Meetings." Unpublished Master's thesis, The University of Kansas Graduate School, 1964.

Morrison, Matthew Clifton, "Daniel Sommer's Seventy Years of Religious Controversy." Unpublished Ph.D. dissertation, University of Indiana, 1972.

Murrell, Arthur Van. "The Effects of Exclusivism in the Separation of the Church of Christ from the Christian Church." Unpublished Ph.D. dissertation, Vanderbilt University, 1972.

Riley, Edgar Carlisle. "A Classified and Annotated List of the Periodicals of the Christian Church (Disciples of Christ) Prior to 1900." Unpublished Master's thesis, The University of Kentucky, 1941.

Thrasher, Byron. "A History of the Instrumental Music Controversy During the Nineteenth Century Restoration Movement." Unpublished Master's thesis, Harding College, 1956.

West, Marion. "Pioneer of the Cumberlands: A History of Burritt College." Unpublished Master's thesis, Tennessee Technological University, 1971.

INDEX

Adamsville Church,14
Aid argument, 27, 28, 89, 90, 94, 97
Allen, James A., 66
Ambrose of Milan, 96
American Christian Evangelizing and
    Educational Association, 44
American Christian Missionary Society, 19,
    22, 42
Appointment of Elders, 138, 139
Armenia, 149
Armstrong, J. N., 83, 126
Autonomy of Church, 135

Bales, James D., 102
Baptisms, Numbers in various years, 132,
    133
Barclay, James T., 19
Barnes, J. M. 29
Baxter, Batsell, 125
Bethlehem Church, 14
Bible Colleges, 153
Bible, N. B. Hardeman and, 70-73
Bible Schools, 142-146
Bible School, census statistics, 143
Boles, H. Leo: 83
    and fellowship with Premillennialists,
    119-121, 123
    and Sunday Schools, 146
    and Unity, 82, 83
    and Unity meetings, 82, 84
    —Boll Debate, 115-122
    —Boll Debate; Evaluation of, 121-122
    —Clubb Debate, 102
    —Explanation about fellowship with
    Premillennialists, 119-121, 123
Boll, R. H.:
    and "Agreement" with *Gospel Advocate*
    publishers, 111-112
    and fair treatment of *Gospel Advocate*
    publishers, 111
    and Otey-Briney Debate, 94
    and articles on Premillennialism, 107-110
    —Boles Debate, 115-122
    —Boles Debate: Evaluation of, 121-122
    Staff writer status on *Gospel Advocate*,
    107, 109, 110
Boswell, Ira, B.:
    —Hardeman Debate, 99-101
    not defend Payne, O. E., 101
Bowling Green, Kentucky and Instrumental
    Music, 35-36
Brewer, G. C.:
    and church organization, 138
    and Premillennialism Debate, 115, 116

and Unity, 82
Medley on the Music Question, 102
Briney, J. B.:
    and Instrumental Music, 54
    and Kurfees, M. C., *Instrumental Music,*
    and Otey Debate, 93-93
    not claim *psallo* demands instrument, 97
    on Payne, O. E., 99
    psallo justifies instrumental music, 98
Brigance, L. L.:
    and "Pastor System", 141-142
    and Unity Meetings, 84
Brightwell, W. E.:
    Church growth report by, 132-133
    Reports on baptisms, 132-133
Bureau of Census 61-63, 132-133
Burritt College 16, 152

Cake, E. B. 49
Calhoun, Hall L.:
    —Kurfees, M. C. exchange, 88-90
Campbell, Alexander:
    and instrumental music, 25-26
    and missionary societies, 19, 20
Campbell, Thomas L., 142
Cathey Creek Church, 14
Cave, R. C., 48, 49
Census Bureau, 61-63, 132-133
Census Reports:
    —1906, 61-63, 132
    —1916, 132
    —1926, 132
    —1936, 133
Chattanooga and missionary society
    work, 45
Christ, Reign of, 117
"Christian Action", 80
Christian Baptist and missionary societies,
    20, 60
Christian Colleges, Enrollment, 1947, 154
Christian Register, 15, 131
Christian Magazine, 16
Christian Women's Board of Missions
    (1874), 44
Church: Emphasis by N. B. Hardeman on,
    67-69
Churches in Tennessee: Statistics, 132-134
Church: Organization of, 138-140
Clement of Alexandria, 96
Clubb, M. D.:
    —Boles Debate, 102
Colleges, supplement to home, 153
Commission on Restudy of the Disciples of
    Christ, 80

Henley, T. M. and cooperation of churches, 20, 21
Hicks, Olan, 133
Holy Spirit: N. B. Hardeman on work of, 71
Home Mission Board, 45
Hudson, John Allen, 88
Humble, Bill J: history of missionary society, 19
Henshall, J. B., 25

"In the New Testament" and *psallo*, 92, 95, 96, 100
Inference and N. B. Hardeman, 72
Indianapolis—Unity meeting in, 82
Instrumental music:
  and churches of Christ, 92, 93
  first notice of in restoration movement, 25,26
  in Bowling Green, Kentucky, 35-36
  in Clarksville, Tennessee, 29
  in Henderson, Tennessee, 29, 30, 90
  in Knoxville, Tennessee, 29
  in Memphis, Tennessee (1869), 29
  in Nashville, Tennessee (Woodland St.), 29
  in Pulaski, Tennessee, 30
  in Tullahoma, Tennessee, 30
  in worship in early years, 26-28
  "in" worship, 89, 90, 91, 92, 94, 97, 98, 100

Jackson, Tennessee and cooperative meeting, 43,44
Janes, Don Carlos, 113
Jorgenson, E. L.:
  regrets about premillennial controversy, 114

Kendrick, Carroll, 88
Kingdom of God, 117
Knoxville, Tennessee: support of missionary society, 36
Koch, E. H. and Commission on Unity, 78
Kurfees, M. C.: 109
  and instrumental music, 94-97
  and unity effort, 77
  and test of fellowship, 78
  —Calhoun, Hall L. exchange, 88-90
  Instrumental Music, 94-97
  response to J. B. Briney, 97
  reviewed by J. B. Briney, 97-98
  reviewed by O. E. Payne, 98-99
  vs. Premillennialism, 112, 121, 123

Ladies' Aid Society, 44

Lanier, Roy H., 145
Lard, Moses vs. instrumental music, 26, 27
Laying on of hands, 139
Lewis, John T., 88
Liberty church, 14
Lipscomb, A. B., 112, 114
Lipscomb, David, editor of *Gospel Advocate:* 33-37
  and Bible schools, 143-146, 152-155
  and R. C. Cave, 48, 49, 56
  and churches in Tennessee, 60-63
  and division, 33-37, 50, 53,59,62
  and liberalism, 48-50, 56
  and Louisville Plan, 35
  and moderation about division, 33-37, 50, 53, 59, 62
  and open fellowship, 47
  and origin of work in Tennessee, 13
  and preachers, 13
  and Sommer, Daniel, 41, 42, 153
  and "The Vital Point", 56
  vs. church statistics, collection, 60, 131
  vs. cooperative meetings, 43, 44
  vs. Henderson meeting (1910), 135
  vs. instrumental music, 29
  vs. instrumental music (1878), 35
  vs. missionary society, 21, 34, 43, 44
  vs. missionary society in Tennessee, 44, 45
  vs. modernism, 48-50, 56
  vs. Thomas Munnell on missionary society, 21
Lipscomb, William, 139
Louisville, Kentucky and Premillennialism, 112-114
Louisville, Plan, 22-23

McCaleb, J. M.: 151
McGarvey, J. W.:
  vs. instrumental music, 27, 28
  vs. F. D. Srygley, 55, 56
McQuiddy, J. C.:
  on Otey-Briney Debate, 94
  on Premillennialism, 109, 123
  on Sand Creek Address and Declaration, 41
Memphis, instrumental music in (1869), 29
Midway, Kentucky church and instrumental music, 26
Milligan, Robert, 88
Minton, J. A.:
  and missionary society defense, 19
  vs. E. A. Elam on missionary society, 19
Miraculous powers: N. B. Hardeman on, 71
Missionary society:
  Defense of, 19, 20

in Tennessee, 36, 42-47
objections to in Franklin, Tennessee, 21
objections to, 20-22
Moderation and division, 33-37, 50, 53, 59, 62
Modern critical approaches, 48-50, 56
Mulkey, John, 16
Munnell, Thomas, 21
Murch, James Deforest:
and Premillennialism, 81
and Witty, Claude F. unity meetings, 80, 81, 84
Music Hall meeting, 125
Myhr, Andres Ivarson:
and missionary society in Tennessee, 45-49
and modernism, 49

Nashville: church in early days: 15
and instrumental music (1890), 29
and Premillennialism, 115
National Teachers' Normal and Business College, 65
Neal, Charles:
and fellowship with Premillennialists, 124
Wallace Debate, 122, 123, 124
Negro Work, 44
New Orleans: Premillennialism in, 110
Nichol, C. R., 115
Nichols, Gus, 140
and Weaver, C. J. Debate, 157
North, S. N. D. and census, 61-63
Numerical strength, 131-134

Objections to Sunday Schools, 143-145
Old Testament Arguments on instrumental music, 90, 94
Olmstead, H. L., 108
Omaha Convention, 47
Open membership, 47, 48
Opinion, N. B. Hardeman on, 73
Otey, W. W. and Briney, J. B. Debate, 93-94
"Pastor System," 140-142
Payne, O. E.:
and unity, 78, 79, 99
retraction of extreme stance on instrumental music, 102
review of M. C. Kurfees on instrumental music, 98, 99, 100, 101
Pendleton, W. K. and Misssionary society, 19
Pinkerton, L. L.:
and instrumental music, 26
and modernism, 48
Post Oak Christian Church, 14

Preachers, 140-142
Preachers, Lists of, 59, 60
Premillennialism:
and *Gospel Advocate,* 108, 109, 111, 112
and N. B. Hardeman, 125
and opinion, 123
and withdrawal of fellowship, 107, 119, 120, 123-127
shift in strategy of advocates,122, 123
Psallo:
and LXX, 91
inherent idea, 96, 99
Kurfees, M. C. on, 94-97
Briney, J. B. on, 97, 98
Payne, O. E. on, 98, 99, 100, 101
Publishers of *Gospel Advocate:*
and R. H. Boll, 107, 108, 109, 110, 111, 112
and Premillennialism, 107, 108, 109, 110, 111, 112

Qualifications of elders 138, 139

Radio programs, 136
Rationalism, 48-50, 56
Reign of Christ, 117
Religious education, 142-146, 154, 155
Restoration movement, 7-10, 13
Restoration of Israel, 116
Restrictive deeds, 40, 137, 140
Roan's Creek church, 14
Roberts, J. W., 102
Rowe, John F. and division, 37
Rubel, R. O.:
Premillennialism, 113
withdrawn from in Louisville, Kentucky, 112
Ryman Auditorium, 66

Sand Creek Illinois church:
Address and Declaration, 39-42
and instrumental music debate (Otey-Briney), 93-94
Second coming of Christ:
imminent, 118
premillennial, 118
Sewell, E. G.:
and division, 54
and Woodland Street church, Nashville, 43, 44, 45
Sewell, Jesse P., 59
Shepherd, J. W., 60, 61, 62
Smith, F. W., 108
Sommer, Daniel, 41, 42, 153
and Hardeman, N. B. proposed debate, 153